STUDIES IN PAUL, EXEGETICAL AND THEOLOGICAL

New Testament Monographs, 2

Series Editor

Stanley E. Porter

Studies in Paul,
Exegetical and Theological

Richard N. Longenecker

SHEFFIELD PHOENIX PRESS

2004

Copyright © 2004 Sheffield Phoenix Press

Published by Sheffield Phoenix Press
Department of Biblical Studies, University of Sheffield
Sheffield S10 2TN

www.sheffieldphoenix.com

A CIP catalogue record for this book
is available from the British Library

Typeset by Fairlie Productions, Fairlie, Ayrshire
Printed on acid-free paper by Antony Rowe, Chippenham,
Wiltshire

ISBN 1-905048-04-1

CONTENTS

The articles in this little volume have been taken over, in the main, as they originally appeared over the span of approximately two decades in various symposium volumes and learned journals. At times an article has been slightly altered, either to bring its content somewhat up to date or to conform its style to what is now current. Likewise, there has been some effort to regularize the form of the articles—as, for example, the use of Greek throughout (rather than Greek script in some articles and English transliterations in others, as originally required), an appended "Select Bibliography" for all of the articles, and the standardization of abbreviations. But apart from these rather slight alterations, all of what follows has appeared earlier in various venues with much the same content and much the same form as it appears here.

Theology is for Lovers

One of the great promotional ads of recent years has been that of the state of Virginia, which proclaims in only four words: "Virginia is for Lovers." What delightful images that little advertisement conjures up in one's mind, heart and imagination. It almost makes one want to drop everything and move to Virginia, expecting that in that major state of the original thirteen American colonies all of the delights of human life will be found.

But that ad is only a publicity gimmick, which attempts to capitalize on our common human delusion that "the grass is always greener" somewhere out there beyond our reach. More importantly, it fails to tell us that love and happiness are to be found in our present relationships and where we are now, not out there in some never-never land.

Nonetheless, when I first heard "Virginia is for Lovers" on the radio, saw it in newspapers, and viewed it on bumper stickers of cars returning from a holiday in Virginia, I couldn't help but transfer the slogan to my own academic study of the New Testament. So I found myself declaring: "Theology is for Lovers." And that's what I'd like to suggest now to the reader in introducing this little volume of collected exegetical and theological studies on Paul.

The Loves of an Academic

It may seem somewhat incongruous, abnormal, anomalous—even a bit peculiar—to speak of the loves of an academic. To some, the joining of scholarship and love may be an oxymoron—perhaps somewhat shocking if wrongly understood. In reality, however, an academic's life is filled with all sorts of loves.

There is, first of all, the love of the subject matter to which an academic has devoted his or her life. Something about the subject originally attracted one's attention, and, on further examination, study and reflection, has come to consume one's entire interest. The true academic wants, above all else, for the area of his or her interest to be developed and prosper, for research and insights pertaining to the subject to be brought together in new and helpful ways, for false starts and dead ends to be identified and eliminated, and to have some sort of a significant part in such endeavors. One has to experience, in fact, a real love relationship with one's subject if one is to be a true academic.

But academics is not only about subject matter. It is also about the conveyance of knowledge regarding that subject to others in meaningful ways. A true academic is also in love with his or her students—with a desire to awaken in them an appreciation of what is vital and important in the area of study, a knowledge of how to move forward in their research, and an understanding of how to convey that subject matter to others. Teaching and counseling go hand in hand with study and research in the life of any academic, whether on an undergraduate, graduate or post-graduate level. In fact, one has to fall in love with students in order to be a true academic—enjoy seeing them "come to life" in a particular discipline, grow in their understanding of the subject matter, mature in their personal lives, and begin to dream dreams and see visions about their own futures.

One could also say that an academic has to be in love with, or at least respect, the institution that supports his or her research and teaching—especially if one is to be happily involved in the various administrative functions and committee responsibilities that must be assumed among any group of people making up an organization. Administration and committee responsibilities are areas that most academics prefer to stay rather clear of. Yet since such activities have important implications for the welfare of their students, the advancement of their own studies, and the health of their respective institutions, academics have also come to develop some type of love relationship with the institutions that employ them and the responsibilities that go with their employment.

Concomitant with all these, however, is the love of developing new ideas, working out new approaches and methods, and proposing new theses in an academic's field of endeavor—and, of course, of having venues available for trying out these new ideas, approaches, methods and theses. Interaction with students in the classroom, with faculty colleagues at one's institution, with peers in the same discipline in a federation of schools or at learned societies, and with broader audiences in the presentation of lectureships are all invaluable to an academic, as well as a source of delight and challenge. Much of what goes on in these various venues, of course, gets eventually published through the normal channels of publication.

What is often lost in these activities, however, are the various articles that an academic produces—sometimes in preparation for his or her more polished publications, sometimes as "spin offs" from larger endeavors, and sometimes just simply because an article was requested by some editor or needed in addressing some particular situation or occasion. It is often these smaller bits-and-pieces that an academic loves more than his or her finished works. For they frequently strike more quickly at the heart of an issue than larger, more inclusive writings, and they often reflect more directly an academic's own approach, methodology, and interests.

Articles of Love in this Collection
The articles included in this volume of collected studies have all been written as expressions of love for the subject. While they all deal exegetically and theologically with some aspect of Paul's teaching, ministry and person, they are not all equal in size, identical in treatment, or originally written with the same intent. Nonetheless, like children and grandchildren of the same family, whatever their differences, they are all loved alike. And while originally composed at various times and with differing purposes, they have all been written with the

hope that they would be stimulating, challenging and helpful to whomever might read them—including whoever will read them in their present form.

The articles for this volume have been arranged in what has seemed to their author a logical order, though, admittedly, logical placement is more evident for some of the articles than for others. Some readers may prefer another arrangement. But the order of the articles is not important, and readers may read them in any order they think best or most helpful.

The first two articles consider matters having to do with Paul's personal life—that is, with (1) the impact of his conversion on his understanding of Jesus, and (2) prayer in his experience, dealing with backgrounds, parallels, forms, contents and significances. To go further in these topics, the reader is encouraged to turn to two of my edited volumes in the McMaster New Testament Studies: *The Road from Damascus: The Impact of Paul's Conversion on His Life, Thought, and Ministry* (Grand Rapids: Eerdmans, 1997) and *Into God's Presence: Prayer in the New Testament* (Grand Rapids: Eerdmans, 2001). Also of pertinence are my earlier monographs *Paul, Apostle of Liberty* (New York: Harper & Row, 1964; repr. Grand Rapids: Baker, 1976; Vancouver: Regent Publishing, 2003) and *The Ministry and Message of Paul* (Grand Rapids: Zondervan, 1971).

The next three articles are exegetical treatments of crucial issues in two of Paul's major missionary letters. The article on Galatians focuses on his use of the pedagogue illustration to clarify the relation of Christians to the Mosaic law, which provides an important insight into the whole of Paul's theology. To go further in this study or on other matters pertaining to Galatians, one could turn to my commentary on *Galatians* (WBC; Dallas: Word, 1990). The two articles on Romans deal with matters regarding the identity and circumstances of the letter's addressees, Paul's purpose or purposes in writing them, his use of early Christian confessional materials, his use of the Old Testament, and the focus of his presentation—all of which are today vital concerns for any proper understanding of Romans. To go further in these areas, one could read my *Biblical Exegesis in the Apostolic Period* (Grand Rapids: Eerdmans, 1975, 2nd ed., 1999), my *New Wine into Fresh Wineskins: Contextualizing the Early Christian*

Confessions (Peabody: Hendrickson, 1999), and my forthcoming commentary on *Romans* (NIGTC) to be published by Eerdmans.

The sixth article on Paul's vision of the church and church order (or, "communityformation") has been written to offer some guidance as we as Christians attempt to contextualize the gospel in ways that are not only true to the proclamation of the New Testament but also meaningful and appropriate in our contemporary situations. To go further, one is encouraged to read my *New Wine into Fresh Wineskins: Contextualizing the Early Christian Confessions* (Peabody: Henrickson, 1999) and my edited symposium volume on *Community Formation in the Early Church and in the Church Today* (Peabody: Henrickson, 2002).

The seventh and eighth articles consider matters of Christian witness and missionary activity. I am not a missiologist. One could certainly learn much more from the honorees of these articles about the subjects of witness and missions than from me. So I urge those who read my articles to read further in the writings of those I have attempted to honor. Nonetheless, I thoroughly enjoyed writing these two articles and trust that what I've said in them will become more and more a part of my own life.

Articles nine, ten and eleven deal with matters of eschatology in Paul's thought—most particularly with his teaching on the resurrection of believers in Jesus. I have written elsewhere on other issues of eschatological concern. But I've wanted to include these three articles because they touch on what I consider to be three of the most important matters with respect to Paul's teaching regarding the resurrection of believers—that is, the basis for his proclamation (article nine); the Jewish background and parallels to his teaching (article ten); and the focus of and developments in his teaching (article eleven). To go further on the subject of the resurrection throughout the New Testament, the reader is invited to study another of my edited McMaster New Testament Studies symposium volumes on *Life in the Face of Death: The Resurrection Message of the New Testament* (Grand Rapids: Eerdmans, 1998).

Only some of the articles included in this volume originally included a bibliography. All of them now, however, have an appended "Select Bibliography." The primary purpose for these selected bibliographies is not to support everything that is said or quoted in the particular article, but to aid the reader's further study of the subject.

The Greater Love

Academics, however, can become so engrossed with all of the above very noble and legitimate loves that they fail to recognize an even greater love, and so turn in on themselves and become quite egoistic. C. S. Lewis in *The Great Divorce*, which Lewis characterized as a "fantasy with a moral," has the spirit of George MacDonald—whom he describes as a "very tall man, almost a giant, with a flowing beard," who spoke even after death with a strong "Scotch" accent, who was "one of the Solid People" of heaven, "an enthroned and shining god," and who was Lewis' "Teacher" in the afterlife—talk about the egoism of various sorts of people during their lifetimes, with each person's own special type of egoism continuing on in his or her existence after death. In particular, Lewis has MacDonald refer to "literary ghosts" whose habit is to "hang about public libraries to see if anyone's still reading their books" (IX.63).

A little later in his fantasy, Lewis imagines MacDonald as bringing him to a place where he overhears another conversation between another heavenly Spirit (i.e., a "Solid Person") and a recently deceased person (i.e., a "Ghost") who had been a famous artist and who laments not being able to continue his painting. Says this other Spirit in rebuke of the artist for his wishes:

> Ink and catgut and paint were necessary down there [i.e., on earth], but they are also dangerous stimulants. Every poet and musician and artist, but for Grace, is drawn away from the love of the things he tells to love of the telling, till, down in Deep Hell, they cannot be interested in God at all but only in what they say about Him. For it doesn't stop at being interested in paint, you know. They sink lower—become interested in their own personalities and then in nothing but their own reputations (IX.79).

With all of our proper loves, may we as Christian academics never forget our greater love: "the love of God"—that is, both his love for us and our love for him—"that is in Christ Jesus our Lord" (Rom 8:39). This little volume, in some small way, is presented to whomever will read it as an expression of its author's greater love.

xi

ORIGINAL LOCATION OF ARTICLES

1. "The Impact of Paul's Conversion on his Understanding of Jesus: A Realized Hope, a New Commitment, and a Developed Proclamation"—Original Article: "A Realized Hope, a New Commitment, and a Developed Proclamation: Paul and Jesus," in *The Road from Damascus: The Impact of Paul's Conversion on His Life, Thought, and Ministry*, ed. R. N. Longenecker. MNTS. Grand Rapids: Eerdmans, 1997, 18-42.

2. "Prayer in the Pauline Letters"—Original Article: "Prayer in the Pauline Letters," in *Into God's Presence: Prayer in the New Testament*, ed. R. N. Longenecker. MNTS. Grand Rapids: Eerdmans, 2001, 203-27.

3. "The Pedagogical Nature of the Law in Galatians 3:19-4:7"—Original Article: "The Pedagogical Nature of the Law in Galatians 3:19-4:7," *Journal of the Evangelical Theological Society* 25 (1982) 53-61.

4. "Prolegomena to Paul's Use of Scripture in Romans"—Original Article: "Prolegomena to Paul's Use of Scripture in Romans," *Bulletin for Biblical Research* 7 (1997) 145-68.

5. "The Focus of Romans: The Central Role of 5:1-8:39 in the Argument of the Letter"—Original Article: "The Focus of Romans: The Central Role of 5:1-8:39 in the Argument of the Letter," in *Romans and the People of God: Essays in Honor of Gordon D. Fee on the Occasion of his 65th Birthday*, ed. S. K. Soderlund and N. T. Wright. Grand Rapids: Eerdmans, 1999, 49-69.

6. "Paul's Vision of the Church and Community Formation in his Major Missionary Letters"—Original Article: "Paul's Vision of the Church and Community Formation in his Major Missionary Letters," in *Community Formation in the Early Church and in the Church Today*, ed. R. N. Longenecker. Peabody: Hendrickson, 2002, 71-88.

7. "The Pauline Concept of Mutuality as a Basis for Luke's Theme of Witness"—Original Article: "The Pauline Concept of Mutuality as a Basis for Luke's Theme of Witness," in *"You Will Be My Witnesses": A Festschrift in Honor of the Reverend Dr Allison A. Trites on the Occasion of His Retirement*, ed. R. G. Wooden, T. R. Ashley, and R. S. Wilson. Macon: Mercer University Press, 2003, 109-26.

8. "'What Does It Matter?': Priorities and the *Adiaphora* in Paul's Dealing with Opponents"—Original Article: "'What Does It Matter?': Priorities and the *Adiaphora* in Paul's Dealing with Opponents in his Mission," in *The Gospel to the Nations. Perspectives on Paul's Mission in Honour of Peter T. O'Brien*, ed. P. G. Bolt and M. D. Thompson. Leicester: Apollos; Downers Grove: InterVarsity, 2000, 147-60.

9. "The Nature of Paul's Early Eschatology"—Original Article: "The Nature of Paul's Early Eschatology," *New Testament Studies* 31 (1985) 85-95.

10. "'Good Luck on Your Resurrection': Beth She'arim and Paul on the Resurrection of the Dead"—Original Article: "'Good Luck on Your Resurrection': Beth She'arim and Paul on the Resurrection of the Dead," in *Text and Artifact in the Religions of Mediterranean Antiquity: Essays in Honour of Peter Richardson*, ed. S. G. Wilson and M. Desjardins. Waterloo: Wilfrid Laurier University Press, 2000, 249-70.

11. "Is There Development in Paul's Resurrection Thought?"—Original Article: "Is There Development in Paul's Resurrection Thought?" in *Life in the Face of Death: The Resurrection Message of the New Testament*, ed. R. N. Longenecker. MNTS. Grand Rapids: Eerdmans, 1998, 171-202.

Acknowledgments

The author and publisher are grateful to the following for permission to reproduce essays first published by them:

Eerdmans Publishing Company for (1) "The Impact of Paul's Conversion on his Understanding of Jesus: A Realized Hope, a New Commitment, and a Developed Proclamation," in *The Road from Damascus: The Impact of Paul's Conversion on His Life, Thought, and Ministry*, ed. R. N. Longenecker (MNTS; Grand Rapids: Eerdmans, 1997), 18-42; (2) "Prayer in the Pauline Letters," in *Into God's Presence: Prayer in the New Testament*, ed. R. N. Longenecker (MNTS; Grand Rapids: Eerdmans, 2001), 203-27; (3) "The Focus of Romans: The Central Role of 5:1–8:39 in the Argument of the Letter," in *Romans and the People of God: Essays in Honor of Gordon D. Fee on the Occasion of his 65th Birthday*, ed. S. K. Soderlund and N. T. Wright (Grand Rapids: Eerdmans, 1999), 49-69; and (4) "Is There Development in Paul's Resurrection Thought?," in *Life in the Face of Death: The Resurrection Message of the New Testament*, ed. R. N. Longenecker (MNTS; Grand Rapids: Eerdmans, 1998), 171-202.

Editor of the *Journal of the Evangelical Theological Society* for "The Pedagogical Nature of the Law in Galatians 3:19-4:7," *JETS* 25 (1982) 53-61.

Editor of the *Bulletin for Biblical Research* for "Prolegomena to Paul's Use of Scripture in Romans," *BBR* 7 (1997) 145-68.

Hendrickson Publishers for "Paul's Vision of the Church and Community Formation in his Major Missionary Letters," in *Community Formation in the Early Church and in the Church Today*, ed. R. N. Longenecker (Peabody: Hendrickson, 2002), 71-88.

Mercer University Press for "The Pauline Concept of Mutuality as a Basis for Luke's Theme of Witness," in *"You Will Be My Witnesses": A Festschrift in Honor of the Reverend Dr. Allison A. Trites on the Occasion of His Retirement*, ed. R. G. Wooden, T. R. Ashley, and R. S. Wilson (Macon: Mercer University Press, 2003), 109-26.

Inter-Varsity Press (UK) for "What Does Its Matter?": Priorities and the *Adiaphora* in Paul's Dealing with Opponents," in *The Gospel to the Nations: Perspectives on Paul's Mission in Honour of Peter T. O'Brien*, ed. P. G. Bolt and M. D. Thompson (Leicester: Inter-Varsity Press; Downers Grove: InterVarsity, 2000), 147-60.

Cambridge University Press for "The Nature of Paul's Early Eschatology," *NTS* 31 (1985) 85-95.

Abbreviations

Wilfrid Laurier University Press for "'Good Luck on Your Resurrection': Beth She'arim and Paul on the Resurrection of the Dead," in *Text and Artifact in the Religions of Mediterranean Antiquity: Essays in Honour of Peter Richardson*, ed. S. G. Wilson and M. Desjardins (Waterloo: Wilfrid Laurier University Press, 2000), 249-70.

ABBREVIATIONS

Reference Works

APOT	*Apocrypha and Pseudepigrapha of the Old Testament*, 2 vols., ed. R. H. Charles (1913, repr. 1963).
BAG	*A Greek-English Lexicon of the New Testament and Other Early Christian Literature*, W. F. Arndt and F. W. Gingrich (1957).
CIJ	*Corpus Inscriptionum Judaicarum*, 2 vols., ed. J. B. Frey (1936–52).
CSEL	*Corpus Scriptorum Ecclesiasticorum Latinorum*, Vienna Academy (1866ff.).
JE	*Jewish Encyclopedia*, 12 vols., ed. I. Singer (1901–1906).
M-M	*The Vocabulary of the Greek Testament, Illustrated from the Papyri and Other Non-Literary Sources*, J. H. Moulton and G. Milligan (1930, 1963).
OTP	*The Old Testament Pseudepigrapha*, 2 vols., ed. J. H. Charlesworth (1983, 1985).
PG	*Patrologia Graeca*, 162 vols., ed. J. P. Migne (1857–86).
PL	*Patrologia Latina*, 221 vols., ed. J. P. Migne (1844–66).
Str-Bil	*Kommentar zum Neuen Testament aus Talmud und Midrasch*, 6 vols., H. L. Strack and P. Billerbeck (1922–61).
TDNT	*Theological Dictionary of the New Testament*, 9 vols., ed. G. Kittel and G. Friedrich, trans. G. W. Bromiley. Grand Rapids: Eerdmans, 1964–74 (from *TWNT*).
TWNT	*Theologisches Wörterbuch zum Neuen Testament*, 10 vols., ed. G. Kittel and G. Friedrich. Stuttgart: Kohlhammer, 1933–78.

Series (Commentaries, Texts and Studies)

AB	Anchor Bible
ACNT	Augusburg Commentary on the New Testament
BNTC	Black's New Testament Commentary
CBC	Cambridge Bible Commentary
EGGNT	Exegetical Guide to the Greek New Testament
EBC	Expositor's Bible Commentary
EtBib	Etudes bibliques
GNC	Good News Commentary

HNT   Handbuch zum Neuen Testament
HNTC   Harper's New Testament Commentary
HTKNT   Herders Theologischer Kommentar zum Neuen Testament
ICC   International Critical Commentary
MKEKNT Meyer Kritisch-exegetischer Kommentar über das Neue Testament
MNTS   McMaster New Testament Studies
MNTC   Moffatt New Testament Commentary
NCB   New Century Bible
NICNT   New International Commentary on the New Testament
NIGTC   New International Greek Testament Commentary
NovTSup   Novum Testamentum Supplements
PNTC   Pelican New Testament Commentaries
SBLMS   Society of Biblical Literature Monograph Series
SP   Sacra Pagina
THNT   Theologischer Handkommentar zum Neuen Testament
TNTC   Tyndale New Testament Commentary
WBC   Word Biblical Commentary

Journals

BBR   *Bulletin for Biblical Research*
Bib   *Biblica*
BJRL   *Bulletin of the John Rylands University Library*
CBQ   *Catholic Biblical Quarterly*
ExpT   *The Expository Times*
JAAR   *Journal of the American Academy of Religion*
JBL   *Journal of Biblical Literature*
JJS   *Journal of Jewish Studies*
JSNT   *Journal for the Study of the New Testament*
JTS   *Journal of Theological Studies*
JTSA   *Journal of Theology for South Africa*
MTZ   *Münchener theologische Zeitschrift*
NTS   *New Testament Studies*
NovT   *Novum Testamentum*
Numen   *Numen: International Review for the History of Religions*
PTR   *Princeton Theological Review*
SJT   *Scottish Journal of Theology*
SR/S   *Studies in Religion / Sciences religieuses*
TSK   *Theologiche Studien und Kritiken*
ZNW   *Zeitschrift für die neutestamentliche Wissenschaft*

The Impact of Paul's Conversion on His Understanding of Jesus
A Realized Hope, a New Commitment, and a Developing Proclamation

"Paul's basic Christian conviction and the starting point for all his Christian theology," as I have argued elsewhere (in concert with many other scholars), "was not apocalypticism but functional christology—that is, his commitment was not first of all to a program or some timetable of events but to a person: Jesus the Messiah" ("Nature of Paul's Early Eschatology," 93). If that be the case, then we need to deal first with how Paul's conversion impacted his understanding of Jesus before we go on to consider how it affected his life, thought and ministry in all sorts of other ways as well. For if his commitment was first of all to Jesus as Israel's Messiah, then all other matters on his agenda as a Christian, while of importance individually, must be seen as dependent on that central conviction.

With respect to method, our procedure will be to work primarily from Paul's own letters. We consider the Acts of the Apostles to be also an important source for understanding Paul's conversion, convictions, preaching and ministry (cf. my "Acts" in *The Expositor's Bible Commentary*, ed. F. E. Gaebelein [Grand Rapids: Zondervan, 1981], 9.207-573; also published separately [1995]; 2nd ed. forthcoming in 2005). But because Acts is an account *about* Paul and not *from* Paul, and so, compared to the apostle's own letters, a secondary historical source and not a primary source, it will be used only in a supplementary manner. Further, due recognition will be given to the facts that (1) Paul's letters were written approximately twenty to thirty years after his conversion, and (2) what he says in his letters about his conversion is set within the respective purpose of each of those letters. We must constantly be aware, therefore, that we are not reading immediate responses to the event itself, but later perceptions that have been nuanced by their author in line with the particular purposes he had in writing the letters under consideration. And what is true of Paul's letters as to their dates and purposes must also be taken into account when dealing with Acts—indeed, since it is a secondary historical source, even more so.

1. *Saul of Tarsus and Jesus of Nazareth*

Before dealing directly with the impact of Paul's conversion on his understanding of Jesus, some consideration must be given to the relationship of Saul of Tarsus to Jesus of Nazareth and his followers. In particular, three rather well-worn questions that have a bearing on Paul's later christology arise: (1) Had Paul personally known the historical Jesus?; (2) What factors impelled him to persecute believers in Jesus?; and (3) How significant for him was what he later called "the scandal of the cross"?

Saul and the Historical Jesus

Extensive debate has taken place over the past century and a half as to whether or not Paul had any interest in the historical Jesus—even, in fact, whether before his conversion Saul of Tarsus had ever met or known Jesus. And often 2 Cor 5:16, which reads "though we once knew [or, 'regarded'] Christ according to the flesh (εἰ καὶ ἐγνώκαμεν κατὰ σάρκα Χριστόν), now we know/regard [him in that manner] no longer (ἀλλὰ νῦν οὐκέτι γινώσκομεν)," has been viewed as the crucial passage in that debate.

On one side of the argument, Ferdinand Christian Baur (1845), Karl von Weizsäcker (1886), Hans Hinrich Wendt (1894), Wilhelm Wrede (1905), Wilhelm Heitmüller (1912), Rudolf Bultmann (1948), and Günther Bornkamm (1969), to cite only a few prominent scholars, have claimed that Paul's kerygmatic Christ displaced all interest in his mind in the historical Jesus, and that 2 Cor 5:16 clearly evidences such a disinterest. On the other side of the argument, however, Heinrich Paret (1858), George Matheson (1881), Adolf Hilgenfeld (1894), Adolf Harnack (1901), Paul Feine (1902), James Moffatt (1908), W. D. Davies (1948), and C. F. D. Moule (1969), again to name only a few representative scholars, have argued (1) that Paul's proclamation of Christ's salvific work on behalf of humanity actually presupposes a knowledge of the events and teaching of Jesus, (2) that various allusions in his letters to Jesus' life and teaching suggest that Paul was indeed interested in the historical Jesus, (3) that where Paul is silent regarding the historical Jesus it is because his letters are pastoral in nature (that is, addressed to specific problems in his churches), and so do not reflect all that he proclaimed in his evangelistic preaching, and (4) that 2 Cor 5:16 has no direct bearing on the question, for the expression "according to the flesh" (κατὰ σάρκα) refers not to a disavowal of interest in the historical Jesus but to a disavowal of a former human or worldly perspective regarding Jesus—just as it does in the first part of that same verse where Paul affirms: "now we regard no one from a human [or, 'worldly'] point of view" (ἡμεῖς ἀπὸ τοῦ νῦν οὐδένα οἴδαμεν κατὰ σάρκα).

In defense of Paul's interest in the historical Jesus, Johannes Weiss went so far as to assert that "the express statement of the apostle himself in 2 Corinthians v.16" clearly reveals that "Paul had actually 'known' Jesus and had been impressed by His human personality and His teaching, though Paul afterwards regarded this impression as external, superficial, and 'carnal'" (*Paul and Jesus*, trans. H. J. Chaytor [London & New York: Harper, 1909], 41, 54). Further, Weiss proposed that "the simplest and most natural assumption is that he had seen Jesus during His last visit to Jerusalem and perhaps had heard Him speak; he may have been a witness of Jesus' Passion and Crucifixion, a supposition likely enough in the case of a passionately enthusiastic pupil of the Pharisees" (*ibid.* 54; see 39-56 for his entire discussion).

Weiss's thesis had some currency among scholars during the first half of the twentieth century (e.g., H. Lietzmann, *An die Korinther I/II* [Tübingen: Mohr, 1923], 125; C. A. A. Scott, *Christianity according to St Paul* [Cambridge: Cambridge University Press, 1927], 11-12). But it has few, if any, contemporary proponents. Rather, most scholars today are prepared to view Paul's pre-conversion knowledge about Jesus as having been obtained entirely from Pharisaic sources, which he trusted. Certainly Saul of Tarsus thought he knew all that needed to be known about Jesus of Nazareth, for he would hardly have persecuted believers in Jesus had he not felt he was in possession of the basic facts about them and their leader—as well, of course, that he possessed the correct interpretation of those facts. But his knowledge then, as he later acknowledged in 2 Cor 5:16b, was from a purely human or worldly perspective.

As a result of his conversion, Paul saw those "facts" in an entirely new light. And while in his mission to the Gentile world Paul's emphasis was on the kerygmatic Christ and the title "Lord," rather than on the historical Jesus and the title "Christ" (as we will later point out), he never denigrated the historical Jesus. Rather, the new interpretation of Jesus' life and teaching that broke into his consciousness when confronted by the risen Christ on the road to Damascus, that he learned by talking with some of Jesus' closest followers (cf. Gal 1:18-19), and that he evidently pondered in studying in some of the church's early confessions (portions of which he quotes in his writings)—and which, of course, must ultimately be credited by Christians to the work of God through his Holy Spirit—underlies all of what he wrote, with portions of that story and its interpretation even serving as the "narrative substructure" for certain significant portions of his letters (cf., e.g., R. B. Hays, *The Faith of Jesus Christ: An Investigation of the Narrative Substructure of Galatians 3:1–4:11* [Chico: Scholars, 1983], esp. 139-91).

Factors Impelling Saul to Persecute

Various factors have been proposed to explain Saul's persecution of the early believers in Jesus. One common explanation, which had its heyday during the latter part of the nineteenth century and the first half of the twentieth, focuses on Paul's supposed hellenistic religious orientation: (1) that he had been heavily influenced by Diaspora Judaism during his youth in Tarsus; (2) that his hellenized Judaism was a poorer religion than existed in Jerusalem; and so (3) that his persecution of Christians reflects his own moral frustrations and misguided sense of logical consistency under such an inferior form of religion, and not at all the tolerance and joy of mainline Judaism (cf. my *Paul, Apostle of Liberty* (New York: Harper & Row, 1964), 21-64, where such views are detailed and evaluated). But Paul expressly refers to himself as "a Hebrew of Hebrews" (Phil 3:5; cf. 2 Cor 11:22). And since W. D. Davies' *Paul and Rabbinic Judaism* (London: SPCK), which was originally published in 1948 and which E. P. Sanders rightly calls "a watershed in the history of scholarship on Paul and Judaism" (*Paul and Palestinian Judaism* [Philadelphia: Fortress, 1977], 7), it has been almost universally accepted that Paul's pre-conversion religious experience—including his persecution of the early followers of Jesus—cannot be simply credited to such a hellenistic orientation.

Another explanation, which had currency for approximately the same period of time as the first, views Saul the Pharisee as generally in line with mainline Pharisaic teaching, as later codified by the rabbis, but interprets the Talmud and its cognate writings as comprising a thoroughly legalistic system of religion, which emphasized external actions over inward piety and elevated the human ego over a theocentric orientation. Coupled with such a view of the rabbinic literature and Saul's Pharisaism, Rom 7:7-25 has often been taken to be an autobiographical account of Paul's pre-conversion struggles under the tyranny of the Mosaic law. Thus various psychological analyses attempted to show how the passage's depiction of an inner spiritual struggle "fit like a glove" Paul's earlier religious experience, where "the shoe pinched" for him, and in what way his persecution of Christians served "to purge the demons in his own soul," which obedience to the law was unable to conquer.

In 1928, however, Werner G. Kümmel argued persuasively that the pronoun "I" in Rom 7:7-25 is a stylistic device meaning "one" or "anyone"—as it often is elsewhere in Paul's letters and in other Greek writings—and so is not to be read autobiographically but rather refers to anyone apart from Christ (*Römer 7 und die Bekehrung des Paulus* [Leipzig: Hinrichs, 1928]). And in 1977 E. P. Sanders captured the day in arguing that the religion of the earlier rabbis quoted in the Talmud (i.e., the *Tannaim*) was not a legalistic system, but rather should be characterized by the expression "covenantal nomism" (cf. his *Paul and Palestinian Judaism*; see also my treatment of "The Piety of Hebraic Judaism" in *Paul, Apostle of Liberty*, 65-85, where earlier I coined the term "nomism" to describe the religion of the better representatives of Early Judaism). "Contemporary New Testament scholars," as Beverly Gaventa points out, "almost universally reject the notion that Paul describes his own conversion here [in Rom 7:7-25]"; in fact, "there is near consensus at this one point: Romans 7 does not provide information about the conversion of Paul" (*From Darkness into Light: Aspects of Conversion in the New Testament* [Philadelphia: Fortress, 1986], 34). So we are properly warned "to be extremely wary of interpretations of Paul that contend that while still a persecutor, he experienced some prolonged period of personal questioning, of either a theological or a moral nature" (*ibid.*, 36).

Paul's own recollections of his pre-conversion experience speak of his impeccable hebraic ancestry, his "extreme zeal" for his ancestral traditions, and his being "blameless" in his worship of God and lifestyle (cf. Gal 1:14; Phil 3:5-6)—with the additional word found in 1 Tim 1:13 (whether by Paul himself, a companion who served as an amanuensis or co-author, or a later Paulinist) that his persecution was done "in ignorance and unbelief." But he does not give even a hint in any of his recollections of his past pre-conversion experience of any theological uncertainty or moral frustration. Rather, it seems that what motivated Saul of Tarsus to persecute early believers in Jesus was his firm commitment to the Jewish religion and his wholehearted acceptance of the Pharisaic interpretation of Israel's faith (cf. my *Paul, Apostle of Liberty*, 86-105, *passim*).

To a great extent, Saul's persecution of Christians must be judged to have been impelled by his Jewish understanding of the Messiah—or, what might be called his "pre-conversion messianology" or "christology." For in addition to being *theocentric* in orientation (that is, focusing on God, who had expressed redemption for his people preeminently in the Exodus) and *nomistic* in lifestyle (that is, observing the law in response to what God had done in establishing his covenant with Israel and redeeming his people from Egyptian bondage, and not, as all-too-often supposed, keeping God's commands in order to gain merit), Saul awaited with eager anticipation "the Coming One" who would be God's "Anointed One"—that is, "the Messiah." He may therefore be seen as having been deeply disturbed by the fragmentation of loyalties that was taking place within the nation because of the rise of a new messianic movement that looked to Jesus of Nazareth as the Messiah.

From his perspective, those who believed in Jesus of Nazareth as God's promised Messiah were terribly mistaken. They were, in fact, sinful, and in their sin were leading many Jews astray. And while such deviant thinking might be allowed for individuals, for early Judaism honored more "orthopraxis" (right living) rather than always "orthodoxy" (right thinking), it could not be tolerated as a movement within the nation—particularly at a time when messianic expectations where high. Joseph Klausner has pointed out that the common view among Pharisees of that day was that "sins cannot completely frustrate the [coming eschatological] redemption; but they can delay it" (*The Messianic Idea in Israel*, trans. W. F. Stinespring [London: Allen & Unwin, 1956], 404). So in days of "Messianic Travail" when the time for the appearance of the Messiah seemed to be drawing close, every effort must be expended to thwart apostasy and to unite the people in a common response to God. Even violent action may have been justified in Saul's mind by such precedents as Moses' order to kill all of the idolatrous and immoral Israelites at Shittim (cf. Num 25:1-5), Phinehas's killing of an immoral Israelite man and Midianite woman in the plains of Moab (cf. Num 25:6-15), and the actions of Mattathias and the Hasidim in rooting out apostasy among the people at the start of the Maccabean rebellion (cf. 1 Macc 2:23-28, 42-48)—perhaps also by the exhortation of 2 Maccabees 6:13: "It is a mark of great kindness when the impious are not let alone for a long time, but punished at once."

The Scandal of the Cross

More particularly, it seems that what repelled Saul most with respect to Jesus of Nazareth—and what ultimately compelled him to act against those who continued to follow Jesus even after his death—was what he later speaks about in Gal 5:11 as "the scandal of the cross" (cf. also 1 Cor 1:23): that an acclaimed Jewish Messiah should have been put to death by crucifixion on a Roman cross. For Deut 21:23 plainly declares that God's curse resides on "anyone who is hung on a tree." This verse originally had reference to the exposure of a criminal executed for a capital offense, whose dead body was hung on a tree for public ridicule. But it came to be viewed by Jews as also referring to the impalement or crucifixion of a living person on a pole or a cross (both a pole and a cross being parts of a tree).

The early Christians and Paul later resolved this problem by viewing God's curse of Christ as "an exchange curse"—that is, a curse that Christ bore on behalf of humanity in exchange for which humanity is offered the righteousness of God by being united with Christ (cf. 2 Cor 5:21; Gal 3:13). Morna D. Hooker has dealt extensively with this concept, most recently and popularly in her *Not Ashamed of the Gospel* (Grand Rapids: Eerdmans, 1994). But before his encounter by Christ on the Damascus road, Saul of Tarsus undoubtedly shared his Jewish compatriots' repugnance to the idea of a crucified Messiah, as suggested by the way in which he nuances his references to that "scandal." And so, again it may be said, his opposition to any messianic claims for Jesus of Nazareth and his persecution of those who would make such a claim were essentially based on his "pre-conversion messianology."

2. The Nature of Paul's Conversion

Much of the hesitancy of scholars to speak about Paul's conversion stems from (1) the brevity and diverse contexts of Paul's own references to his conversion, (2) suspicions about the accuracy of the portrayals of his conversion in Acts 9, 22 and 26, particularly when compared to the apostle's own statements but also when comparisons are made between the three accounts themselves, and (3) the difficulty of developing a general definition of conversion and then applying that definition to Paul's experience, for he speaks of that event in ways that are not always compatible with our standard definitions and reflects a consciousness of having never left his ancestral faith. Nonetheless, as Alan Segal rightly maintains, "Conversion is an appropriate term for discussing Paul's religious experience, although Paul did not himself use it" (*Paul the Convert: The Apostolate and Apostasy of Saul the Pharisee* [New Haven: Yale University Press, 1990], 72).

Paul's Own References
As Beverly Gaventa has pointed out regarding Paul's own references to what might be called his conversion experience: "Paul tells us very little about himself. Paul is not self-preoccupied, self-reflective, intro-spective, or narcissistic" (*Darkness into Light*, 20; citing J. Christiaan Beker, *Paul the Apostle: The Triumph of God in Life and Thought* [Philadelphia: Fortress, 1980], 3-5, who builds on Krister Stendahl's "Call Rather Than Conversion," in *Paul among Jews and Gentiles and Other Essays* [Philadelphia: Fortress, 1976]). In fact, Paul refers to his own experience only in contexts where he deals with other issues—that is, in defending the gospel that he proclaimed to his Gentile converts in Gal 1:13-17; in countering certain "supra-spiritual" believers who were evidently attempting to denigrate him in 1 Cor 9:1 and 15:8-10; and in rebutting certain Jewish Christians who were trying to "judaize" his converts in Phil 3:4-11.

Yet even in those brief, allusive references, Paul sets out the essen-tial features of what can legitimately be called a conversion experience: (1) He had personally "seen Jesus our Lord" (1 Cor 9:1). (2) What he saw was on a par with all of Jesus' other post-resurrection appearances, whether to Peter and "the Twelve," as referred to in the early confessional portion quoted in 1 Cor 15:3b-5, or to five hundred other believers at one time, to James, and to all the other apostles, as he enumerates in 15:6-7—even though that appearance was highly usual because of his own spiritual condition (i.e., even though he was a spiritual "abortion," as he characterizes his conversion in 1 Cor 15:8). (3) What he experienced was of the nature of a revelation (Gal 1:11-12, 16a). (4) Jesus Christ was the agent of that revelation (Gal 1:12, understanding Ἰησοῦ Χριστοῦ as a subjective genitive). (5) The content of that revelation was "his [God's] Son," who was also the agent of the revelation (Gal 1:16b). (6) The ultimate purpose of that revelation was "so that I might preach him [God's Son] among the Gentiles" (Gal 1:16c). And (7) Christ's appearance to him had a revolutionary effect on his life, so that he came to consider "everything [particularly his past Jewish credentials and accomplishments] a loss compared to the surpassing greatness of knowing Christ Jesus my Lord" and to focus only on "knowing Christ," with all that such a consuming passion involved (Phil 3:7-11).

Paul's few references to his own experience make no use of such terms as "repentance" (μετάνοια) or "turning/conversion" (ἐπιστροφή), as one might expect in a conversion account—though he uses the verbs "to turn around/convert" (ἐπιστρέφειν) and "to believe" (πιστεύειν) with respect to the reception of the gospel by others (cf. 2 Cor 3:15-16; 1 Thess 1:9-10; conversely Gal 4:8-9) and the verb "to be transformed" (μεταμορφοῦσθαι) in admonition of believers (Rom 12:1-2). Rather, by saying in Gal 1:15 that "God set me apart from my mother's womb" (ὁ θεὸς ἀφορίσας με ἐκ κοιλίας μητρός μου) and "called me by his grace" (καλέσας διὰ τῆς χάριτος αὐτοῦ), he appears to lay all of the import of that experience on being called to a particular service—that is, his Gentile ministry—which he seemingly compares to the call of the prophets of Old Testament times (cf. Jer 1:5) and the Isaian Servant of Yahweh (cf. Isa 49:1-6). But Paul's language regarding his conversion, it needs to be recognized, was neither as precise nor as restrictive as our modern definitions seem to require. His reference in 1 Cor 1:26 to the conversion of believers at Corinth, for example, is expressed in terms of their being "called": "For consider your call (τὴν κλῆσιν ὑμῶν), brothers and sisters (ἀδελφοί), because not many of you were wise by human standards; not many were influential; not many were of noble birth, etc."

Likewise, in Paul's own references to his conversion there is no mention of a trip to Damascus in order to persecute followers of Jesus (though a later trip to Damascus as a Christian is spoken about in 2 Cor 11:32 and Gal 1:17) and no narrative detailing what took place on the way, as in Acts. No light, no voice, no companions, no blindness, and no Ananias to interpret the significance of it all. But there is certainly an impression given in the dramatic shift depicted in both Gal 1:13-17 and Phil 3:4-11—that is, from a description of his earlier life to an immediate portrayal of his present stance—that what Paul experienced in that event was a change of commitment, values and identity that was sudden and unexpected.

Portrayals in Acts

There are three accounts of Paul's conversion in Acts, in chapters 9, 22 and 26. That may seem a trivial matter to note, but it is actually highly significant. For, as Ernst Haenchen observes: "Luke employs such repetitions only when he considers something to be extraordinarily important and wishes to impress it unforgettably on the reader. That is the case here" (*The Acts of the Apostles*, trans. R. McL. Wilson [Philadelphia: Westminster, 1971], 327).

Source criticism has had a field day with these accounts, often attributing the repetitions to a plurality of sources and the differences to divergent perspectives among those sources. The differences between the three accounts, of course, are notorious, with such questions as the following being repeatedly asked: Who heard the voice? Who saw the light? What did the heavenly voice say? Was Saul's conversion an objective or a subjective experience? How did he learn of his future ministry to Gentiles, and to what extent was that ministry revealed to him? Likewise, there are differences between Paul's allusive references and Luke's explicit accounts, as we have noted above. The materials are impossible to harmonize completely. Yet taking into consideration the redactional purposes of both Paul in his letters and Luke in his portrayals, it is possible to understand why certain matters were included and other matters omitted in their respective presentations (cf. my Acts commentary, *loc. cit.*).

Most important to note, however, is the fact that in all three of his accounts, Luke makes one dominant point: that Christ was the one who brought about the change in the strategy of divine redemption that occurred in Paul's Gentile ministry—that is, that it was not a plan Paul thought up or a program given him by another; rather, it was instigated by a commission that came directly from the risen Christ (just as Christ had commissioned the Eleven for their ministries in Acts 1:4-8). Therefore Luke emphasizes the miraculous circumstances of Saul's conversion and the supernatural nature of his call. And with that point, though with variations in spelling out the details, Paul was in full agreement.

Definitions and Applications

What, then, should we call what Paul experienced? Certainly it involved a "paradigm shift" in his life and thought—that is, a different way of looking at what he had previously known, a different set of questions than he had previously asked, and a different way of evaluating all that he had previously accepted. It could, therefore, be called simply an "alternation" (i.e., a shift in perspective and practice, without distancing oneself from one's past) or perhaps a "transformation" (i.e., a new perception and a marked change in outward form or appearance, but not necessarily a break with the past). For now he viewed everything from the perspective of fulfilled messianism, with Jesus of Nazareth being identified as Israel's Messiah and the realization of the nation's ancestral hopes. Now having received a revelation from God, he could no longer live or think only in the old ways. The revelation of "his Son in me" had taken precedence over all that he had previously ever experienced or contemplated.

Yet the grammatical counterpoint between *formerly* a persecutor of "the church of God" but *now* a persecuted teacher of "the faith he once tried to destroy" (1 Cor 15:9-11; Gal 1:13-17, 23, and Phil 3:6-7) indicates quite clearly, as Alan Segal has rightly insisted, that Paul's own self-consciousness was that of having undergone a conversion (cf. his *Paul the Convert*, 117). Admittedly, at a time when Christianity was not yet defined as being different from Judaism, Paul had no desire to disassociate himself from his ancestral faith. Rather, viewing commitment to Jesus as the fulfillment of his people's ancient expectations, he thought of his post-Damascus stance as being in direct accord with the ancient promises of God (cf. Gal 3:6-18; 4:21-31; Rom 9:6–10:33) and of his relationship to his nation as that of being part of the "remnant" or "elect" of Israel (cf. Rom 9:6; 11:1-10). Still, in that his own self-consciousness and sense of identity had been radically altered by Christ's encounter on the road to Damascus, Paul can properly be understood as having experienced a conversion.

It was, in reality, a new commitment that Paul made when he responded affirmatively to Christ's encounter. It was a new identity that he took on as a follower of Christ. It may have been difficult for him to relinquish his ties with Pharisaism or to think of himself as anything other than a fulfilled Jew. The Jewish world of his day, however, seems to have been more perceptive than Paul in this regard, for they evidently recognized—even more clearly than he—that he had broken with the past.

In 2 Cor 11:24 there is the statement: "From the Jews five times I received forty lashes less one." Just where and when Paul received these lashings is uncertain. But there is no doubt that they were "synagogue whippings" or "stripes" that were administered by synagogue officials as a severe form of punishment for some type of serious deviation from Jewish thought or practice (cf. L. N. Dembitz, "Stripes," *JE*, 11.569-70). And there is no doubt that Paul viewed them as afflictions that he suffered as a "servant of Christ" and because of his witness for Christ (cf. the whole passage of 1 Cor 11:23-29).

2 Cor 11:24, in fact, speaks quite dramatically of how reticent Paul was to separate himself from his Jewish past and how far he would go in being "to those under the law as one under the law" (1 Cor 9:20). But it also suggests how the Jewish world, even at such an early time, viewed his commitment to Jesus, and how for them that commitment was *anathema* to the Jewish religion (cf. 1 Thess 2:14). Likewise, Acts depicts how Paul attempted at various times to minister in Diaspora synagogues, but how he was repeatedly opposed by Jews and forced to leave those synagogues—often even forced to leave the respective cities and areas as well—if he wanted to continue to express his new identity as a missionary of Jesus Christ (cf. Acts 9:20-25, 28-30; 13:14-51; 14:1-7, 19-20).

The principal factor when one deals with conversion is that of one's identity. Paul never forgot his Jewish past or his Jewish training, and emotionally he still identified with his Jewish compatriots (cf. Rom 9:1-5; 10:1-2). A great deal of his past, in fact, he brought into his new experience. But while Paul carried over into Christianity much of what he learned in Judaism, "he inverts the values of his past in a way that is consonant with his new commitments" (Segal, *Paul the Convert*, 125). And chief among those new commitments was his commitment to Jesus as Israel's Messiah—from which, then, sprang his new identity as being no longer simply a Jewish Pharisee or even a fulfilled Jew, but a "Christ follower" or "Christian" (cf. the parallel consciousness reflected in the use of "Christian" in Acts 11:26; 26:28; 1 Pet 4:16).

3. *Immediate Christological Implications*

All that he learned and experienced in Judaism was considered by Paul, in one way or another, to have been important, for he seems to have viewed it all as a pre-stage for his Christian life, thought and ministry. But his conversion, which he characterized as God's revelation of "his Son in me" (Gal 1:16), was, as James S. Stewart rightly identified it, "far and away the most vital and formative influence of Paul's life" (*A Man in Christ: The Vital Elements of St Paul's Religion* [London: Hodder & Stoughton, 1935], 82).

Like the first disciples, who began from their Easter experience and viewed everything from the standpoint of that historical and existential occasion, Paul looked back on his former hopes, life and thought in the light of Christ's encounter, and from that perspective (1) affirmed everything that the earliest believers held to be true about Jesus, (2) transposed some of their statements into language that would be more meaningful for Gentiles, and (3) developed his own distinctive christological proclamation. The straining of his ancestral faith had suddenly given way to realization and fulfillment, as is most readily seen in his affirmation, transposition, and development of the early church's christology.

Reaffirmed Theocentricity

As a Jew, Paul well knew that it is the God of holy Scripture, the One who is both Creator and Redeemer, who alone is to be credited as the initiator, sustainer, and final agent of human redemption. What took place in Paul's conversion, therefore, was not a setting aside of God in favor of Jesus, as though espousing a "Unitarianism of the Second Person" or a "Jesus Only" theology. Rather, what occurred was an overwhelming realization that God's salvific purposes for both creation in general and humanity in particular are now to be understood as focused in the work and person of Jesus of Nazareth. Thus in words undoubtedly drawn from some of the church's early confessions (for the delineation and use of early Christian confessional materials, see my *New Wine into Fresh Wineskins: Contextualizing the Early Christian Confessions* [Peabody: Hendrickson, 1999]), Paul affirms the basic theocentricity of the Christian gospel: (1) that Christ's redemptive work was "according to the will of our God and Father" (Gal 1:4); (2) that "God sent his Son" (Gal 4:4-5); (3) that "God was in Christ reconciling the world to himself" (2 Cor 5:19); (4) that believers are "being justified freely by his [God's] grace" (Rom 3:24); (5) that "God presented him [Christ] as a sacrifice of atonement" (Rom 3:25); (6) that it is God who shows "justice," is himself "just," and "justifies sinners"

(Rom 3:26); (7) that "God exalted him [Jesus Christ] ... and gave him the name that is above every name" (Phil 2:9); (8) that the worship of Jesus and the confession "Jesus Christ is Lord" are "to the glory of God the Father" (Phil 2:10-11); and (9) that "God was pleased to have all his fullness dwell in him [Christ], and through him to reconcile all things to himself" (Col 1:19-20).

Messiah / Son of God / Lord

Understanding that God's redemptive purposes are now to be seen as focused in Jesus, the most immediate implication of Paul's conversion was the conviction that "Jesus is Israel's Messiah ['the Christ']," who acted as God's agent in inaugurating the Messianic Age and bringing about divine redemption. Most often, of course, Paul used the Greek term Χριστός as a proper name and not a title (which is a phenomenon we will speak about more fully later). Yet there are a number of places in his letters where his reference to Christ reflects a Jewish understanding of messiahship. Most clearly such a titular usage comes to the fore in Rom 9:5, where, at the conclusion of a list of Israel's advantages, he says: "From them [the people of Israel] comes the Christ [the Messiah], according to the flesh."

Connected with the theme of Jesus as the Messiah is the theme of Jesus as the Son of God. Many early comparative religionists have claimed that "Son of God" was an alien import into the New Testament, being derived from polytheistic notions that were then circulating in the hellenistic world. But with its appearance in some of the writings of Second Temple Judaism that express their authors' messianic expectations—in particular, in *1 Enoch* 105:2; *4QFlorilegium* on 2 Sam 7:14; and *4 Ezra* 7:28-29; 13:32, 37, 52; 14:9 (all of which may be roughly dated between 200 BCE and 100 CE)—the title "Son of God" when used of Jesus in the New Testament is today being viewed in a more Jewish and functional manner to denote Jesus' unique relationship with God and his obedience to the Father's will. For just as Israel was understood to be uniquely God's "son" (or, "child") among all the peoples of the earth and Israel's anointed king to be in a special manner God's "son"—with both the nation and its king pledged to a relationship with God of loving obedience—so Jesus, who exemplified obedience to God in an unparalleled manner, was seen to be the Son of God *par excellence*.

Sixteen times in his letters Paul speaks of Christ as God's Son: three times as "Son of God" (Rom 1:4; 2 Cor 1:19; Gal 2:20); twice as "the Son" (1 Cor 15:28; Col 1:13); and eleven times as "his Son" (Rom 1:3, 9; 5:10; 8:3, 29, 32; 1 Cor 1:9; Gal 1:16; 4:4-6 [twice]; 1 Thess 1:10). Four times his reference to Christ as God's Son appears in a quoted confessional portion (i.e., Rom 1:3-4 [twice]; Gal 4:4-6 [twice]); once in a traditional eschatological climax (i.e., 1 Thess 1:10); and at other times in polemical contexts (e.g., Gal 1:16; 2:20)—all of which seems to suggest that not only did Paul use "Son" with regard to Christ relatively infrequently (as compared to its use elsewhere in the New Testament), but also that his use of that title was fairly traditional and often quite circumstantial.

An additional immediate result of Paul's conversion was that he came to affirm the lordship of Jesus. The preaching of Jesus' earliest disciples had made this connection between "Christ" and "Lord," as Luke's report of Peter's exhortation at the close of his sermon on the Day of Pentecost evidences: "Therefore let all the house of Israel know assuredly that God has made him both Lord and Christ, this Jesus whom you crucified" (Acts 2:36). And Paul's quotation of various early Christian confessional statements that speak of the lordship of Christ testifies to his own acceptance of what the church was confessing about Jesus (cf., e.g., Rom 10:9; 1 Cor 12:3; 2 Cor 4:5; Phil 2:11; see also Col 2:6).

Thus in Luke's first account of Paul's conversion in Acts 9, the newly converted apostle is portrayed as almost immediately proclaiming in Damascus that "Jesus is the Christ" (v 22) and "Jesus is the Son of God" (v 20), and soon afterwards in Jerusalem as "speaking boldly in the name of the Lord" (v 28). Undoubtedly Paul's immediate perceptions and first attempts at preaching his new convictions were dominantly functional in nature—that is, with an emphasis on the supremacy of Jesus in the divine strategy of redemption and on what God had done redemptively through Jesus, as Peter is portrayed doing in his Pentecost sermon of Acts 2:14-36. And undoubtedly he called for a response of repentance and faith, as Peter did at the conclusion of his sermon in Acts 2:38-39. For both as a former Pharisee and a new believer in Jesus, Paul knew that being justified before God was not a matter of human endeavor, but that it had to do with a person's response of faith in God who has acted redemptively for his people (cf. Gal 2:15-16).

4. *Transposed Christological Language and Features*

As time went on after his conversion, however, certain ways of expressing those immediate christological convictions became, it seems, transposed—that is, became altered as to sequence or changed as to order, if we understand "transposed" in a literary fashion; though probably it is better to think along musical lines of a composition that is arranged or performed in a key other than originally written. Most obvious of these transpositions is the move in Paul's letters from the single name "Jesus" and the title "Christ" (or, "Messiah") to the use of "Christ" (or, in compound form, "Jesus Christ" or "Christ Jesus") as a proper name and an emphasis on "Lord" as the associated title. But there are other identifiable transpositions as well.

"Jesus is the Christ/Messiah" to "Christ is Lord"
In the four canonical Gospels, the use of the name "Jesus" is, by far, most common, usually with the article (ὁ Ἰησοῦς). Likewise, in Hebrews the common designation is "Jesus," which appears ten times (2:9; 3:1; 4:14; 6:20; 7:22; 10:19; 12:2, 24; 13:12, 20), as opposed to "Jesus Christ," which appears three times (10:10; 13:8, 21). And in the early Christian confessional portions quoted by Paul in his letters, the usual designation is also simply "Jesus"—as, for example, in Phil 2:10 ("that at the name of Jesus every knee should bow, in heaven and on earth and under the earth"); 1 Thess 4:14a ("that Jesus died and rose again"); Rom 10:9 ("that if you confess with your mouth 'Jesus is Lord'"); and 1 Cor 12:3 ("no one can say by the Spirit of God 'Jesus is cursed', and no one can say 'Jesus is Lord' except by the Holy Spirit"; cf. also Rom 3:26b; 1 Cor 11:23; 2 Cor 4:8-11, 14; 11:4; 1 Thess 1:10).

In Paul's letters, however, apart from the confessional material he quotes, "Jesus" is usually transposed into "Christ," "Christ Jesus," or "Jesus Christ." There are, of course, exceptions to this pattern. But often the exceptions are to be found in such portions as a traditional grace benediction at the close of his letters (cf. Rom 16:20; 1 Cor 16:23), a traditionally conditioned doxological statement (cf. 1 Thess 3:11, 13), a comment on confessional material previously quoted (cf. 1 Thess 4:14b), a reference to something historical, such as Jesus' afflictions, death and resurrection or Paul's own conversion (cf. Rom 4:24; 1 Cor 9:1; 2 Cor 4:10, 14; Gal 6:17; 1 Thess 2:15), or in roughly parallel statements, with "Jesus" and "Christ" (or "Christ Jesus"/"Jesus Christ") appearing in the parallelism as equivalent names (cf. Rom 8:11; Eph 4:20-21; also 2 Thess 1:12). Only a handful of other exceptions can be cited—such as in Rom 14:14; 1 Cor 5:4 (twice); 2 Cor 1:14; 11:31; Eph 1:15; Phil 2:19; Col 3:17; 1 Thess 4:1, 2; 2 Thess 1:7, 8; 2:8; and Philem 5. The use of the single name "Jesus" in Paul's letters, therefore, while not scorned by the apostle, must be seen as being exceptional in comparison to his much more abundant use of the name "Christ," "Christ Jesus," or "Jesus Christ."

Likewise, Paul's frequent reference to Christ as "Lord" should be seen as something of a transposition on his part. For while the early church confessed that "Jesus is Lord" (e.g., Acts 2:36; Rom 10:9; 1 Cor 12:3), it is in Paul's letters that the title "Lord" receives particular prominence and that the lordship of Christ resounds in a higher key and with greater explication. The situation is somewhat comparable to Luke's use of "Lord" for Jesus in his Gospel (forty-two times) vis-à-vis the christological use of that title in Mark (four times) and Matthew (nineteen times)—also to Luke's use of the synonym "Master" (ἐπιστάτης) on the lips of the disciples in addressing Jesus in his Gospel (seven times) and his use of "Lord" in his Acts (fifty-three times, though since "Lord" is used in Acts for both God and Jesus it is sometimes difficult to determine when it specifically refers to Jesus).

Why this transposition of name and title in Paul's letters? Probably it had much to do with the ways in which "Jesus," "Christ," and "Lord" were perceived by Gentiles living in the Greco-Roman world, whom Paul was attempting to evangelize. For the name Jesus, which carried a distinctly Jewish flavor, Paul probably thought it best to tone down such a Jewish nuance when addressing Gentiles by using Christ as a name, or the double name Christ Jesus or Jesus Christ. Further, the title Christ, which like the Jewish title Messiah means "anointed one," would likely have been understood by Gentiles to signify someone who had been medicinally anointed or rubbed with oil in preparation for an athletic contest. It may very well, in fact, not have suggested to them the significant notion of "God's Anointed One" or any idea of supremacy. The title Lord, by contrast, would certainly have conveyed to Gentiles the note of supremacy, needing then only clarification regarding the nature of that supremacy.

But any postulated rationale for such transpositions of name and title should also include Paul's own consciousness. For his relationship with Jesus had not been historical in nature, as was true of the earliest believers portrayed in the Gospels. Indeed, it was what can only be called supra-historical. It came about originally by means of a heavenly encounter at his conversion, it included various mystical experiences during the period of his Christian ministry (cf. 2 Cor 12:1-6; also Acts 22:17-21; 23:11), and it was nourished by continued personal communion between himself and his risen Lord. Further, his Christian understanding of all of the Jesus traditions that he quotes (e.g., 1 Cor 15:3b-5; 1 Thess 4:1-9; Phil 2:6-11) and all of the Jesus narrative substructure that he builds on in his letters (e.g., 2 Cor 1:5; 4:10; 5:14; 8:9; 10:1; Gal 1:4; 3:1, 13; 4:4-5) was probably mediated to him through the church's leading figures (e.g., Peter and James, as referred to in Gal 1:18-20) and the church's confessions. Thus the title "Lord" would have been more appropriate in his own consciousness, with "Christ" retained but used by Paul mostly as a name.

Other Identifiable Transpositions

Other christological images and titles used by Jewish Christians could also be cited as having been transposed by Paul in his Gentile mission (cf. the discussion of "Distinctive Imagery and Motifs" in my *Christology of Early Jewish Christianity*, 25-62; also note some of the titles spelled out under the caption "Messiahship and Its Implications," *ibid.*, 63-119). Representative of such christological ascriptions is the title "God's Salvation," "Israel's Salvation," or simply "The Salvation," which was used in messianic fashion by Jews during the Second Temple period (cf. *Jubilees* 31:19; *1 QIs^a* 51.4-5; *1QH* 7.18-19; *CDC* 20:20 [9.43]; 20:34 [9.54]; also note the rabbinic tractate *b. Berakoth* 56b-57a) and is reflected in some of the materials of the New Testament (cf. Luke 1:69, 71, 77; 2:30; 3:6; John 4:22; Acts 4:12). Paul, however, seems to have transposed that ancient title by speaking of "the Lord Jesus Christ" as "Savior" (Phil 3:20; cf. Eph 5:23; 2 Tim 1:10; Tit 1:4; 2:13; 3:6; Acts 13:23). It may also be argued that he transposed the christological image "Son of man," which appears extensively in the Gospels (cf. also Acts 7:56; Rev 1:13; 14:14), into a "Second Adam" typology or a "Son of God" ascription. But I doubt the validity of both those latter views.

More to the point is the transposition that seems to take place in Paul's shift from the theme of Jesus' obedience, which appears prominently elsewhere in the New Testament (especially in the confessional materials that he quotes, as well as in Matthew's Gospel and the Epistle to the Hebrews), to his use of the expression πίστις Χριστοῦ, which appears to be the dominant way in which he highlights that obedience (cf. my article on "The Foundational Conviction of New Testament Christology"). The expression is admittedly difficult, as witness the extensive discussion currently taking place as to its meaning. But when Χριστοῦ is read as a subjective genitive and πίστις is understood in terms of the Hebrew word אֱמוּנָה, which means both "faith" and "faithfulness," then it is not too difficult to view Paul as talking about "the faith" or "faithfulness of Christ" in Rom 3:22; Gal 2:16 (twice); 3:22; Eph 3:22, and Phil 3:9 (cf. also Gal 3:26 in P[46]) in much the same way as he speaks about "the faithfulness of God" in Rom 3:3 and "the faith of Abraham" in Rom 4:16.

That Paul found this expression already rooted in the vocabulary of early Jewish Christianity can be argued from the appearance of the phrase ἐκ πίστεως Ἰησοῦ at the conclusion of the quoted material in Rom 3:24-26. And that Paul also, at least once, spoke directly of Christ's "obedience" (ὑπακοή) can be seen by reference to Rom 5:19. But his more usual way of speaking of Christ's obedience was, it seems, by the use of the expression "the faith" or "faithfulness of Christ" (πίστις Χριστοῦ), thereby transposing that theme into another key. And so by transposing the theme in this manner, he was, it appears, able to set up a parallel between (1) the objective basis of the Christian gospel, that is, Christ's "faith" or "faithfulness," understood as his perfect response of obedience to God the Father, both actively in his life and passively in his death, and (2) the subjective response of "faith" that is required of all human beings whom God reconciles to himself through the work of Christ.

5. *Distinctive Christological Proclamation*

In addition to his affirmation of the early church's acclaim of Jesus and his transposition of some of the ways in which that acclaim took form, Paul also can be said to have developed certain distinctive christological emphases. Some of the nuancing of these emphases may be credited to the catalyst of his Gentile mission, for he needed to make his preaching not only understandable but also relevant to his Gentile audiences. In the main, however, it seems that many of the distinctive christological features in Paul's proclamation were rooted primarily in his conversion experience and developed by means of his own reflection on that experience.

Paul's letter to Christians at Rome provides us with an excellent source for identifying some of the particularly significant and distinctive features of his proclamation. For not only is Romans the longest, most systematic, and least overtly polemical writing among the apostle's extant letters, it also—and more importantly for our present purposes—(1) addresses Gentile believers whom Paul had not evangelized and probably never met, (2) tells them in the opening thanksgiving section that he wants to include them among his converts and to give them a "spiritual gift" (χάρισμα πνευματικόν) in order to make them strong, implying that in so doing he was giving them the essence of what he had been proclaiming to all Gentiles throughout his missionary activities (1:11-15), and (3) speaks in an early part of the letter and its concluding doxology of what he was presenting to them as being "my gospel" (2:16; 16:25), thereby suggesting that it was something fairly distinctive that he was giving them. But while Romans may be declared to be an excellent source of material for our purposes, it must also be admitted that the letter is extremely difficult to analyze, with numerous proposals being offered today for most of the major issues of provenance and interpretation.

My own understanding of the issues involved—which, of course, informs my interpretation here, but must await a forthcoming commentary to explicate—includes two important points. First, that the addressees, while ethnically both Jews and Gentiles, were predominantly Gentile believers in Jesus who (1) had been evangelized by Jewish believers from Jerusalem, (2) continued to look to the Jerusalem church for inspiration and guidance, and (3) "kept up some Jewish observances and remained faithful to part of the heritage of the Jewish Law and cult, without insisting on circumcision" (to quote R. E. Brown, *Antioch and Rome: New Testament Cradles of Catholic Christianity* [New York, Toronto: Paulist Press, 1983], 104, whose thesis J. A. Fitzmyer has agreed with in his *Romans* [New York: Doubleday, 1993], 33-34, though without drawing out the hermeneutical implications of such a position). Second, that Paul's primary purposes in writing were (1) to give Christians at Rome, whom he had not evangelized and did not know personally, but who as mainly Gentiles ethnically were within the orbit of his Gentile mission, teaching that he considered to be uniquely his, which he characterizes as his "spiritual gift" to them (cf. 1:11-15; 15:15-18), and (2) to seek their assistance for his proposed ministry to the western regions of the Roman empire (cf.

1:10b, 13; 15:23-32)—with the setting out of "my gospel," as he calls it in 2:16 and 16:25, meant not only to prepare them for his coming, but also so that they might understand and appreciate what he is preaching in his ministry to Gentiles.

He may, of course, have had other reasons for writing as well, which many scholars have found by means of "mirror reading" such passages as 14:1–15:13 (on "the strong" and "the weak"), 13:1-7 (on a Christian's relations with civil governments and on paying taxes), and 16:17-19 (on those who cause divisions and set up obstacles in the church). Perhaps he also wanted to correct certain misconceptions circulating at Rome about him and his ministry, as well as counter accusations against him in the empire's capital city. All of these matters need further investigation and explication in a full-blown commentary. All I want to signal here is that in this chapter I am working from a particular understanding of the letter's addressees and a particular understanding of Paul's primary purposes in writing, as indicated in the paragraph above.

An additional problem that confronts interpreters of Romans, and one that is of pertinence for our discussion here, is the rather decided difference that exists between the first major section of the letter, that is 1:16–4:25 (or wherever the body of the letter begins, whether at 1:13, 1:16 or 1:18), and the second major section, that is 5:1–8:39 (or possibly 5:12–8:39, with 5:1-11 being a hinge section between the two). For whereas 1:16–4:25 contains some fifteen to eighteen biblical quotations located at eight or nine places, biblical quotations in 5:1–8:39 are notoriously lacking (only at 7:7, used illustratively, and at 8:36, within a quoted confessional portion). Further, these two sections seem fairly different in their overall presentations. For 1:16–4:25 is quite Jewish in its vocabulary, rhetoric and argumentation—with those same Jewish features carried on in the third section of 9:1–11:36—but 5:1–8:39 is seemingly devoid of distinctly Jewish features and given over more to the universal themes of "death," "life," "peace," and "reconciliation" and to such distinctive emphases as being "in Christ" and being "in the Spirit."

Perhaps the differences between 1:16–4:25 and 5:1–8:39 should be seen as supporting the thesis that chapters 1–11 of Romans contain two Pauline sermons: one to a Jewish audience, which was originally made up of material now in chapters 1–4 and 9–11 but whose parts have somehow become separated; the other to a Gentile audience, which is represented in chapters 5–8 (as proposed by R. Scroggs, "Paul as Rhetorician: Two Homilies in Romans 1-11," in *Jews, Greeks, and Christians (Festschrift* W. D. Davies), ed. R. Hammerton-Kelly and R. Scroggs [Leiden: Brill, 1976], 271-98). More likely, however, is the view that in 5:1–8:39 Paul is presenting what he spoke of in the thanksgiving section of the letter as his "spiritual gift" to his Roman addressees, which was being given for their strengthening (1:11)—that is, the form of the gospel that he customarily proclaimed within his Gentile mission, which in the concluding doxology he calls "my gospel" (16:25; cf. also 2:16).

Approaching the relationship of chapters 1–4 and 5–8 from the perspective of this latter thesis, 1:16–4:25 can be seen as the type of proclamation that Paul knew was held in common by all Jewish believers in Jesus—including, as well, Gentile believers who traced their origins back to the Jerusalem church and who looked to Jerusalem Christianity for their inspiration and support. That form of Christian proclamation, it may be posited from 1:16-17 and 3:21-26, laid great stress on such Jewish concepts as "the righteousness of God," "the witness of the law and the prophets," "justification," "redemption," and "expiation/propitiation," seeking only to focus attention on Jesus as Israel's Messiah and on faith as one's proper response to God—features that both Jewish Christians and Paul believed were inherent in Israel's religion (cf. Gal 2:15-16). It proclaimed the fulfillment of God's promise to Abraham in Jesus' ministry and the church's message, honored the Mosaic law as the God-ordained "pedagogue" for the nation Israel, cherished the traditions of the Jerusalem church, and supported its proclamation by a christocentric reading of holy Scripture.

With this form of Christian proclamation Paul was thoroughly in agreement, and so he begins Romans with a section that presents his agreements with his addressees (i.e., 1:16–4:25) before then going on to set out his distinctive message (i.e., 5:1–8:39). By way of comparison, it may be noted that Paul did something similar in his letter to the Galatians, presenting in his proposition statement of Gal 2:15-21 (the *propositio*) first the points on which he and his addressees agreed (i.e., vv 15-16, which are spelled out in 3:1-18) and then the points on which they differed (i.e., vv 17-20, which are spelled out in 3:19– 4:11), with a summary of the issues involved appended (i.e., v 21). And probably

Paul often preached the gospel in the manner he does in 1:16–4:25 when the occasion demanded, particularly before a Jewish audience.

In Rom 5:1–8:39, however, it may be claimed, Paul details the distinctive features of the gospel that he proclaimed in his Gentile mission, to those who had no Jewish heritage and no biblical instruction. The material in 5:1-11 may be seen either as a thesis statement for what follows in 5:12–8:39 or as a hinge between chapters 1–4 and 5–11—or, in fact, as both. But what seems evident is that in 5:12-21 Paul lays out before his predominantly Gentile Christian addressees what could be called a "new constitutive story" that has universal dimensions, as opposed to the more limited story of redemption from bondage in Egypt that Jews held as being central. Paul's constitutive story speaks of (1) sin coming into the world through "one man," (2) death and its effects reigning over all people, but (3) grace and life being available to everyone "through Jesus Christ our Lord." And throughout 5:1–8:39 Paul highlights, in explication of this more universal narrative of the human situation and God's salvific action, such matters as "peace with God," "reconciliation" with God and others, deliverance from sin and death, being "in Christ," being "in the Spirit," and being unable to be separated from "Christ's love," and so from God's love and protection.

Chapters 5–8 have frequently been viewed as the apex of Paul's argument in Romans. They deal with the central factors of human existence—that is, with sin, death, life, and relationship with God and others. These are matters that can, by analogy, be based on God's past dealings with Israel as recorded in Scripture. But they are also matters that, evidently, were not directly demonstrable to Gentiles by specific biblical texts. Nor, it seems, would such an approach have been meaningful or appreciated by Gentiles. Rather, Paul's emphases on "peace with God," "reconciliation," life "in Christ," life "in the Spirit," etc. (as in chapters 5–8) appear to have stemmed primarily from his conversion experience and his own reflections on the significance of that experience—with his practice in his Gentile mission being to present such matters without any necessary reference to the Jewish Scriptures.

Christ's confrontation of Paul, with all that went into the apostle's subsequent understanding of it, confirmed for him what the early Jewish believers in Jesus were proclaiming—which, of course, he also proclaimed (so Rom 1:16–4:25). In addition, however, it gave him a new understanding of (1) relationship with God, (2) relationships with others, and (3) the logistics for a Gentile mission (so Gal 1–2). Therefore in writing to Gentile Christians at Rome, who, it may be postulated, were largely dependent on the theology and traditions of the Jerusalem church, he speaks at the beginning of his letter as wanting to given them a "spiritual gift" (1:11) and refers at its closing to "my gospel" (16:25; see also 2:16). And in 5:1–8:39 he presents that spiritual gift and his gospel, which, we propose, turns out to be his own distinctive and developed christological proclamation that has to do with "death," "life," "peace," "reconciliation," being "in Christ," being "in the Spirit," and being unable to be separated from "the love of God that is in Christ Jesus our Lord."

6. *Is Paul's Conversion a Paradigm for Christian Experience?*

At least one further question, however, needs to be asked when we consider the impact of Paul's conversion on his view of Jesus: Did Paul understand his conversion experience to be a paradigm for the experience of every Christian? And if so, in what way and to what extent?

In 1 Cor 4:16 and Phil 3:17 Paul exhorts his converts: "Be imitators of me!" (συμμιμηταί μου γίνεσθε). His exhortation in 1 Corinthians has reference to the attitudes of his addressees toward their present life "in Christ Jesus" vis-à-vis their former lives, for now they are not to boast about their past attainments but to boast "in the Lord" (cf. 1 Cor 1:26-31). His exhortation in Philippians has also to do with a radical change of perspective, for now "having been taken hold of by Christ Jesus" his addressees are asked to follow Paul's example in counting everything from their past as garbage in comparison to "the surpassing greatness of knowing Christ Jesus [their] Lord" (cf. Phil 3:4-16). And in 1 Cor 11:1 and 2 Thess 3:7, 9 Paul asks his converts to imitate him in other matters as well (also in Gal 4:12 and Phil 4:9, though without the use of the term "imitate").

Further, in Gal 3:26-29 Paul says that those who have expressed "faith in Christ Jesus" and have been "united with Christ in baptism," and so in their conversion have been "clothed with Christ," have come into an entirely new relationship with God and with others. It is, as he spells it out in that passage, a relationship where one's identity is changed (i.e., now "children of God," those who "belong to Christ," and those who are truly "Abraham's seed" and "heirs according to the promise") and where social relationships are altered, with judgments no longer to be made on the basis of traditional human categories but on the basis of new redemptive categories (i.e., now "no longer Jew or Greek, slave or free, male and female, for you are all one in Christ Jesus").

As a result of his conversion, Paul's self-identity and thinking were dramatically changed. With respect to his understanding of Jesus of Nazareth, he saw him in an entirely new way, affirming as true all that the early church had claimed him to be: Israel's Messiah, the Son of God, and humanity's redemptive Lord. Also on the basis of his conversion—coupled with his own reflections on that experience and the needs of his Gentile mission—Paul came to transpose some of the language of those early affirmations and to develop his own distinctive christological proclamation.

But Paul's conversion experience is never portrayed as a paradigm for Christian experience with respect to the specific details of that event, as those details are narrated in Luke's Acts. He never, for example, asks his converts to travel a "road to Damascus," either actually or metaphorically; nor to consider their conversion legitimate only if they had been the recipients of a "heavenly vision"; nor to view ecstatic "visions and revelations from the Lord," which were part of his own experience, as normative for the Christian life (cf. 2 Cor 12:1-13). Nonetheless, Paul does present his own conversion experience in his letters as paradigmatic for all Christians in terms of a radical reorientation of thought about Jesus and of life now lived "in Christ." Further, there is the suggestion of the need to follow his example in (1) transposing the gospel proclamation into forms more readily understandable and relevant for today, and (2) developing a distinctive proclamation that better explicates the truths of the gospel in various situations and to various audiences addressed. For, as seen in Paul's practice, contextualization of the gospel must always take place—both by way of transposing certain traditional features and by way of developing certain new significances, with those transpositions and developments being always in line with the testimony of Scripture and Christ's transforming and illuminating encounter.

SELECT BIBLIOGRAPHY

Boyarin, Daniel. *A Radical Jew: Paul and the Politics of Identity.* Berkeley: University of California Press, 1994.

Davies, W. D. *Paul and Rabbinic Judaism: Some Rabbinic Elements in Pauline Theology.* London: SPCK, 1948, 1955², 1970³; Philadelphia: Fortress, 1980⁴.

Dietzfelbinger, Christian. *Die Berufung des Paulus als Ursprung seiner Theologie.* WMANT, 58. Neukirchen–Vluyn: Neukirchener Verlag, 1985.

Donaldson, Terence L. "Zealot and Convert: The Origin of Paul's Christ–Torah Antithesis," *CBQ* 51 (1989) 655-82.

Gaventa, Beverly R. *From Darkness into Light: Aspects of Conversion in the New Testament.* Philadelphia: Fortress, 1986.

Dunn, James D. G. "The New Perspective on Paul," *BJRL* 65 (1983) 95-122.

_____. "'A Light to the Gentiles': The Significance of the Damascus Road Christophany for Paul," in *The Glory of Christ in the New Testament*, ed. L. D. Hurst and N. T. Wright. Oxford: Clarendon, 1987, 251-66.

_____. "How New was Paul's Gospel? The Problem of Continuity and Discontinuity," in *Gospel in Paul. Studies on Corinthians, Galatians and Romans for Richard N. Longenecker*, ed. L. A. Jervis and P. Richardson. Sheffield: Sheffield Academic Press, 1994, 367-88.

Hooker, Morna D. *Not Ashamed of the Gospel.* Grand Rapids: Eerdmans, 1994.

Hurtado, Larry W. "Convert, Apostate or Apostle to the Nations: The 'Conversion' of Paul in Recent Scholarship," *SR/SR* 22 (1993) 273-84.

Jeremias, Joachim. "The Key to Pauline Theology," *ExpT* 76 (1965) 27-30.

Kim, Seyoon. *The Origin of Paul's Gospel.* Tübingen: Mohr–Siebeck, 1981; Grand Rapids: Eerdmans, 1982.

Longenecker, Richard N. *Paul, Apostle of Liberty.* New York: Harper & Row, 1964; repr. Grand Rapids: Baker, 1976; repr. Vancouver: Regent College Publishing, 1993, 2003.

_____. *The Christology of Early Jewish Christianity.* London: SCM Press, 1970; repr. Grand Rapids: Baker, 1981; repr. Vancouver: Regent College Publishing, 2001.

_____. "The Nature of Paul's Early Eschatology," *NTS* 31 (1985) 85-95.

_____. "The Foundational Conviction of New Testament Christology: The Obedience/ Faithfulness / Sonship of Christ," in *Jesus of Nazareth: Lord and Christ. Essays on the Historical Jesus and New Testament Christology (Festschrift* I. H. Marshall), ed. J. B. Green and M. Turner. Carlisle: Paternoster; Grand Rapids: Eerdmans, 1994, 473-88.

_____. *New Wine into Fresh Wineskins: Contextualizing the Early Christian Confessions.* Peabody: Hendrickson, 1999.

Sanders, E. P. *Paul and Palestinian Judaism.* Philadelphia: Fortress, 1977.

Segal, Alan F. *Paul the Convert: The Apostolate and Apostasy of Saul the Pharisee.* New Haven, London: Yale University Press, 1990.

Stendahl, Krister. *Paul among Jews and Gentiles and Other Essays.* Philadelphia: Fortress, 1976.

2

PRAYER IN THE PAULINE LETTERS

The Acts of the Apostles portrays Paul as a man of prayer. As Paul's story in Acts begins, Ananias is told by God to go into Damascus and search out a man from Tarsus named Saul, "for he is praying" (9:11). Throughout his ministry as a Christian apostle, Paul is represented in Acts as praying frequently: when called by God at Syrian Antioch to begin his missionary journeys (13:2-3); when appointing elders in the newly established churches of Asia Minor (14:23); when thrown into a Roman dungeon at Philippi because of his Christian witness (16:25); when leaving Ephesus on his final journey to Jerusalem (20:36); and when healing Publius's father on the island of Malta (28:8). Further, when speaking to a rioting crowd from the steps of the Antonian · fortress in Jerusalem, Paul is depicted as saying that it was while he "was praying at the temple" that God told him to leave Jerusalem and go to the Gentiles (22:17). Indeed, throughout Luke's Gospel and Acts to be an apostle of Jesus, as was Paul—or, to be a follower of Jesus, as are all those who claim Christ's name—is to be a person of prayer, as was Jesus himself.

All of the reports of Paul praying in Acts, however, are second-hand reports, whatever might be thought about their accuracy. What is needed is an investigation of the Pauline letters themselves for reflections of the apostle's prayer life and the nature and content of his prayers. This is what we will endeavor to do in what follows, focusing on (1) the Pauline prayer vocabulary, (2) major methodological issues in dealing with the Pauline references to prayer, (3) the background of Paul's prayers, (4) the structure of Paul's prayers, (5) Paul's prayers of adoration, (6) Paul's prayers of thanksgiving, (7) Paul's prayers of petition, and (8) some significant features of Paul's prayers, with a concluding epilogue.

1. *The Pauline Prayer Vocabulary*

Terms having to do with prayer appear more frequently in Paul's letters than in the writings of any other New Testament author. Robert Morgenthaler's *Statistik des neutestamentlichen Wortschatzes* (Zürich, Frankfurt: Gotthelf, 1958) lists 16 words for prayer (see those cited in the following paragraphs), which occur some 133 times in the thirteen canonical Pauline letters. In comparison, Matthew has 8 of these words, which occur 60 times; Mark has 8 prayer words, which are used 32 times; Luke has 10 used 57 times; John has 3 used 15 times, Acts has 10 used 80 times; Hebrews has 7 used 18 times; while in the rest of the New Testament these explicit prayer terms appear 59 times. The place to begin any study of the prayers of Paul, therefore, is with a scanning of the apostle's prayer vocabulary.

Primary expressions for the adoration of God in the Pauline letters are "to bless" or "blessed" (εὐλογεῖν, εὐλογία, εὐλογητός; cf. Rom 1:25; 9:5; 1 Cor 14:16; 2 Cor 1:3; 11:31; Eph 1:3), "to praise" or "praise" (αἰνεῖν, ἐξομολογεῖν, ἔπαινος; cf. Rom 14:11; 15:9-11; Eph 1:6, 12, 14; Phil 1:11; 2:11), and "to worship" (προσκυνεῖν; 1 Cor 14:25). They occur in quotations of Scripture and in citations of early Christian hymns and confessions. More commonly, however, they appear in Paul's own statements with reference to prayers of adoration to God.

Paul's use of thanksgiving terminology in prayer contexts is also noteworthy. The verb "to give thanks" (εὐχαριστεῖν) appears twenty-four times (Rom 1:8, 21; 14:6 [twice]; 16:4; 1 Cor 1:4, 14; 10:30; 11:24; 14:17, 18; 2 Cor 1:11; Eph 1:6; 5:20; Phil 1:3; Col 1:3, 12; 3:17; 1 Thess 1:2; 2:13; 5:18; 2 Thess 1:3; 2:13; Philem 4), the noun "thanksgiving" (εὐχαριστία) appears twelve times (1 Cor 14:16; 2 Cor 4:15; 9:11, 12; Eph 5:4; Phil 4:6; Col 2:7; 4:2; 1 Thess 3:9; 1 Tim 2:1; 4:3, 4), and the adjective "thankful" (εὐχάριστος) used substantively appears once (Col 3:15). Further, when one takes into consideration the nine times that the noun "thanks" (χάρις) is used to signify gratitude to God (Rom 6:17; 7:25; 1 Cor 15:57; 2 Cor 2:14; 8:16; 9:15; Col 3:16; 1 Tim 1:12; 2 Tim 1:3), the total number of instances of thanksgiving vocabulary in the Pauline prayer materials comes to forty-six—with those instances being distributed fairly evenly throughout the Pauline corpus, except for Galatians and Titus.

Paul's usual expressions for intercessory prayer are (1) the verb "to pray" (προσεύχεσθαι), which appears seventeen times (Rom 8:26; 1 Cor 11:4, 5, 13; 14:14 [twice], 15 [twice]; Eph 6:18; Phil 1:9; Col 1:3, 9; 4:3; 1 Thess 5:17, 25; 2 Thess 1:11; 3:1), (2) the noun "prayer" (προσευχή), which appears fourteen times (Rom 1:10; 12:12; 15:30; 1 Cor 7:5; Eph 1:16; 6:18; Phil 4:6; Col 4:2, 12; 1 Thess 1:2; 1 Tim 2:1; 5:5; Philem 4, 22, (3) the noun "entreaty" or "request" (δέησις), which appears ten times (Rom 10:1; 2 Cor 1:11; 9:14; Eph 6:18; Phil 1:4, 19; 4:6; 1 Tim 2:1; 5:5; 2 Tim 1:3), and (4) the verb "to call upon" (ἐπικαλεῖν or παρακαλεῖν), which appears in prayer contexts seven times (Rom 10:12, 13, 14; 1 Cor 1:2; 2 Cor 1:23 [probably]; 12:8; 2 Tim 2:22). In several places non-prayer terms are also used in connection with prayers of petition—for example, the noun "mention" or "remembrance" (μνεία; cf. Rom 1:9; Eph 1:16; Phil 1:3; 1 Thess 1:2; Philem 4), the verb "to assist" (συναγωνίζεσθαι, Rom 15:30), the verb "to help" (συνυπουργεῖν, 2 Cor 1:11), and the verb "to mention" or "remember" (μνημονεύειν,1 Thess 1:3; perhaps also Col 4:18).

The greeting "grace and peace to you" (χάρις ὑμῖν καὶ εἰρήνη), which appears in the salutation of every Pauline letter, and a peace benediction (e.g., "The God of peace be with you all. Amen"), which often begins the concluding section of a Pauline letter, may also reflect the language of Jewish prayers generally and Paul's prayers in particular. In the Pauline corpus, however, such a greeting and bene-diction function primarily as an epistolary *inclusio* to bracket or enclose the contents of the respective letters, and so—even though echoing the language of prayer—they will not be treated here as prayers. Likewise, the evocative expression "By no means!" (μὴ γένοιτο; "Far from it!," "Never!," "Absolutely not!," or the KJV's "God forbid!") is an emotionally charged exclamation, which usually appears in Paul's letters after a rhetorical question (cf. Rom 3:4, 6, 31; 6:2, 15; 7:7, 13; 9:14; 11:1, 11; 1 Cor 6:15; Gal 2:17; 3:21; the only exception being Gal 6:14), and so will not be treated as a prayer. Nor will the cursing statement "Let that one be eternally accursed by God!" (ἀνάθεμα ἔστω of Gal 1:8, 9; or, ἤτω ἀνάθεμα of 1 Cor 16:22), for similar reasons. And while future indicative verbs are often to be taken as equivalent to optative verbs, the statements of Rom 16:20a ("The God of peace will soon crush Satan under your feet"), 1 Cor 1:8 ("He will keep you strong to the end so that you will be blameless on the day of our Lord Jesus Christ"), 2 Cor 13:11b ("The God of love and peace will be with you"), Phil 4:7 ("The peace of God, which transcends all understanding, will guard your hearts and minds in Christ Jesus"), Phil 4:9b ("The God of peace will be with you"), Phil 4:19 ("My God will meet all your needs according to his glorious riches in Christ Jesus"); 1 Thess 5:24b ("The one who calls you is faithful and he will do it"), and 2 Thess 3:3 ("The Lord is faithful, and he will strengthen and protect you from the evil one") should probably be viewed more as declarations than as prayers.

2. *Major Methodological Issues*

Any study of prayer in the Pauline letters is immediately faced with a number of issues regarding the identification, classification and interpretation of the above references to prayer. Most obvious is the delineation of the Pauline corpus. The safest way, of course, is to consider only the prayer materials of the seven letters most assuredly attested critically and most commonly accepted as authentic—that is, Romans, 1 and 2 Corinthians, Galatians, Philippians, 1 Thessalonians, and Philemon (to list them in their canonical order). But prayers are traditional in nature. So the prayer materials found throughout the Pauline corpus might reasonably be expected to contain many similar features, whether expressed directly by Paul, mediated through an amanuensis or secretary, or reflected by his followers. And, as a matter of fact, though questions about Paul's authorship, his use of amanuenses, and/or the composition of one or more letters by a later Paulinist will certainly affect how one understands many matters within the Pauline corpus, the prayer materials in the thirteen canonical letters have a consistency of pattern and content (as we will see as we proceed) that permits them to be treated together—even while procedurally one must always begin with those most assuredly authentic before turning to those more problematic.

More serious, however, is the fact that in treating the prayer materials of the Pauline letters we are dealing not with liturgical texts (though such a text may be reflected in 1 Cor 16:22: Μαρανα θα, "O Lord, Come!") but with letters—that is, not with prayers addressed to God but with reports about prayers that are addressed to the letters' recipients. In liturgical texts, God is addressed in the second person and people are spoken about in the third person, whereas in letters the recipients are addressed in the second person and God is spoken about in the third person. Thus prayers of adoration and thanksgiving in the Pauline letters are recast to provide a précis of what has been prayed, but do not address God directly or provide the recipients of the letters with the prayers themselves. Likewise, prayers of petition have been recast so that, while they express the central concerns of the writer in his praying, they refer to God in the third person and only set out the essence of what has been prayed for.

Further, it often becomes difficult to delineate the exact boundaries of the prayer materials in Paul's letters. Reports about what Paul has prayed for are often merged with descriptions about his addressees' situations, and prayer wishes expressed on behalf of the recipients are often combined with exhortations to work out in their lives what has been prayed for. This is particularly true in the opening thanksgiving sections of Paul's letters, where praise, prayer reports, prayer wishes, references to particular situations, and exhortations are frequently intermingled.

Other questions regarding method also arise when we try to interpret the Pauline prayer materials. Chief among such questions are these: What criteria of form, content, or function are to be used in classifying the prayer materials of the Pauline letters? How should the similarities and differences in the Pauline prayer vocabulary be evaluated? What features from his background and experience has Paul incorporated—whether consciously or unconsciously—into his prayers, and how have these features been blended in his praying? And to what extent have Paul's convictions regarding Jesus affected his use of traditional prayer materials?

3. *The Background of Paul's Prayers*

Jews have always been a people of prayer. It is, therefore, to the Jewish practice of prayer, particularly Jewish prayer practices of the first century CE, that we must first turn in order to understand Paul's prayers as reflected in his extant letters. For Paul was probably nowhere more traditional than in his prayer life.

Judaism gives high priority to prayer. The Jewish Scriptures contain many prayers, as do also the Jewish apocryphal and pseudepigraphical writings and the Dead Sea Scrolls. The rabbinic tractate *Berakoth* ("Benedictions")—which is the first tractate of the Mishnah, and therefore also the first tractate of the Talmud—is devoted to the subject of prayer. The Jerusalem temple was called a "house of prayer" (cf. Isa 56:7; Mark 11:17, par.) because the sacrifices were accompanied by prayers (cf. *Sirach* 50:19; Josephus, *Contra Apion* 2.196; Luke 1:10), and so the times of the evening and morning sacrifices were called simply "the hour of prayer" (cf. Acts 3:1). The Jewish synagogue was also called a "house of prayer" (cf. Josephus, *Contra Apion* 2:10; *Life* 277)—as well, of course, a "house of study," "assembly house," "little sanctuary," and "school" (*schul*)—because there prayers were voiced by one appointed by the ruler of the synagogue and the people responded with "Amen" after each benediction or blessing (cf. Neh 8:6; 1 Chron 16:36; *Tobit* 8:8; *1QSerek* 1.20; *Mishnah Berakoth* 8:8; *Mishnah Ta'anith* 2:5; 1 Cor 14:16).

Jews also gave thanks to God before their meals, and frequently after them as well (cf. Deut 8:10; *1QSerek* 6.4-5; Josephus, *War* 2.131; *Mishnah Berakoth* 6:1–8:8). The *Kiddush* ("sanctification" or ceremonial blessing) was recited over each of the different kinds of food in a Jewish home. And since in olden times strangers were often fed in the synagogue, the custom arose of also reciting the *Kiddush* as part of the evening service on Sabbath and festival days in the synagogue (except on the first night of Pesah, when strangers were to be given hospitality in private homes). A typical blessing over the bread would be: "Blessed art thou, O Lord, who brings forth bread from the earth"; a typical blessing over the wine: "Blessed art thou, O Lord, who has created the fruit of the vine" (cf. *Mishnah Berakoth* 6:1-8). Further, short prayers were to be directed to God in every situation of life that a Jew encountered—as, for example, when a rabbi entered and left a synagogue or "house of study" (cf. *Mishnah Berakoth* 4:2), or when a traveler faced some danger on the way (cf. *Mishnah Berakoth* 4:4).

There is no commandment in the Jewish Scriptures that says simply "Thou shalt pray!" Rather, what one finds is a verse like Deut 11:13, which calls on Israel "to love the Lord your God and to serve him with all your heart and with all your soul." The rabbis of the Talmud asked about this verse: "What kind of service is it that takes place in the heart?" And they answered their own question: "It is prayer!" (*b. Ta'anith* 2a). Therefore as "the service that takes place in the heart," Jewish teachers concluded that prayer is to be understood as "the free outpouring" of a person's heart before God, "the spontaneous expression" of a person's "deepest concerns" and "highest aspirations"—not just something that one is commanded to do, but something that a person *feels* like doing or is *moved* to do from the heart (cf. J. J. Petu-chowski, *Understanding Jewish Prayer* [New York: KTAV, 1972], 3, 17).

Nonetheless, though it is to be freely given and voluntarily expres-sed, prayer is also regarded by Jews as a divine commandment, an obligation or *mitzvah*, since God commands his people to serve him with all their heart. This dual understanding of the nature of prayer means that in Judaism prayer is viewed as both an inward response of devotion and an outward act of obedience—that is, a reflection of individual spontaneity and an ordinance of community tradition; a voluntary outpouring of human emotion and an obligatory expression of a statutory rite (cf. *ibid.*, 3-25).

Many Jews have assumed that all the prayers in the *Siddur* or Jew-ish prayer book were not only condoned by the ancient rabbis but also commanded by God's prophets in Scripture. Prominent among them is the *Shema*, which is the subject of the first two chapters of the tractate *Berakoth*, the first tractate (as noted above) of the Mishnah and Talmud. The *Shema* begins with the words "Hear, O Israel (ישׂראל שׁמע): The Lord our God, the Lord is one." It consists of Deut 6:4-9, Deut 11:13-21 and Num 15:37-41, with these passages then followed by benedictions that enunciate the great Jewish affirmations of God's creation, revelation and redemption (cf. *Daily Prayer Book* [Orthodox], ed. P. Birnbaum [New York: Hebrew Publishing Com-pany, 1949], 191-97 [Evening Service], 71-81 [Morning Service]; *Sabbath and Festival Prayer Book* [Conservative] [The Rabbinical Assembly of America and The United Synagogue of America, 1946], 15-19 [Evening Service], 87-95 [Morning Service]; *Union Prayer Book, Revised* [Reform] [Cincinnati: The Central Conference of American Rabbis, 1940], 13-17 [Evening Service], 125-41 [Morning Service]). The obligation to recite the *Shema* twice a day, both evening and morning, was derived from the first paragraph of the *Shema* itself: "Impress them [these commandments] on your children. Talk about them when you sit at home and when you walk along the road, *when you lie down and when you get up*" (Deut 6:7). Midday prayer, which also includes the *Shema*, has some biblical precedent (cf. Ps 55:17, "Evening, morning and noon I cry out in distress, and he hears my voice"; Dan 6:10, "Three times a day he [Daniel] got down on his knees and prayed, giving thanks to his God"). But as Jakob Petuchowski points out, the reciting of the *Shema*, with its attendant benedictions, was to the ancient rabbis "not a matter of 'prayer,' but of 'declaration' or 'proclamation'," with these affirmations or confessions of faith only later turned into statutory prayers (*ibid.*, 20). Originally the *Shema* was not meant so much to be prayed as to be affirmed or confessed as a declaration or proclamation of Israel's faith.

The only prayer commanded to be prayed in ancient rabbinic lore is the *Shemoneh Esreh*, or "Eighteen Benedictions." It is designated in the Talmud as *Tefillah*, which means "intercession" and signifies "the Prayer" *par excellence*. It functions as the central feature in the daily services of the synagogue and the basic prayer for every Jew (cf. *Daily Prayer Book*, 81-97 [Weekday], 265-73, 349-59, 391-405, 449-59 [Sabbath], 585-97, 609-25 [Festival]; *Sabbath and Festival Prayer Book*, 230-37 [Weekday], 21-25, 96-101, 137-45, 169-76 [Sabbath], 29-33, 146-56 [Festival]; *Union Prayer Book, Revised*, 320-26 [Weekday], 19-25, 125-41 [Sabbath], 193-201, 225-43 [Festival]).

The *Shemoneh Esreh* is commonly known as the *Amidah* ("standing"), since it is to be recited while standing. Jewish tradition has it that it was composed by Ezra in the fifth century BCE (*b. Megillah* 18a; *Sifre on Deuteronomy* 343). Modern Jewish scholars, however, dispute such an early date and have demonstrated various stages in its development (cf. K. Kohler, "The Origin and Composition of the Eighteen Benedictions," in *Contributions to the Scientific Study of Jewish Liturgy*, ed. J. J. Petuchowski, 52-90; L. Finkelstein, "The Development of the Amidah," in *ibid.*, 91-133; J. Heinemann, *Prayer in the Talmud*, 13-76). All that can be said with confidence is that the formulation of the *Shemoneh Esreh* began sometime before the first century CE and that its inclusion of eighteen benedictions antedates the destruction of the Jerusalem temple.

The first three benedictions of the *Shemoneh Esreh* have to do with the adoration of God; its intermediate twelve comprise petitions to God concerning the community's circumstances and the people's needs; its last three constitute prayers of thanksgiving. A number of reasons are given in the Talmud for the fact that the *Shemoneh Esreh* has eighteen benedictions: that God's name is mentioned eighteen times in Psalm 29 and eighteen times in the *Shema*; that the three patriarchs of the Jewish people, Abraham, Isaac, and Jacob, are mentioned together eighteen times in the Bible; and that the number eighteen corresponds to the eighteen main vertebrae in the human

spinal column (cf. *b. Berakoth* 28b). The prayer for the restoration of
the Davidic monarchy ("and speedily establish in [Jerusalem] the
throne of David"), which was evidently first voiced in Babylon and
known in Palestine during the first century CE, did not, however,
become a nineteenth benediction, but was combined with the fourteenth, which is a prayer for the rebuilding of Jerusalem (cf. J.
Heinemann, *Prayer in the Talmud*, 22, 67, 225). Similarly, the *birkat
ha-minim*, or prayer against "apostates" and "betrayers," which was
composed under the direction of Rabbi Gamaliel II at Jamnia about 80
CE, did not become an additional benediction, but was combined with
the twelfth and then later revised to speak more generally against
"slanderers" and the "arrogant" (cf. R. A. Pritz, *Nazarene Jewish
Christianity* [Jerusalem: Magnes; Leiden: Brill, 1988], 102-107). And
a number of other developments in the wording of the *Shemoneh
Esreh*—particularly the petitions of its central section—have been
identified as well.

Whenever it was first formulated and however it developed over the
course of history, the *Shemoneh Esreh* seems to have been the basic
statutory prayer of Judaism in the first century CE. Yet while it was the
prescribed prayer of Paul's day, it was never viewed by Jews to be
without flexibility or spontaneity. It may be that its first three
benedictions of adoration and its final three benedictions of thanksgiving were always considered rather fixed. But its intermediate
twelve intercessory benedictions seem to have changed and developed
over the years—depending, always, on the circumstances of the nation
and the needs of the people. The great medieval Jewish scholar
Maimonides (1135–1204 CE, who in Jewish writings is usually called
"Rambam" from the initials of his name, Rabbi Mosheh ben
Maimon)—commenting on prayer generally ("the service that takes
place in the heart"), but particularly on the *Shemoneh
Esreh*—encapsulated the Jewish attitude when he said:

> A man should entreat God and pray every day, and proclaim the praise
> of the Holy One, praised be He [i.e., the first three benedictions].
> Afterwards he should voice his needs in petitionary prayer [i.e., the
> next twelve benedictions, expressed in terms of the community's
> circumstances and the people's needs]. And, after that, give praise and
> thanksgiving to God for the goodness which He has abundantly
> bestowed upon him [i.e., the last three benedictions]. Everybody does
> so in accordance with his own ability. If, however, he was inhibited in
> speech, he would merely speak according to his ability and whenever

he desired to do so. Similarly, the number of prayers would depend upon the ability of every individual. Some would pray once every day, while others would pray many times (quotation from J. J. Petuchowski, *Understanding Jewish Prayer*, 19).

Paul's background of prayer in Judaism, therefore, had within it large elements of inwardness, spontaneity and voluntarism, as well as features of obligation, statutory ritual, and community tradition. Further, Paul's Jewish background provided him with an understanding that in responding to God's mercy and grace, one was both (1) to affirm one's faith in God's creation, revelation and redemption (as in the *Shema*), and (2) to pray to God in adoration, petition and thanksgiving (as in the *Shemoneh Esreh*). All of these matters seem to have been intertwined in Paul's Jewish prayer experience. And, as will be highlighted in what follows, they are features that resonate throughout the references and allusions to prayer in the extant Pauline letters as well.

The phenomenon of prayer in Paul, however, is not to be understood only in terms of his Jewish practice of prayer, important as that background is. Paul's prayer life was also rooted in the piety of the Jewish Scriptures, the traditions of the emerging Christian church, and his own personal relationship with the risen Christ. Thus, though he claimed a large measure of independence as an apostle of Christ in his mission to Gentiles (cf. Gal 1:16b–2:14), Paul also acknowledged his indebtedness to (1) the Scriptures of the Old Testament, which he quoted extensively and whose language he used in his prayers (cf. my *Biblical Exegesis in the Apostolic Period*, 2nd. ed. [Grand Rapids: Eerdmans, 1999], 88-116), and (2) an existing body of Christian confessional material, which he incorporated at various places into his letters and whose theological perspectives influenced his praying (cf. my *New Wine into Fresh Wineskins: Contextualizing the Early Christian Confessions* [Peabody: Hendrickson, 1999], 9-106). Further, his commitment to Jesus as Israel's Messiah and humanity's Lord had a profound impact on the nature and content of his prayers, as will be evident in our analysis of the Pauline prayer materials below.

4. *The Structure of Paul's Prayers*

We do not, as noted earlier, have any verbatim reproductions of Paul's prayers, for the Pauline corpus does not include any liturgical texts addressed to God but only letters addressed to the apostle's recipients.

Commentators, therefore, have tried to classify Paul's prayers either according to content or according to form.

Attempting to classify the Pauline prayer materials in terms of content, some have based their analyses on comparative studies of prayer in the human experience and proposed such categories for prayer as (1) "primitive," (2) "ritual," (3) "cultural," (4) "philosophical," (5) "mystical," and (6) "prophetic"—with Paul's prayers, seen as more private, spontaneous and emotional, being classed as "personal," "mystical" and/or "prophetic" (e.g., F. Heiler, *Prayer: A Study in the History and Psychology of Religion*, trans. S. McComb and J. E. Park [London: Oxford University Press, 1938]). Others have drawn from the Old Testament Psalms such prayer categories as (1) "petitions of the people," (2) "petitions of an individual," (3) "declarative praise of the people," (4) "declarative praise of an individual," (5) "descriptive praise of the people," (6) "descriptive praise of an individual," and (7) "enthronement prayers" (cf. C. Westermann, *Praise of God in the Psalms*)—with Paul's prayers, when correlated with these categories, declared to be either "prayers of praise" or "prayers of petition."

More common today, however, is the classification of the Pauline prayer materials according to their form: (1) "prayer reports," which address the recipients of the letters in the second person and tell them what Paul has prayed for them—or, at times, what he has prayed for others (Rom 10:1) or what others have prayed for them (2 Cor 9:14), and (2) "wish prayers," which refer to God in the third person and address the recipients using the optative "may" when speaking about what is desired for them (e.g., G. Harder, *Paulus und das Gebet* [Gütersloh: Bertelsmann, 1936]; P. Schubert, *Form and Function of the Pauline Thanksgivings* [Berlin: Töpelmann, 1939]).

Each of these methods of cataloguing has some descriptive merit. Yet little is achieved by classifying Paul's prayers as being "personal," "mystical" or "prophetic." And probably less by speaking of them as simply "prayers of praise" and "prayers of petition," for praise and petition are features that run concurrently through many of them. Nor is it sufficient to classify them as either "prayer reports" or "wish prayers," though that terminology may often be appropriate as a subcategory.

A better way of understanding the structure of Paul's prayers, we propose, using a methodology that could be called "phenomenological historiography" (i.e., the tracing out of parallels in the thought patterns and expressions of related groups of people in history), is to situate the prayer materials of his letters in the context of the Jewish patterns of prayer of his day. That means, in particular, to seek to understand the structure of Paul's prayers vis-à-vis the *Shemoneh Esreh*, the prayer *par excellence* of the Jewish world, which contains prayers of adoration (Benedictions 1–3), prayers of petition (Benedictions 4–15), and prayers of thanksgiving (Benedictions 16–18). We have, of course, no single, comparable prayer text from Paul to support such a proposal. But all of the features of the *Shemoneh Esreh* appear in the prayer materials of the Pauline letters. And it is highly likely that their presence reflects a basic structuring of Paul's thought, which had been conditioned by his Jewish experience.

The closest one gets to one Pauline passage that exhibits all of these features is Ephesians 1, which, after the salutation, (1) expresses adoration to God (εὐλογητὸς ὁ θεός) in verses 3-12 (or, possibly, through verse 14), (2) offers thanksgiving for the addressees (εὐχαριστῶν ὑπὲρ ὑμῶν) in verses 15-16, and (3) sets out in the optative mood and second person plural (ἵνα … δώῃ ὑμῖν) prayers for the readers in verses 17-23 (possibly also verses 13-14, which use the second person plural in direct address as well). In the long adoration section of verses 3-12, God is extolled for his blessings of salvation "in Christ" (v 3), with affirmations made about his election (v 4), adoption (v 5), predestination (v 6), redemption (v 7), wisdom (v 8), the mystery of his will (v 9), and the consummation of all things "under the one head, even Christ" (v 10). Further, believers are reminded of their status as chosen and predestined by God "in Christ" (v 11) in order that they "might be for the praise of his glory" (v 12). In the thanksgiving section of verses 15-16 the writer assures his addressees of his prayers for them, highlighting the fact that he prays for them continually. And in the petition section of verses 17-23, the details of what the writer prays for them come tumbling out in terms of their growth in wisdom, insight, understanding and power, with then closing statements about how God will bring about the final culmination of their salvation. Intertwined throughout 1:3-23, in fact, are most (if not all) of the distinctive features of the *Shemoneh Esreh*—though, of course, with all of what is presented set in the matrix of commitment to Jesus as Christ (Messiah) and Lord.

The language of Ephesians 1 reflects the theology and piety of the Jewish / Old Testament Scriptures. It also reflects the christological confessions of the early church. And it expresses personal commitment to Jesus as Christ and Lord, as well as direct involvement with God's Spirit. The structure of the passage, however, suggests that its author was conditioned by patterns established by praying the *Shemoneh Esreh*. It is probably best, therefore, to understand Eph 1:3-23 in the following manner: first, in terms of its structure, which seems to have been inherited from the writer's Jewish background; then in terms of its content, which reflects a coming together of basic Jewish theology and piety, distinctive Christian confessional materials, personal commitment to Jesus, and direct involvement with God's Spirit.

It may be, of course, that Ephesians was written by a Pauline follower. Or it may be that Paul, through an amanuensis or secretary, wrote what we know as "Ephesians" as something of a circular letter (however defined) to believers in Christ who lived in some of the cities and towns of western Asia Minor. Either hypothesis would account for many of the features that distinguish this letter from other letters of Paul. But whatever is thought about provenance, canonical Ephesians must be viewed in some manner as "Pauline." And since the same features of the prayer materials found in Ephesians 1 appear in various places and contexts in the other Pauline letters, we may assume that the same explanation given for their appearance in Ephesians is also to be proposed for their appearance elsewhere in the Pauline corpus. In what follows, therefore, the prayer materials of the Pauline letters will be discussed in terms of the structure provided by the *Shemoneh Esreh*, "the Prayer" *par excellence* of Paul's Jewish background.

5. *Paul's Prayers of Adoration*

The Hebrew noun *berakah* (ברכה) means "blessing" or "praise." It appears in every prayer of the *Siddur*, the Jewish prayer book—usually at the beginning of a prayer in praise to God, but also at the end of long prayers as a eulogy extolling God. Two types of adoration prayers, therefore, can be identified in the Jewish prayer materials. The first is the "*berakah*-formula prayer," wherein (1) praise to God is declared in the opening address ("Blessed art Thou, O Lord" or "Blessed be the Lord"), (2) statements are made about God's person and what he has done on behalf of his people, which are introduced by a relative clause or substantival participle ("who" or "the One who"), (3) the verb in those statements is cast in the perfect tense ("has"), and (4) the content regarding God's activity is expressed either briefly or in extended fashion. The second may be called a "eulogy-type prayer," wherein a statement extolling God comes at the end of a long prayer, expresses itself not in the perfect tense but by an active verb or participle, and is mostly brief—usually no more than a few words of praise that reflect in summary fashion what has been prayed in the longer prayer.

Numerous instances of the *barakah*-formula prayer can be found in the Old Testament. For example, the words of Abraham's servant after he had requested a sign from God and the request was granted, begin with "Blessed be the Lord (ברוך יהוה), the God of my master Abraham, who has not withheld his steadfast kindness from my master Abraham" (Gen 24:27). The words of Jethro on hearing from Moses "all that the Lord had done to Pharaoh and to Egypt" are similar: "Blessed be the Lord (ברוך יהוה), who has rescued you from the hand of the Egyptians and of Pharaoh, and who has rescued the people from the hand of the Egyptians" (Exod 18:10). Other examples can be found in Gen 14:20; Ruth 4:14; 1 Sam 25:32, 39; 2 Sam 18:28; 1 Kgs 1:48; 5:7; 8:15, 56; 2 Chron 2:12; 6:4; Ezra 7:27; Pss 66:20; 124:6; and Dan 3:28.

Eulogies at the end of prayers, however, have much less biblical precedent than *berakah*-formula prayers. One clear example is the conclusion of David's prayer to God, which was expressed "in the presence of the whole assembly" when gifts had been generously given by the people for building the temple: "Now, O God, we give you thanks, and praise your glorious name!" (1 Chron 29:13). Another example is the praise expressed toward the conclusion of the second section of Psalm 119, that great teaching psalm: "Praise to you, O Lord; teach me your decrees" (Ps 119:12). In most cases, eulogy-type praise at the conclusion of a longer prayer seems to have been derived in later Judaism from *berakah*-formula praise at the opening of prayers (cf. J. Heinemann, *Prayer in the Talmud*, 77-103).

Two rather explicit *berakah*-formula type prayers of adoration in the Pauline letters are:

> Blessed be the God and Father of our Lord Jesus Christ (εὐλογητὸς ὁ θεὸς καὶ πατὴρ τοῦ κυρίου Ἰησοῦ Χριστοῦ), the Father of

compassion and the God of all comfort, who comforts us in all our troubles! (2 Cor 1:3-4a).

Blessed be the God and Father of our Lord Jesus Christ (εὐλογητὸς ὁ θεὸς καὶ πατὴρ ἡμῶν Ἰησοῦ Χριστοῦ), who has blessed us in the heavenly realms with every spiritual blessing in Christ! (Eph 1:3).

Statements about what God has done on behalf of his people are then given briefly in 2 Cor 1:4b-7 (following the first) and quite extensively in Eph 1:4-12 (following the second).

This type of adoration address is also reflected in Paul's letters in Rom 1:25 ("The Creator, who is to be praised/blessed [εὐλογητός] forever. Amen"), in Rom 9:5 ("God over all, who is to be praised/blessed [εὐλογητός] forever. Amen"), in 2 Cor 11:31 ("The God and Father of the Lord Jesus, who is to be praised/blessed [εὐλογητός] forever"), and, probably, in 1 Cor 14:16 ("If you are praising/blessing God [εὐλογῇς] with your spirit ...")—as it is also in such LXX passages as 1 Kgs 1:48; 2 Chron 2:12; 6:4; and Ps 71[72]:18 and such other New Testament passages as Luke 1:68 and 1 Pet 1:3.

Examples of closing eulogy-type prayers in the Pauline letters include the following:

To him [God] be the glory (ἡ δόξα) for ever! Amen" (Rom 11:36).

To the only wise God be glory (ἡ δόξα) forever through Jesus Christ! Amen" (Rom 16:27).

To whom [our God and Father] be glory (ἡ δόξα) for ever and ever! Amen" (Gal 1:5).

To him [God] be glory (ἡ δόξα) in the church and in Christ Jesus throughout all generations, for ever and ever! Amen" (Eph 1:21).

To our God and Father be glory (ἡ δόξα) for ever and ever! Amen" (Phil 4:20).

Probably to be coupled with these eulogy type prayers are expressions of praise that use (1) the verb ἐξομολογέω ("confess"), which came to mean "praise directed to God in prayer" (cf. LXX 2 Kgs 22:50; 1 Chron 29:13; Pss 85[86]:12; 117[118]:28), in Paul's quotations in Rom 14:11 (quoting Isa 45:23), "every tongue will confess [give praise in prayer] to God," and in Rom 15:9 (quoting Ps 17:50 [18:49]), "I will confess [give praise in prayer] to you [God] among the Gentiles"; and (2) the noun ἔπαινος ("praise"), which came to mean "praise given in prayer to God" (cf. LXX Ps 21:26 [22:25];

34[35]:28; *Sirach* 39:10), as found in Eph 1:6, 12, 14 and Phil 1:11 and 2:11.

6. *Paul's Prayers of Thanksgiving*

The thanksgiving sections of Paul's letters have been the focus of extensive scholarly attention. In 1939 Paul Schubert noted that most of Paul's letters, after an epistolary greeting, have a thanksgiving section, and that these sections exhibited certain common structural and functional traits (cf. Schubert, *Form and Function of the Pauline Thanksgivings*). And Schubert's observations and analyses have been accepted and developed by many today.

Structurally, the Pauline thanksgivings are of two types. Type I*a* begins with the principal statement, "I thank God" (εὐχαριστῶ τῷ θεῷ) or its equivalent, and continues on with one or more participial constructions that modify the principal verb εὐχαριστέω. The fact that these participles are always in the nominative masculine (whether singular or plural) makes it clear that it is the apostle himself (though sometimes in conjunction with his associates) who has offered the prayer. Type I*b* also commences with the verb of thanksgiving (εὐχαριστέω). But instead of being followed by participles, εὐχαριστέω is succeeded by a causal ὅτι-clause that spells out the basis for the apostle's thanksgiving. The first type, in which both a thanksgiving and intercessory prayer reports are featured, is the more elaborate and appears the greater number of times in the Pauline letters (i.e., Eph 1:15ff.; Phil 1:3ff.; Col 1:3ff.; and Philem 4ff., with 2 Cor 1:11 being viewed as an inverted instance of this same type). The second type is briefer and appears only two times in the Pauline corpus (i.e., 1 Cor 1:4ff.; 2 Thess 2:13f.). Three of the Pauline thanksgivings Schubert saw as being mixed forms of these two basic types (i.e., Rom 1:8ff.; 1 Thess 1:2ff.; 2 Thess 1:3ff.).

Functionally, Schubert argued that the purpose of the Pauline thanksgivings was "to indicate the occasion for and the contents of the letters which they introduce" (*ibid.*, 26). Thus they serve both epistolary and didactic purposes—that is, (1) they establish contact with the recipients, remind them of previously given instructions, and set the tone and atmosphere for each of the writings, and (2) they indicate the main themes or topics to be presented in the respective letters.

But while the Pauline thanksgivings are, indeed, to be understood as having epistolary and didactic functions, they also should be seen as expressing the apostle's deep pastoral and apostolic concerns for those he addresses. They do this by reporting, in summary fashion, on (1) his prayers of thanksgiving expressed to God for the addressees, and (2) his prayers of petition offered on their behalf. So when speaking of his prayers, Paul tells his addressees that they were directed "to God" (1 Cor 1:4; 1 Thess 1:2; 2:13; 3:9; 2 Thess 1:3; 2:13) or "to my God" (Rom 1:8; Phil 1:3; Philem 4), who is known to Paul as "the Father of Jesus Christ" (Col 1:3), and that they have been offered "always" (1 Cor 1:4; Phil 1:4; Col 1:3; 1 Thess 1:2; 2 Thess 1:3; 2:13; Philem 4) or "unceasingly" (1 Thess 1:2; 2:13) on their behalf—which does not mean that Paul was continuously in a state of prayer, but that he always included references to his addressees in his regular times of prayer (cf. Harder, *Paulus und das Gebet*, 8-19).

Some of those for whom Paul gives thanks were well known to him (e.g., those at Corinth, at Philippi and at Thessalonica). Others had been converted through the ministry of a colleague or colleagues (e.g., those at Colosse; perhaps also those referred to in some manuscripts as "at Ephesus"). Still others he considered to be within his Gentile mission, even though they were outside the scope of his own evangelistic ministry (e.g., those at Rome). The bases for Paul offering prayers of thanksgiving are: (1) God's redemptive actions on behalf of his addressees, which stem from God's own eternal counsels, were manifest in the work and person of Jesus, and continue to be expressed in the ministry of the Holy Spirit (cf. 1 Cor 1:4-9; Phil 1:6; Col 1:12-14; 1 Thess 1:4; 2 Thess 2:13-14); (2) the proclamation of the gospel and his addressees' reception of it (1 Cor 1:6; Phil 1:5; Col 1:6; 1 Thess 1:3-10; 2:13-14; 2 Thess 2:14); and (3) his addressees' continued spiritual growth (Rom 1:8; Eph 1:15; Col 1:4-5; 1 Thess 1:3; 2 Thess 1:3-4; Philem 5).

There are also eight instances of the expression "thanks be to God" (χάρις τῷ θεῷ) in the Pauline letters (Rom 6:17; 7:25; 1 Cor 15:57; 2 Cor 2:14; 8:16; 9:15; 1 Tim 1:12; 2 Tim 1:3), sometimes appearing as a spontaneous outburst of praise. This shorter thanksgiving formula probably reflects, as Reinhard Deichgräber has argued, a mixture of Greek and Jewish features, since the expression is found also in the Greek papyri and is comparable to the short eulogies of praise at the close of many Jewish prayers of adoration (*Gotteshymnus und*

Christushymnus, 43). Further, thirty-five times Paul uses the verb καυχᾶσθαι, "to boast," "glory," or "pride oneself in," in a manner that suggests the idea of thanksgiving before God (cf. Rom 5:2, 3, 11; 15:17; 1 Cor 1:29-31; 2 Cor 1:12-14; chs 10–12 *passim*; Phil 2:16; 1 Thess 2:19). And on six occasions the giving of thanks over food is referred to in the Pauline letters (εὐχαριστέω in Rom 14:6 [twice]; 1 Cor 10:30; 11:24; εὐχαριστία in 1 Tim 4:3, 4).

7. Paul's Prayers of Petition

The twelve intercessory benedictions of the *Shemoneh Esreh* are framed by the first three prayers of adoration and the last three prayers of thanksgiving. These prayers of petition, however, are not without praise or thanksgiving. Each of them includes expressions of praise and thanksgiving to God. And each of them ends (as do also the first three prayers of adoration and the last three prayers of thanksgiving in the *Shemoneh Esreh*) with the eulogistic formula, "Blessed art Thou, O Lord," which is then followed by a brief statement that summarizes the content of the respective prayer (e.g., "Blessed art Thou, O Lord, gracious Giver of knowledge" [Benediction 4]; "Blessed art Thou, O Lord, who is pleased with repentance" [Benediction 5]; "Blessed art Thou, O Lord, who heals the sick among your people Israel" [Benediction 8]; etc.).

The first three prayers of adoration and the last three prayers of thanksgiving in the *Shemoneh Esreh* express timeless words of praise, and so have probably remained from very early times relatively fixed. The intermediate twelve prayers, which are intercessory in nature, have, however, evidently been revised from time to time in accordance with the nation's circumstances, the community's experiences, and the people's needs. Further, while Benedictions 1–3 (prayers of adoration) and Benedictions 16–18 (prayers of thanksgiving) were always to be prayed in full, Benedictions 4–15 (prayers of petition) could be reworded to fit particular situations (e.g., a changed cultural situation or new oppression) or could be abbreviated (e.g., when one was in physical danger or the pressures of work required brevity)—or they could even be omitted (particularly where it was feared they might cause people to think more of themselves than God). In fact, when necessitated because of circumstances, all of the twelve intercessory benedictions could be condensed into a single prayer, such as "Save, O Lord, Thy people, the remnant of Israel. In every time of crisis let their needs be before Thee!" or "Do Thy will in heaven above, and grant equanimity to those who bear Thee before, and do that which is good in Thine eyes!" or "The needs of Thy people Israel are many, and their understanding is limited. May it be Thy will, O Lord our God, to give to each one his sustenance and to each body what it lacks!" Every prayer, however, whether abbreviated or in full, was to be concluded with the formulaic eulogy: "Blessed art Thou, O Lord, who hearest prayer" (*b. Berakoth* 29b).

Paul's intercessory prayers are often referred to in the Pauline corpus. They are mentioned most directly in the "prayer reports" found in the nine thanksgiving sections that use the εὐχαριστῶ formula, "I give thanks" (i.e., Rom 1:8-12; 1 Cor 1:4-9; 2 Cor 1:10b-11 [elliptically after the *berakah* of 1:3-4a]; Eph 1:15-23 [after the *berakah* of 1:3-12]; Phil 1:3-11; Col 1:3-14; 1 Thess 1:2-10; 2 Thess 1:3-12; and Philem 4-6), being omitted only in Galatians. And they are alluded to in the two thanksgiving sections of the Pastoral Epistles that use the noun χάρις in expressing "thanks" to God (1 Tim 1:12-14; 2 Tim 1:3-7), being omitted only in Titus.

In the thanksgivings that use the εὐχαριστῶ formula, the following prayer reports on behalf of the addressees appear:

> Constantly I remember you in my prayers at all times, and I pray that now at last by God's will the way may be opened for me to come to you (Rom 1:9b-10).

> I always thank God for you (1 Cor 1:4a).

> I remember you in my prayers. I keep asking that the God of our Lord Jesus Christ, the glorious Father, may give you a spirit [or, the Spirit] of wisdom and revelation, so that you may know him better. I pray also that the eyes of your heart may be enlightened in order that you may know the hope to which he has called you, the riches of his glorious inheritance in the saints, and his incomparably great power for us who believe (Eph 1:16b-19a).

> In all my prayers for all of you, I always pray with joy because of your partnership in the gospel from the first day until now (Phil 1:4-5).

> We always thank God, the Father of our Lord Jesus Christ, when we pray for you … We have not stopped praying for you and asking God to fill you with the knowledge of his will through all spiritual wisdom and understanding (Col 1:3, 9).

> We always thank God for all of you, mentioning you in our prayers. We continually remember before our God and Father your work produced by faith, your labor prompted by love, and your endurance inspired by hope in our Lord Jesus Christ (1 Thess 1:2-3).

> We constantly pray for you, that our God may count you worthy of his calling, and that by his power he may fulfill every good purpose of yours and every act prompted by your faith (2 Thess 1:11).

> I always thank my God as I remember you in my prayers (Philem 4).

And in the thanksgiving sections where χάρις is used to express thanks to God, there are these prayer reports:

> I thank Christ Jesus our Lord, who has given me strength, that he considered me faithful, appointing me to his service (1 Tim 1:12).

> I thank God, whom I serve, as my forefathers did, with a clear conscience, as night and day I constantly remember you in my prayers (2 Tim 1:3).

Elsewhere in the Pauline letters there are further instances of reports as to what Paul has prayed on behalf of his addressees and others:

> Brothers, my heart's desire and prayer to God for them [the people of Israel] is for their salvation (Rom 10:1).

> We pray to God that you will not do anything wrong (2 Cor 13:7).

> Our prayer is for your perfection (2 Cor 13:9b).

> I pray that out of his glorious riches he [God] will strengthen you with power through his Spirit in your inner being, so that Christ dwells in your hearts through faith (Eph 3:16-17a).

> I pray that you, being rooted and established in love, will have power, together with all the saints, to grasp how wide and long and high and deep is the love of Christ, and to know this love that surpasses knowledge—so that you become filled to the measure of all the fullness of God (Eph 3:17b-19).

Further, Paul's concerns and prayers for his addressees are reflected in the following "wish prayers," which use the optative "may":

> May the God who gives endurance and encouragement give you a spirit of unity among yourselves as you follow Christ Jesus, so that with one heart and mouth you may glorify the God and Father of our Lord Jesus Christ (Rom 15:5-6).

> May the God of hope fill you with great joy and peace as you trust in him, so that you may overflow with hope by the power of the Holy Spirit (Rom 15:13).

> May the grace of the Lord Jesus Christ, and the love of God, and the fellowship of the Holy Spirit be with you all (2 Cor 13:14).

> May our God and Father himself and our Lord Jesus clear the way for us to come to you. May the Lord make your love increase and overflow for each other and for everyone else, just as ours does for you. May he give you inner strength that you may be blameless and holy in the presence of our God and Father when our Lord Jesus comes with all his holy ones (1 Thess 3:11-13).

> May God himself, the God of peace, sanctify you through and through. May your whole spirit, soul and body be kept blameless at the coming of our Lord Jesus Christ (1 Thess 5:23).

> May our Lord Jesus Christ himself and God our Father, who loved us and by his grace gave us eternal encouragement and good hope, encourage and strengthen you in every good deed and word (2 Thess 2:16-17).

> May the Lord direct your hearts into God's love and Christ's perseverance (2 Thess 3:5).

> May the Lord of peace himself give you peace at all times and in every way (2 Thess 3:16a).

> May it not be held against them [those who did not come to Paul's aid at his "first defense" but "deserted" him] (2 Tim 4:16).

There are also places in the Pauline letters where the addressees are exhorted to pray (e.g., Rom 12:12; Eph 5:20; 6:18; Phil 4:6; Col 4:2; 1 Thess 5:16-18; 1 Tim 2:1-2) and where prayer is requested on behalf of Paul himself (e.g., Rom 15:30-32; 2 Cor 1:11; Eph 6:19-20; Phil 1:19; Col 4:3-4; 1 Thess 5:25; 2 Thess 3:1-2; Philem 22).

8. *Significant Features of Paul's Prayers*

In concluding his discussion of early Christian hymns, Reinhard Deichgräber has aptly commented:

> The praise of the church is the response to God's act of salvation ... praise is never the first word, but always occurs in the second place ... [it is] never *prima actio*, but always *reactio*, *reactio* to God's saving activity in creation and redemption, to his orderly working in nature and history (*Gotteshymnus und Christushymnus*, 201; trans. by P. T.

O'Brien, "Thanksgiving within the Structure of Pauline Theology,"
50).

And this sense of response to God resonates throughout all the prayer
materials of the Pauline letters as well. Prayer in the Pauline letters is
never viewed as something initiated by humans in order to awaken a
sleeping or reluctant deity. Nor is it understood as negotiating or
bargaining with God. Rather, it is always an acknowledgement of
dependence on God, a response to what God has done in both creation
and redemption, and a declaration of God's goodness in inviting
people to present their praise and petitions before him.

Paul's prayers of adoration, as reflected in his letters, evidently
began with the acclamation: "Blessed be God" (εὐλογητὸς ὁ
θεός)—as do also the prayers of the Old Testament ("Blessed be the
Lord") and the prayers of Judaism ("Blessed art Thou, O Lord"). This
is a statement of praise that proclaims God to be the source of all
human blessings. Yet while God is the Creator of all that exits and the
Redeemer of all who turn to him for salvation, the One who alone is
worthy to receive glory (ἡ δόξα), he has made himself known to his
people as "Father." Thus they are to address him as "Father" (ἀββά,
πατήρ)—as also in the Old Testament (cf. Isa 63:16: "But you are our
Father; ... you, O Lord, are our Father"), in Second Temple Judaism
(cf. *Sirach* 51:10: "O Yahweh, my Father art Thou"), in Rabbinic
Judaism (cf. *Shemoneh Esreh*, Benediction 6: "Forgive us, our
Father"), and in Jesus' teaching (cf. Matt 6:9: "Our Father in heaven";
Luke 11:2: "Father").

Distinctive to Paul's prayers (as well as Christian prayer generally),
however, are the dual convictions (1) that prayer to God is through
Jesus Christ, and (2) that because of being "in Christ" the Christian
has a more intimate relationship with God the Father than was ever
possible before (cf. esp. Rom 8:15-17 and Gal 4:6-7). Thus when Paul
prays to God the Father, it is to "the Father of our Lord Jesus Christ"
(πατὴρ τοῦ κυρίου Ἰησοῦ Χριστοῦ; cf. 2 Cor 1:3-4a; 11:31; Eph
1:3). And when Paul speaks to his addressees about their relationship
to God, he urges them to recognize their more intimate relation as
God's children, which has been brought about by God's Spirit, and so
to pray to God more consciously in terms of "Abba, Father" (Αββα ὁ
πατήρ; cf. Rom 8:14-17; Gal 4:6-7).

Paul's prayers of thanksgiving, as reported in his letters, have
principally to do with (1) God's redemptive actions through the work

of Christ and the ministry of the Holy Spirit on behalf of his addressees, (2) the proclamation of the gospel and his addressees' reception of it, and (3) his addressees continued spiritual growth. There is even something of a holy *chutzpah* ("brazenness" or "nerve") in Paul's thanksgiving prayers when he "boasts (καυχάομαι) in the hope of the glory of God" (Rom 5:2), "boasts in afflictions" (Rom 5:3), "boasts in God through our Lord Jesus Christ" (Rom 5:11), "boasts in the Lord" (1 Cor 1:31), "boasts" in his ministry for God (2 Cor 1:12-14, chs 10–12 *passim*), and tells his converts that he expects to "boast" about them "in the day of the Lord Jesus" or "in the presence of our Lord Jesus Christ when he comes" (2 Cor 1:14; Phil 2:16; 1 Thess 2:19).

Paul's prayers of petition, as deduced from his "prayer reports" and his "wish prayers," are focused primarily on the spiritual welfare of his addressees. He also, of course, repeats in 1 Cor 16:22 an eschatological petition, which was evidently drawn from the liturgy of the early church, that asks for the culmination of God's salvation: "O Lord, Come!" Further, he prays in Rom 10:1 for those who have spurned the gospel of Christ ("My heart's desire and prayer to God for them [the people of Israel] is that they may be saved") and requests prayer for himself and his missionary activities in Rom 15:30-32; 2 Cor 1:11; Eph 6:19-20; Phil 1:19; Col 4:3-4; 1 Thess 5:25; 2 Thess 3:1-2; Philem 22. But the main thrust of his intercessory praying was, it seems, for the welfare of his converts and those he considered within his Gentile mission. And while prayers for wisdom, revelation, knowledge, insight, and discernment (e.g., Eph 1:16b-19a; Phil 1:9-11; Col 1:9-10) might have been rather traditional, and so to be expected (cf. *Shemoneh Esreh*, Benediction 4, which is a prayer for "knowledge, understanding and insight"), most of the requests voiced in Paul's prayers of petition stem from his perceptions of his addressees' circumstances, seem to be suited to their particular spiritual needs, and are intertwined with his exhortations to them.

An Epilogue

To converts at Philippi and Thessalonica, whom Paul seems to have viewed as some of his best friends, the apostle gave the following exhortations:

> Do not be anxious about anything, but in everything, by prayer and petition, with thanksgiving, present your requests to God (Phil 4:6).

Be joyful always; pray continually; give thanks in all circumstances, for this is God's will for you in Christ Jesus (1 Thess 5:16-18).

Similar exhortations appear in the other Pauline letters as well—even in letters where Paul might not have personally known the addressees:

Be joyful in hope, patient in affliction, faithful in prayer (Rom 12:12).

Be always giving thanks to God the Father for everything, in the name of our Lord Jesus Christ (Eph 5:20).

Pray in the Spirit on all occasions with all kinds of prayers and requests; to that end, be alert and always keep on praying for all the saints (Eph 6:18).

Devote yourselves to prayer, being watchful and thankful (Col 4:2).

I urge, first of all, that requests, prayers, intercession and thanksgiving be made for everyone (1 Tim 2:1).

I want people everywhere to lift up holy hands in prayer, without anger or disputing (1 Tim 2:8).

Prayer, therefore, was not only significant in Paul's life and ministry, he also viewed it as of great importance for those to whom he wrote—whether well known to him or more distantly related. For prayer in the Pauline letters is not only the hallmark of true piety in the presence of God, it is also the lifeblood of every Christian and the wellspring of all Christian ministry. And what was true for Paul and his addressees in that day remains true for us, his readers, today.

SELECT BIBLIOGRAPHY

Charlesworth, James H. "A Prolegomenon to a New Study of the Jewish Background of the Hymns and Prayers in the New Testament," *JJS* 33 (1982) 265-85.
Cullmann, Oscar. "Basic Characteristics of the Early Christian Service of Worship," in *Early Christian Worship*, trans. A. S. Todd and J. B. Torrance. London: SCM, 1953, 7-36.
———. *Prayer in the New Testament*. London: SCM; Minneapolis: Fortress, 1995.
Daniélou, Jean. *Prayer: The Mission of the Church*, trans. D. L. Schindler, Jr. Grand Rapids: Eerdmans, 1996.
Deichgräber, Reinhard. *Gotteshymnus und Christushymnus in der frühen Christenheit: Untersuchungen zu Form, Sprache und Stil der frühchristlichen Hymnen*. Göttingen: Vandenhoeck & Ruprecht, 1967.
Gebaurer, Roland. *Das Gebet bei Paulus: Forschungsgeschichte und exegetische Studien*. Giessen, Basel: Brunnen, 1989.

Harder, G. *Paulus und das Gebet*. Gütersloh: Bertelsmann, 1936.

Heinemann, Joseph. *Prayer in the Talmud. Forms and Patterns*, trans. R. S. Sarason. Berlin, New York: de Gruyter, 1977.

Hunter, W. Bingham. "Prayer," in *Dictionary of Paul and His Letters*, ed. G. F. Hawthorne, R. P. Martin, and D. G. Reid. Downers Grove: InterVarsity, 1993, 725-34.

Kopciowski, Elias, compiler. *Praying with the Jewish Tradition*, trans. P. Clifford. Grand Rapids: Eerdmans, 1997.

O'Brien, Peter T. "Thanksgiving and the Gospel in Paul," *NTS* 21 (1974) 144-55.

——. *Introductory Thanksgivings in the Letters of Paul*. Leiden: Brill, 1977.

——. "Ephesians 1: An Unusual Introduction to a New Testament Letter," *NTS* 25 (1979) 504-16.

——. "Thanksgiving within the Structure of Pauline Theology," in *Pauline Studies: Essays Presented to Professor F. F. Bruce on his 70th. Birthday*, ed. D. A. Hagner and M. J. Harris. Grand Rapids: Eerdmans, 1980, 50-66.

Petuchowski, Jakob J., ed. *Contributions to the Scientific Study of Jewish Liturgy*. New York: KTAV, 1970.

——. *Understanding Jewish Prayer*. New York: KTAV, 1972.

Schubert, Paul. *Form and Function of the Pauline Thanksgivings*. Berlin: Töpelmann, 1939.

Stanley, David M. *Boasting in the Lord: The Phenomenon of Prayer in Saint Paul*. New York: Paulist, 1973.

Westermann, Claus. *The Praise of God in the Psalms*, trans. K. R. Crim. Richmond: John Knox, 1965.

Wiles, Gordon P. *Paul's Intercessory Prayers: The Significance of the Intercessory Prayer Passages in the Letters of St Paul*. Cambridge: Cambridge University Press, 1974.

THE PEDAGOGICAL NATURE OF THE LAW IN GALATIANS 3:19–4:7

In the discussion of Christians and the Mosaic law, the analogy of the pedagogue in Gal 3:24-25 and the illustration of a son in a patrician household in Gal 4:1-7 provide significant, though somewhat puzzling, points of reference. There is no doubt that the analogy and illustration are meant to be taken together. Our difficulties have to do with (1) what Paul meant by them, (2) what areas in the discussion they apply to, and (3) how seriously they should be taken. The analogy and illustration require careful explication if we are to grasp Paul's point aright.

1. *The Analogy of the Pedagogue*

We think today of pedagogues as teachers. In the Greco-Roman world, however, a pedagogue (παιδαγωγός) was distinguished from a teacher (διδάσκαλος or καθηγητής) and had more custodial and disciplinary functions than educative or instructional. The pedagogue was a well-known figure not only in the Greco-Roman world but also in Judaism, where the term *pedagog* (פדגוג) appears as a Greek loan word. He was generally a trusted slave charged by the father of the family to supervise his son's (or sons') activities and conduct—that is, as the etymology of the words suggests (παῖς meaning "child"; ἀγωγός meaning "custodian" or "supervisor"), a "child custodian" or "supervisor."

Plato (c. 427–347 BCE), the younger friend of Socrates and himself an important Greek philosopher, speaks in *The Republic* of "pedagogues (παιδαγωγῶν), nurses wet and dry, beauticians, barbers, and yet again cooks and chefs" as part of the retinue of Greek patrician households (*Rep.* 373C) and characterizes pedagogues as "not those who are good for nothing else, but men who by age and experience are qualified to serve as both leaders (ἡγεμονάς) and custodians (παιδαγωγούς) of children" (*Rep.* 467D). In chapter 4 of *Lysis*, Plato provides us with a fascinating glimpse into the rearing of a son in a Greek family, from which the following dialogue between the boys Socrates and Lysis is an excerpt (with Socrates the questioner):

> Do they [i.e., Lysis's father and mother] let you control your own self, or will they not trust you in that either? Of course they do not, he replied. But someone controls you? Yes, he said, my pedagogue (παιδαγωγός) here. Is he a slave? Why certainly; he belongs to us, he said. What a strange thing, I exclaimed: a free man controlled by a slave! But how does this pedagogue (παιδαγωγός) exert his control over you? By taking me to the teacher (εἰς διδάσκαλον), he replied (*Lysis* 208C).

And in *The Laws* he writes of children:

> Just as no sheep or other witless creature ought to exist without a herdsman, so children cannot live without pedagogues (παιδαγωγῶν), nor slaves without masters. And of all wild creatures, the child is the most intractable; for insofar as it, above all others, posesses a fount of reason that is yet uncurbed, it is a treacherous, sly and most insolent creature. Wherefore the child must be strapped up, as it were, with many bridles—first, when he leaves the care of nurse and mother, with pedagogues (παιδαγωγοῖς) to guide his childish ignorance, and after that with teachers (διδασκάλοις) of all sorts of subjects and lessons, treating him as becomes a freeborn child. On the other hand, he must be treated as a slave; and any free man that meets him shall punish both the child himself and his pedagogue (παιδαγωγόν) or his teacher (διδάσκαλον), if any of them does wrong (*Laws* VII. 808D-E).

Aristotle (384–322 BCE), one of the greatest of the Greek philosophers, alludes to such a custodial function of a pedagogue when he says that "the appetitive part of us should be ruled by principle, just as a boy should live in obedience to his pedagogue (παιδαγωγόν)" (*Nicomachean Ethics* 3.12.8). And Xenophon (c. 431–355 BCE), the Athenian soldier, historian and essayist, who was a disciple of Socrates, writes: "When a boy ceases to be a child, and begins to be a lad, others release him from his pedagogue (παιδαγωγόν) and from his teacher (διδάσκαλον); he is then no longer under them, but is allowed to go his own way" (*Laced.* 3.1).

Reflecting more directly the New Testament period, Josephus (37–100/110 CE), the Jewish historian, uses παιδαγωγός six times in contexts having to do with biblical history (*Antiq.* 1.2.1 §56; 9.6.5

§125; 10.10.1 §186), with Greco-Roman households (*Antiq.* 18.6,9 §212; 20.8.10 §183), and in speaking about his own son's pedagogue, whom he describes as "a slave, a eunuch," and who was punished by the emperor Domitian for an accusation made against Josephus (*Life* 76 §429). The Greek Stoic philosopher Epictetus (first–second century CE) referred to brothers having not only the same father and mother but also commonly the same pedagogue (παιδαγωγός) (cf. Arrian's account in *Dissertations* 2.22.26). He also spoke of pedagogues cudgeling the family cooks when their charges would overeat, and exhorts them: "Man, we did not make you the cook's *paidagogos*, did we?, but the child's. Correct *him*; help *him*!" (*Dissertations* 3.19.5). And in a late-second- or early-third-century CE papyrus letter, on hearing of the departure of her son's teacher, a mother writes: "So, my son, I urge both you and your pedagogue (μελησάτω σοί τε καὶ τῷ παιδαγωγῷ σου) that you go to a suitable teacher (κατήκοντι κατηγητῷ)"—and then closes her letter with the words: "Salute your esteemed pedagogue Eros (ἄσπασαι τὸν τειμιώτατον παιδαγωγόν σου Ερωτα)" (*POxy.* 6.930).

A pedagogue is frequently encountered in rabbinic writings, where the term *pedagog* (פדגוג) most often appears in parables having to do with the household of a king and where the prince is under custodial supervision. *Genesis Rabbah* 28:6, for example, reads:

> R. Judan said: This may be illustrated by the case of a king who entrusted his son to a pedagogue (*pedagog*) who led him into evil ways, whereat the king became angry with his son and slew him. Said the king, "Did any lead my son into evil ways save this man? My son has perished and this man lives!" Therefore [God destroyed] "both man and beast."

Or again, *Genesis Rabbah* 31:7 reads:

> It is as if a royal prince had a pedagogue (*pedagog*), and whenever he did wrong, his pedagogue was punished; or as if a royal prince had a nurse, and whenever he did wrong, his nurse was punished. Similarly, the Holy One, blessed be He, said, "Behold, I will destroy them with the earth!" (cf. also *Exodus Rabbah* 37:2; 42:9; *Deuteronomy Rabbah* 2:11; *Lamentations Rabbah* 4:12; *Sifre Deuteronomy* 19 on Deut 1:20-21).

There are also several places in the Talmud where Moses is depicted as Israel's pedagogue (e.g., *Exodus Rabbah* 21:8; 42:9), or where Moses, Aaron and Miriam are so presented (*Numbers Rabbah* 1:2), or

Moses, David and Jeremiah (*Deuteronomy Rabbah* 2:11). But no passage in the extant Jewish literature has been found where the Mosaic law itself is spoken of as a pedagogue. *Fourth Maccabees* comes close in referring in 1:17 to the law as bringing *paideia* ("instruction," "discipline") and in speaking in 5:34 of the law as a *paideutes* ("teacher," "instructor"), yet without expressly calling the law a *paidagogos*.

From such a collection of Greek and Jewish references it can be seen that Paul's use of παιδαγωγός in Gal 3:24-25, though creatively applied, is not an isolated phenomenon. The pedagogue, though usually a slave, was an important figure in ancient patrician households, being charged with the supervision and conduct of one or more of the sons in the family. He was distinguished from the teacher (διδάσκαλος or καθηγητής), for he gave no formal instruction but administered the directives of the father in a custodial manner—though, of course, indirectly he taught by the supervision he gave and the discipline he administered. The characterization of the pedagogue as having "the bad image of being rude, rough, and good for no other business," one for whom "the public did not have much respect," and "a comic type," as Hans Dieter Betz portrays him (*Galatians*, 177), arises from caricatures drawn by ancient playwrights. But it is a caricature and entirely ignores passages that speak of him as a trusted figure in antiquity who commanded respect and even affection. Plutarch (c. 46–120 CE), the Greek essayist and Pythian priest, considered the term appropriate for a good political leader when he wrote of Aratus in his *Parallel Lives*: "And all the world thought that Aratus was a good pedagogue for a kingdom no less than for a democracy, for his principles and character were manifest, like color in a fabric, in the actions of the king" (*Parallel Lives* on *Aratus* 48.3).

The depiction of the ancient pedagogue as a grim and ugly character is, indeed, a caricature, and must not be imported into Paul's statements in Gal 3:24-25. Yet, on the other hand, it is not possible to interpret Gal 3:24-25 as assigning a positive preliminary or preparatory role to the law. The point of the analogy for Paul is not that the law was a preparation for Christ. Rather, the focus is on the inferior status of one who is under a pedagogue and the temporary nature of such a situation.

2. *The Illustration of a Son in a Patrician Household*

There can be no doubt that the illustration of Gal 4:1-7 of a son in a patrician household is meant to illumine what is said in 3:23-29 and to carry on the analogy of the pedagogue in 3:24-25. The titles ἐπίτροπος ("manager," "foreman," "guardian") and οἰκονόμος ("steward," "manager," "trustee") of 4:2 have given rise to a great deal of discussion as to their precise meaning and the exact law that the apostle had in mind. But they are certainly meant in some way to be synonymous with παιδαγωγός. This is particularly clear for ἐπίτροπος, which was a frequent term in Greek and became a loan word in Hebrew for the guardian of a minor. And while there is no certain instance of the use of οἰκονόμος in the literature of antiquity for one who has charge of the person or estate of a minor, nor any case of the terms ἐπίτροπος and οἰκονόμος being used together, οἰκονόμος appears frequently in Greek and as a loan word in Hebrew for a slave acting as a household steward or administrator for his master.

Some have argued from the combination of titles that Paul had in mind the Roman law (known to us from a later period) that decreed that a minor was under a παιδαγωγός or ἐπίτροπος until his fourteenth year, and thereafter under a κουρατώρ ("curator") until his twenty-fifth year. Against this, however, it must be noted (1) that Paul could have said explicitly ἐπίτροπος καὶ κουρατώρ, thereby using the precise legal terms, rather than ἐπίτροπος καὶ οἰκονόμος, if he had this in mind, (2) that Paul adds "until the time set by his father," whereas Roman law itself fixed the time during which a child was under the supervision of a παιδαγωγός or ἐπίτροπος and then under that of a κουρατώρ, and (3) that among Greeks there seems to have been no such distinction between an ἐπίτροπος and a κουρατώρ. Thus like Demosthenes (384–322 BCE), the greatest of the Greek orators, who in his *Against Nausimachus* used "guardian" (ἐπίτροπος) and "caretaker" (κηδεμῶν) as a double title for the one man Aristaechmus (*Nausimachus* 12. 988[2]), we should probably regard οἰκονόμος as being roughly synonymous with ἐπίτροπος, with the plural forms appearing as qualitative plurals. Perhaps Paul's joining of these titles came about because of his references to imprisonment in 3:22-23 and to slavery in 4:1, 3, for οἰκονόμος was also used in antiquity of a household administrator who supervised slaves.

In the Greco-Roman world the words κληρονόμος ("heir"), νήπιος ("young child," "minor") and κύριος ("lord," "master," "owner") were also legal terms, as was, as we noted, ἐπίτροπος ("guardian," "manager")—all of which suggests that Paul's illustration was drawn from some legal practice of the day known both to him and to his readers. The precise details of that practice may be unclear to us today, simply because our texts come from various periods and represent various jurisdictions (i.e., Roman, Athenian or provincial). To further complicate matters, being more interested in the application than the details Paul could have made the illustration conform to his desired purpose, for no illustration is required to represent precisely every aspect of a situation in order to be meaningful or telling. But however we identify the source of the illustration and the exact significance of the terms in antiquity, Paul's meaning is clear: The guardianship of the Mosaic law was meant to be for a time when God's people were in their spiritual minority, but now with the coming of Christ the time set by the Father has been fulfilled and Christians are to live freely as mature sons apart from the law's supervision.

All of the nuances in Paul's analogy of the pedagogue in 3:24-25 are picked up in his illustration of 4:1-7: sons of a household, kept under restraint during the period of their minority, but destined to be mature, truly free and heirs of the estate through the father's action and at a time set by the father. The only feature in the illustration that goes beyond the analogy is the idea of υἱοθεσία ("adoption"), which was a legal term for the adoption of children. Here, evidently, Paul's theology of grace has outrun his illustration, yet without setting aside the main point of the illustration: that custodial care under an appointed guardian comes to an end at a time set by the father, resulting in mature freedom and the full possession of all that has been promised by the father.

3. *The Argument of Galatians 3:19–4:7*

When Paul raises the question "Why then the law?" (τί οὖν ὁ νόμος) in Gal 3:19, he does so both because his previous argument has brought him to it and because a proper Christian attitude toward the law is at the heart of the problem he is addressing. Having argued that righteousness comes by faith and not by observing the law—and in the process seeming to leave no function at all for the law—Paul turns in 3:19–4:7 to a consideration of the law's purpose and function. And here, undoubtedly, the law he has in mind is the Mosaic law, for it is identified in 3:17 as "the law that was given 430 years later," is spoken of in 3:19b as having been "ordained through angels by the hand of a mediator," and is equated in 3:22 with "the Scripture" (ἡ γραφή).

Of this Mosaic law Paul makes four opening statements in 3:19 by way of defining its purpose and function: (1) "it was added because of transgressions" (τῶν παραβάσεων χάριν προσετέθη), (2) "until the Seed to whom the promise referred should come" (ἄχρις οὗ ἔλθη τὸ σπέρμα ᾧ ἐπήγγελται), (3) "it was ordained through angels" (διαταγεὶς δι' ἀγγέλων), (4) "by the hand of a mediator" (ἐν χειρὶ μεσίτου). Now certainly there are a number of matters here that may be taken in any one of several ways, particularly the expression "because of transgressions" (τῶν παραβάσεων χάριν) and the comment of 3:20 that arises from the word "mediator": "A mediator, however, is not of one; but God is one" (ὁ δὲ μεσίτης ἑνὸς οὐκ ἔστιν, ὁ δὲ θεὸς εἷς ἐστιν). J. B. Lightfoot has commented (certainly in hyperbolic fashion) on these words of 3:20: "The number of interpretations of this passage is said to mount up to 250 or 300 (*St Paul's Epistle to the Galatians* [London: Macmillan, 1865], 147). Thankfully, Lightfoot never attempted to list all of those 250 to 300 interpretations. But our uncertainties regarding some matters must not be allowed to divert attention from Paul's main point. Nor should these statements be considered just four unconnected statements given *seriatim* without any apparent cohesion, as many commentators have tended to treat them. Rather, what ties all four of these statements together is the emphasis on the inferior status of the Mosaic law vis-à-vis the promise given in the Abrahamic covenant—an inferiority expressed in terms of the law's temporary status, its purpose and function, and the manner in which it was given. In these four statements, in fact, Paul sets the theme for all that follows in 3:19–4:7.

Ernest deWitt Burton has rightly caught the thrust of Paul's four statements and so says of the first: "προσετέθη marks the law as supplementary and hence subordinate to the covenant"; in fact, "the law in the apostle's thought forms no part of the covenant, [it] is a thing distinct from it, in no way modifying its provisions" (*A Critical*

and Exegetical Commentary on the Epistle to the Galatians [Edin-
burgh: T. & T. Clark, 1921], 188). As for the second statement,
Burton observes: "The whole clause, ἄχρις, etc., sets the limit to the
period during which the law continues. Thus the covenant of promise
is presented to the mind as of permanent validity, both beginning
before and continuing through the period of the law and afterwards;
the law on the other hand is temporary, added to the permanent
covenant for a period limited in both directions" (*ibid.* 189). And on
the third and fourth statements (which Burton treats together),
particularly in commenting on the pejorative references to "angels,"
"hand" and "mediator," he says: "The intent of the whole phrase is to
depreciate the law as not given directly by God" (*ibid.*).

Having set the theme, Paul goes on in 3:21 to insist that the law and
the promises of God are neither the same, as the Judaizers evidently
claimed, nor opposed to one another, as antinomians would hold—that
is, neither complementary nor contradictory, neither in continuum nor
in contrast—but that they function on different levels in the economy
of God or "operate in different spheres" (*ibid.* 193). Then in 3:22-23
Paul sets out a twofold purpose for the Law: (1) to condemn sin and
declare all mankind guilty, so that men and women might turn to God
by faith and thereby receive what is promised (v 22), and (2) to
supervise and have custodial care over the righteous (note the change
to the first person plural in the verb ἐφρουρούμεθα, "we were held
prisoners," and the participle συγκλειόμενοι, "we were locked up")
until "the intended faith" (τὴν μέλλουσαν πίστιν), which came in
Jesus Christ, should be revealed (v 23). Of both purposes he uses
συγκλείω ("lock up, hem in, imprison"), first as a finite verb and then
as an adverbial participle, to portray the way the law works, for in
both cases the feature of constraint is prominent—in the first, by
condemning sin; in the second, by supervising life. Of the second, the
supervision and custodial care of the righteous, he uses the analogy of
the pedagogue in 3:24-25 and the illustration of a son in a patrician
household in 4:1-7, for these figures were particularly suggestive (as
we have seen) in nuancing what he means by "we were held prisoners
by the law" (ὑπὸ νόμον ἐφρουρούμεθα συγκλειόμενοι).

With regard to the first purpose, God's law—as given at the dawn
of human consciousness, as reiterated and clarified in the law of
Moses, and as intensified and heightened in the teachings and example
of Jesus—continues to provide the standard necessary for an

intelligent and realistic act of repentance. It calls on us to recognize how far from God's demands even our best thoughts and actions are, thereby providing an objective standard for self-criticism. It brings home God's judgment on us. To accept this judgment is, in fact, the first step in what the New Testament calls "repentance" (cf. C. H. Dodd, *Gospel and Law: The Relation of Faith and Ethics in Early Christianity*. New York: Columbia University Press, 1951], 61). It is, as Martin Luther called it, "God's strange work" as compared to "God's proper work," for it brings us down that we might then by faith look up to receive God's gift of righteousness ("Treatise on Christian Liberty," *Works of Martin Luther*, 2.317).

With regard, however, to the second purpose for the law, Paul says quite clearly that it functioned in this manner "until the intended faith" (εἰς τὴν μέλλουσαν πίστιν, i.e., "the faith" that came with Christ) should be revealed" (3:23; cf. v 19). This suggests that some difference in the divine economy took place with the coming of Christ, with that difference being that righteousness is now apart from the law (cf. Rom 3:21)—yet without in any way nullifying the promise. Or, as Burton expresses it:

> That the relation of men to God was different after the period of law was ended from what it had been under the law is implied in v. 23. But that the promise with its principle of faith was in no way abrogated or suspended in or after the period of the law is the unequivocal affirmation of vv. 15-18, and clearly implied in the quotation in v. 11 of Hab. 2:4, which the apostle doubtless ascribed to this period (*Galatians*, 189).

In the analogy of the pedagogue used to represent this supervisory function of the law, Paul's emphasis appears in 3:25: "But now with the coming of 'the intended faith' we are no longer under the pedagogue." And in his illustration of a boy in a patrician household his conclusion in 4:7 highlights his main concern: "So you are no longer a slave, but a son; and since you are a son, God has made you also an heir."

In light of this we must reject the interpretation of εἰς Χριστόν in 3:24 as suggesting the idea of a positive educational development from the religion of Israel to Christianity. That is what is said elsewhere of the Mosaic law in such passages as Rom 3:21b ("being witnessed to by the law and the prophets") and Rom 3:31b ("we establish the law"). But it is not what is being said here. Rather, εἰς

Χριστόν must be taken here in the temporal sense of "until Christ." With the coming of Christ the supervisory function of the law ended, just as the services of a pedagogue end when his charge comes to maturity. Any endeavor on the part of a son who has reached maturity and come into possession of his inheritance to revert back to the supervision of an administrative guardian would be a reversion to childishness—it would, in fact, be a return to what Paul calls "the elemental principles/teachings of the world" (τὰ στοιχεῖα τοῦ κόσμου). For when God moves forward in his redemptive economy, any reversion or standing still becomes a "worldly" act, no matter how good or how appropriate such a stance once was (cf. the reference to the tabernacle as "a worldly sanctuary" in Heb 9:1, it being so because God's economy of redemption had moved beyond even what he had graciously provided earlier.)

4. *The Relevance of All This for the Question of Christians and the Mosaic Law*

What then should we say as to the relevance of Paul's pedagogue analogy of Gal 3:24-25, his illustration of a son in a patrician household in Gal 4:1-7, and his overall argument of Gal 3:19–4:7 for the question of Christians and the Mosaic law? Some hold that we should say very little, because 3:19–4:7 is only a digression from the main argument in 3:1-18. Others hold that we should say little, because here Paul has gotten carried away in the heat of controversy and has overstated his position. Many ignore Gal 3:19–4:7 almost entirely, evidently believing that all that is necessary for the topic resides in 3:1-18 and in certain statements to be found in the letter to the Romans. Such disparaging attitudes, however, I consider to be wrongheaded, believing that in Gal 3:19–4:7 Paul has given us an important answer to a perennial problem of Christian theology and life-style—an answer that needs to be highlighted, particularly in evangelical circles today.

Three points, briefly, need to be made by way of bringing this all together and in conclusion. In the first place, it needs to be stressed that Paul is not denying that God's self-revelation (be it defined as Torah, "instruction" or "law") stands as the external standard for all human thought and action. Paul implies as much in 3:19 when he says that the law "was added because of transgressions," and he says it directly in 3:22 when he declares that "the Scripture consigns (or, 'imprisons') all things under sin." Yet while Paul holds to the eternal validity of God's law as the standard of righteousness that condemns sin and thereby brings us to an intelligent and realistic act of repentance, he sees that law as having reached its zenith in the teachings and example of Jesus Christ. Thus he tells the Corinthians that though he is "free" and "not under the law," he is "not free from God's law" because he is "under Christ's Law" (1 Cor 9:19-21, ἔννομος Χριστοῦ; "in-lawed of Christ").

Second, it needs to be insisted that Paul always was against any idea of soteriological legalism—that is, that false understanding of the law by which people think they can turn God's self-revelation to their own advantage, thereby gaining divine favor and acceptance. This, too, the prophets of Israel denounced, for legalism in this sense was never a legitimate part of Israel's religion. But it was, it appears, part of the Judaizers' message—whether overtly or unintentionally. And it is this that Paul opposes when he speaks pejoratively of "the works of the law" (ἔργα νόμου). Thus in Gal 2:15-21, recalling his words to Peter among Christians at Syrian Antioch, he writes: "We who are Jews by birth and not 'sinners of the Gentiles' know that a person is not justified by observing the Law (ἐξ ἔργων νόμου), ... because by observing the law (ἐξ ἔργων νόμου) no one will be justified... I do not set aside the grace of God, for if righteousness could be gained through the law (διὰ νόμου) Christ died for nothing." And so in Gal 3:1-18 he argues from his converts' experience of the Spirit, from God's promise to Abraham, and from the priority of the Abrahamic covenant against the Judaizers' soteriological legalism.

A third point, however, needs also to be emphasized—particularly because it is so often neglected—and that is that Paul not only opposes in Galatians a soteriological legalism but also the necessity for a nomistic lifestyle. The Jewish religion at its best was never, nor is it today, legalistic in the sense we have defined that term above. The decalogue, for example, was not understood as ten prescriptions for attaining God's favor, but as (1) a declaration of God's personal relationship with his people and his salvific action on their behalf (Exod 20:2: "I am the LORD your God, who brought you out of Egypt, out of the land of slavery") and then (2) a list of statements as to how God's people were to live in response to such a relationship and act. Yet while not legalistic, the religion of Israel, as well as all forms of ancient and modern Judaism, are avowedly nomistic—that is, they view the Torah, both Scripture and tradition, as supervising the lives of God's own, so that all questions of conduct are ultimately measured against the touchstone of the Mosaic law and all of life is to be directed in one way or another by the law. While the prophets denounced legalism, they never sought to set aside the custodial function of the law for the righteous. The Mosaic law was for Israel, therefore, not only the standard by which righteousness was defined and sin denounced, it was also a system by which the lives of God's people were regulated. The law did not make people righteous, but it served as (1) the standard for an intelligent and realistic act of repentance, and (2) a system to supervise the lives of God's people as they responded by faith to divine mercy. In such ways the law was associated formally with righteousness in Israel's experience.

The Judaizers at Galatia were evidently attempting to foist upon Paul's converts both a soteriological legalism and a nomistic lifestyle, arguing that both were pragmatically important and theologically necessary. Like the prophets of old, Paul denounces their legalism (Gal 2:16-21; 3:1-18). And like the prophets of old, he affirms that one of the purposes of the Mosaic law was to set the standard for righteousness and thereby condemn sin (Gal 3:19a, 22)—though he also sees that standard as expressed preeminently in the teachings and example of Jesus, and so appeals to "the law of Christ" (ὁ νόμος τοῦ Χριστοῦ) in his final exhortation to his Galatian converts "to bear each other's burdens" (Gal 6:1-2). But unlike the prophets, the Judaizers, and all forms of ancient and modern Judaism, Paul's argument in Gal 3:19–4:7 is against any necessity for a nomistic lifestyle. For, as he sees it, such a life controlled by law was instituted by God only for the period of his people's spiritual minority and meant to last only until "the Christ" (Messiah) should come.

God's purpose in redemption has always been to bring his people to a full realization of their personal relationship with him as his sons and daughters, which includes a full possession of their promised inheritance. So with the coming of Christ, Paul insists that "we are no longer under the supervision of the law" (3:25) and "no longer a slave, but a son ... and also an heir" (4:7). It is for this reason that Judaism speaks of itself as being Torah-centered and Christianity declares that it is Christ-centered. For in Christ the Christian finds not only God's law as *standard* preeminently expressed, but also the law as a *system of conduct* set aside in favor of guidance by reference to Jesus' teachings and example and through the direct action of God's Spirit. Thus Paul proclaims that "Christ is the end of the law in its connection with righteousness to everyone who believes" (Rom 10:4, understanding the much disputed word τέλος as including the idea of "termination" and not to be understood as just "goal"). It is such a concept that Paul has nuanced by his use of the pedagogue analogy of Gal 3:24-25 and by his illustration of a son in a patrician household of Gal 4:1-7, and it is such a concept that Christians need to recapture today. Otherwise we are in danger of being "half-Judaizers"—that is, of denying the Judaizers' soteriological legalism but retaining their insistence on the necessity for a nomistic lifestyle. The argument of Gal 3:19–4:7, however, was given as a corrective to such thinking. It sets before us one important feature of the answer to the question concerning Christians and the Mosaic law.

SELECT BIBLIOGRAPHY

Betz, Hans Dieter. *Galatians: A Commentary on Paul's Letter to the Churches in Galatia*. Hermeneia. Philadelphia: Fortress, 1979.
Burton, Ernest deWitt. *A Critical and Exegetical Commentary on the Epistle to the Galatians*. ICC. Edinburgh: T. & T. Clark, 1921.
Callan, Terrance. "Pauline Midrash: The Exegetical Background of Gal. 3:19b," *JBL* 99 (1980) 549-67.
Dodd, C. H. *Gospel and Law: The Relation of Faith and Ethics in Early Christianity*. New York: Columbia University Press, 1951.
Goldin, Judah. "Not by Means of an Angel and Not by Means of a Messenger," in *Religions in Antiquity. Essays in Memory of Erwin Ramsdell Goodenough*. Numen Supplements, 14. Ed. J. Neusner. Leiden: Brill, 1968, 412-24.
Hübner, Hans. *Das Gesetz bei Paulus*, 2nd ed. Göttingen: Vandenhoeck & Ruprecht, 1980.
Lightfoot, Joseph B. *Saint Paul's Epistle to the Galatians*. London: Macmillan, 1865; 10th ed. 1890.
Longenecker, Richard N. *Galatians*. WBC. Dallas: Word, 1990.
Lull, David J. "'The Law Was Our Pedagogue': A Study in Galatians 3:19-25," *JBL* 105 (1986) 481-98.
Luther, Martin. "A Treatise on Christian Liberty," *Works of Martin Luther*, vol. 2, trans. W. A. Lambert. Philadelphia: Holman, 1916.
Matera, Frank J. *Galatians*. SP. Collegeville: Liturgical Press, 1992.
Mussner, Franz. *Der Galaterbrief*. Freiburg: Herder, 1974.
Räisänen, Heikki. *Paul and the Law*. Tübingen: Mohr, 1983, 1987[2].

Sanders, E. P. *Paul, the Law, and the Jewish People*. Philadelphia: Fortress, 1983,
     esp. 65-70.
Westerholm, Stephen. *Israel's Law and the Church's Faith: Paul and his Recent
     Interpreters*. Grand Rapids: Eerdmans, 1988, esp. 174-222.
Young, Norman H. "παιδαγωγός: The Social Setting of a Pauline Metaphor,"
     NovT 29 (1987) 150-76.

4

PROLEGOMENA TO PAUL'S USE OF SCRIPTURE IN ROMANS

Paul's letter to the Romans has always been highly regarded by Christians. It has been, in large measure, the heartland of Christian theology and piety. Throughout the two millennia of its existence, its status in the church has been more highly acclaimed than that of any other New Testament writing.

Yet despite its importance and status, Romans is probably the most difficult letter of the New Testament to analyze and interpret. It can hardly be called a simple writing. Augustine, for example, began in the winter of 394–395 to write a commentary on Romans. But after producing materials on 1:1-7 (see his *Epistolae ad Romanos inchoata expositio* [*PL*, 35.2087-2106]), he felt unable to proceed, saying that the project was just too large for him and that he would return to easier tasks (cf. *Retractationes* 1.25 [*CSEL*, 84.183-85]).

Erasmus in 1517, when introducing his *Paraphrase of Romans* with a discussion on "The Argument of the Epistle of Paul to the Romans," said of the letter: "The difficulty of this letter equals and almost surpasses its utility!"—citing Origen and Jerome, who also found the letter difficult (Erasmus, *Opera* 7.777). As Erasmus saw it, its difficulty stems from three causes: (1) its literary style, for "nowhere else is the order of speech more confused; nowhere is the speech more split by the transposition of words; nowhere is the speech more incomplete through absence of an apodosis," (2) its content or the "obscurity of things which are hard to put into words," for "no other letter is handicapped by more frequent rough spots or is broken by deeper chasms," and (3) its "frequent and sudden changes of masks" or shifting stances on the part of the author, for "he considers now the Jews, now the Gentiles, now both; sometimes he addresses believers, sometimes doubters; at one point he assumes the role of a weak man, at another of a strong; sometimes that of a godly man, sometimes of an ungodly man" (*ibid.* 7.777-78).

In addition to style, content and shifting stances, Erasmus could have referred to the difficulty of understanding Paul's use of Scripture. And it is this feature of the letter that we intend to examine in this chapter.

1. *Questions Arising from Paul's Use of Scripture*

Paul's use of Scripture in Romans presents the interpreter with a number of perplexing questions. Eight, in particular, are important here. One set of questions focuses on issues that may be classed as being more introductory in nature—that is, questions that concern the concentration, distribution and purpose of the biblical quotations in the letter. First of all, one must ask: (1) Why did Paul use so many Old Testament quotations in Romans, when elsewhere in his letters he is more reserved in the use of Scripture? For of the approximately 83 places in the Pauline corpus where quotations are to be found—totaling some 100 biblical passages, if one disengages the conflated texts and separates the possible dual sources—well over half appear in this letter: 45 of 83 in Romans (or 55–60 biblical passages of about 100 total, if the conflated texts and dual sources are unpacked and counted separately). Elsewhere in the Pauline letters there are 15 such places in 1 Corinthians, 7 in 2 Corinthians, 10 in Galatians, 4 in Ephesians, 1 in 1 Timothy, 1 in 2 Timothy, but none in 1 Thessalonians, 2 Thessalonians, Philippians, Colossians, Philemon, or Titus. Also to be asked is: (2) Why is the distribution of Old Testament quotations in Romans so uneven? For about 18 quotations appear in eight or nine places in 1:16–4:25 and about 30 quotations in 25–26 places in 9:1–11:36—with an additional ten to be found in the exhortations of 12:1–15:13 and one more in the so-called Apostolic Parousia of 15:14-32—whereas biblical quotations occur only twice, and then somewhat tangentially, in what has seemed to most interpreters to be the apex of Paul's argument in 5:1–8:39 (once in 7:7, citing in illustrative fashion the tenth commandment "Do not covet" of Exod 20:17 and Deut 5:21; once in 8:36, in what appears to be a traditional confessional portion that makes use of Ps 44:22).

Further, one might ask, (3) Why did Paul use the Old Testament at all in writing to Christians at Rome, particularly when his addressees are identified as being within the orbit of his Gentile ministry (1:5-6;

13-15; 15:15-16), explicitly addressed as Gentiles (11:13), and distinguished in their ancestry from his own Jewish ancestry (9:3; 11:14)? One could understand why Paul used Scripture so extensively in writing to Gentile believers at Galatia and Corinth, particularly if the problem at Galatia stemmed from "Judaizers" who themselves were using the Old Testament for their own purposes and if the "Peter party" at Corinth represented some form of Jewish Christian propaganda. The use of Scripture in Ephesians and the letters to Timothy, though more infrequent, might even be justified on the basis of Ephesians being a circular letter to mixed congregations and Timothy having been trained in the Scriptures by his mother. But Romans cannot easily be "mirror read" so as to identify any Jewish or Jewish-Christian protagonists or opponents. And Paul's more common practice when writing Gentile believers, particularly those not affected by a problem of Jewish origin, was not to quote Scripture at all in support of his arguments (though, of course, his language was always informed by biblical idioms and expressions)—as witness his letters to the Thessalonians, Philippians and Colossians, as well as to Philemon and Titus.

A second set of questions regarding the use of Scripture in Romans focuses on comparative issues. Here one must ask: (4) How do Paul's exegetical procedures in Romans compare to those of Second Temple Judaism and early Rabbinic Judaism, and what effect do such cognate exegetical practices have on our understanding of Paul's treatment of the Old Testament?, and (5) How does Paul's use of the Old Testament compare to his use of Scripture in his other writings, particularly in Galatians where there is an overlap of topics and similar treatments?

A third set of questions brings us to the very heart of matters in dealing with interpretive issues: (6) Why do the textforms of Paul's biblical quotations differ from those attributed to Jesus in the four Gospels and those credited to the earliest preachers in the Book of Acts? For in Paul's quotations, both in Romans and throughout his other letters, there appears a rather peculiar mix of textual readings. Over half of the Pauline textforms are either absolute or virtual reproductions of the LXX, with about half of these at variance with the MT. But almost another half vary from both the LXX and the MT to a greater or lesser extent—and once in Romans (11:35, citing Job 41:11 in a traditional theocentric doxology) and three times elsewhere in the Pauline corpus (1 Cor 3:19, citing Job 5:13; 2 Cor 9:9, citing Ps 112:9; and 2 Tim 2:19, citing Num 16:5) the texts are in agreement with the MT against the LXX. By contrast, the texts used by Jesus and the earliest Christian preachers are reported as having been dominantly septuagintal in form.

Likewise it must be asked: (7) How can the wide scope of Paul's treatment of Old Testament texts be understood, ranging, as it does, from his quite literal "pearl-stringing" approach in Rom 3:10-18 to his seeming disregard of the original text and context in Rom 10:6-8 (where Deut 30:12-14 is cited in an inexact and possibly proverbial manner to his own advantage; cf. Eph 4:8, where Ps 68:18 is cited in a similar fashion). And, finally, it needs to be asked: (8) What does it mean to speak of Paul's "christocentric exegetical orientation," and how did such a perspective affect his interpretation of holy Scripture?

2. Preliminary Considerations Regarding Addressees and Purpose

The above questions cannot be treated in isolation or in any atomistic fashion. Rather, much depends on how one views (1) the addressees and their circumstances, and (2) Paul's purpose in writing the letter. These are matters that are being extensively debated today, with many finding it necessary to "go back to square one." But such a reevaluation is absolutely necessary, particularly if Romans is to be read as a letter and not as a theological tractate or a compendium of the Christian religion. For as a letter, it cannot be accurately interpreted—and its use of Scripture rightly appreciated—unless the nature and circumstances of its addressees are correctly identified and its purpose properly understood.

The Addressees and Their Circumstances

The usual way of determining the identity and circumstances of Paul's Roman addressees has been by "mirror reading" the letter itself. It is impossible here to identify all of the positions that have been taken using this approach, or to list all of the data that have been cited in attempting to justify the various views proposed. Suffice it only to say that, using a mirror-reading method, some have found the Jewish features of the letter and what they take to be the letter's contra-Jewish polemics (esp. vis-à-vis Galatians) to be the controlling factors in their determination of the identity and circumstances of the letter's addressees. Others, however, have insisted that the facts that Gentiles are directly addressed and that there are a number of gentilistic features in the letter to be decisive for determining the addressees' identity. Still others have proposed a mixed audience of Jewish and Gentile believers, though with the Gentiles in the majority and the Roman church experiencing some difficulties—either of a doctrinal or an ethical nature, or both—arising from the interaction between these two groups.

But mirror reading only works well where one is dealing with either polemics (i.e., an aggressive explication that seeks to counter specific errors, whether doctrinal or ethical) or apology (i.e., a defensive response to accusations)—that is, where one can be reasonably sure that the agenda of a particular writing is driven by some error, need or situation that was present among the addressees, and not just by a desire for contact or communication on the part of the author himself. The problem, however, is that it is not always easy in a letter to distinguish between (1) polemic, (2) apology, and (3) exposition. In particular, the problem in applying this method to Romans is that, while the letter is forthright in its exposition, it is notoriously vague when it comes to matters of polemic and apology.

We need not deny that circumstances at Rome played a part in motivating Paul to write, or that some knowledge of the situation of the Roman Christians can be derived from mirror reading his letter to them. But something of a dead end seems to have come about in the identification of Paul's addressees and their circumstances through a mirror-reading approach—with data derived from external sources only being utilized later in order to supplement conclusions reached by such an internal process. It is, therefore, probably better to start the other way around: first, by giving attention to external considerations; then to note how a mirror reading of the letter might support the hypotheses proposed from such an external approach.

As Wolfgang Wiefel has pointed out, questions regarding the origin of Roman Christianity, its character, and the identity and circumstances of Paul's addressees in Romans "cannot be clarified without considering the entire phenomenon of Judaism in Rome" ("The Jewish Community in Ancient Rome and the Origins of Roman Christianity," in *The Romans Debate: Revised and Expanded Edition*, ed. K. P. Donfried [Peabody: Hendrickson, 1991], 85-101 [86]). It is impossible here to enter into a full discussion of Jews and Judaism at Rome. But three matters drawn from Wiefel's article seem especially important as background for any consideration of the identity and circumstances of Paul's addressees: (1) that of Roman Jewry's decentralized situation administratively and socially; (2) that of Roman Jewry's religious dependence on Palestinian Jewry; and (3) that of the continued existence of Jews in Rome even after Claudius's edict of expulsion in 49 CE. With regard to the first two of these matters, undoubtedly the decentralized situation of the Jews at Rome and their close ties with Palestinian Jewry had an impact on the character of Christianity at Rome as it arose within the city's various synagogues. So it may be postulated, what with Roman Christianity coming to birth within the context of Roman Jewry, that the first Christians of the city of Rome, though in fellowship with one another, probably did not develop any central governing structure or agency, but looked primarily to the Jerusalem church for their spiritual direction.

And with regard to the third of the above matters, the continued existence of Jews in Rome after the Edict of Claudius, it may also be postulated that the emperor's order of expulsion was directed primarily against those Jews who were in Rome's eyes stirring up trouble and causing dissension among the Jewish populace of the city, whether in defense of traditional Judaism or in proclaiming Jesus of Nazareth as the Jewish Messiah (cf. Suetonius, *Vita Claudii* 25.4, interpreting "Chresto" as a reference to Christ, whether intended or inadvertent). It seems likely, for a number of reasons, that many Jews continued to live in Rome or returned to Rome during the latter years of Claudius's reign. Their existence in the city after Claudius's edict, of course, would have been severely restricted, for with the emperor's edict they also lost the right of free assembly in their various synagogal groupings. But it need not be held that a Jewish component was no longer part of a Christian presence at Rome, for many Jewish believers in Jesus may have remained in the city and have had some influence within the developing Christian congregations, whatever might be postulated regarding their numbers compared to Gentile believers within that community.

The question to be asked regarding the identity and character of Christians at Rome when Paul wrote them, however, is not, "Were they Jews or Gentiles, or, if ethnically mixed, dominantly one or the other?"—with the implications being that if Jewish believers, then they should be viewed as non-Pauline in outlook, but if Gentile believers, then adherents to Paul's teaching. Undoubtedly the addressees constituted both Jewish and Gentile believers in Jesus. And probably the Gentiles were in the majority, for Paul considered the Roman church to be within the orbit of his Gentile ministry. But rather than trying to determine the addressees' character on the basis of their ethnicity, "the crucial issue," as Raymond Brown has pointed out, "is the theological outlook of this mixed Jewish/Gentile Christianity" ("The Beginnings of Christianity at Rome" and "The Roman Church near the End of the First Christian Generation (A.D. 58—Paul to the Romans)," in R. E. Brown and J. P. Meier, *Antioch and Rome: New Testament Cradles of Catholic Christianity* [New York: Paulist, 1983], 92-127 [109, n. 227]).

The testimony of the fourth century commentator "Ambrosiaster" (as dubbed by Erasmus) is that believers at Rome, both Jews and Gentiles, "came to embrace faith in Christ ... according to the Jewish rite (*ritu licet judaico*)" (*Commentarium ... ad Romanos* [*CSEL*, 81.1.6], as per codex K). Closely aligned with this view is the suggestion of the early second century Roman historian Tacitus that Judean Christianity and Roman Christianity are to be seen as being directly related:

> This pernicious superstition [i.e., Christianity, which Tacitus had earlier said arose in Judea during the reign of Tiberius] had broken out again [i.e., during Nero's reign], not only in Judea (where the mischief had originated) but even in the capital city [i.e., Rome] where all degraded and shameful practices collect and become the vogue (*Annals* 15.44).

Therefore we should probably highlight as being of major importance the axis that ran from Roman Christianity back to the Jerusalem church in Judea. And if that be true, then we should understand Paul's Roman addressees—even though dominantly Gentile believers, and so within the orbit of his Gentile ministry—to be principally influenced in their thought, traditions and religious practices by Jewish Christianity as centered in Jerusalem.

In addition, as Brown has further pointed out, the witness of the Acts of the Apostles needs here to be taken into account:

> According to Acts, for the first two Christian decades, Jerusalem and Antioch served as the dissemination points of the Gospel. Because of his interest in Paul, the author keeps us well informed of missions to the West moving out from Antioch, but there is never a suggestion that a mission went from Antioch to Rome. (Indeed, in the first 15 chapters of Acts the only mention of Rome/Roman is 2:10, which

notes the presence of Roman Jews at Jerusalem on the first Pentecost.)
There are no arguments from Acts for a site other than Jerusalem as
the source for Roman Christianity, and Acts 28:21 relates that Jews in
Rome had channels of theological information coming from Jerusalem
("Beginnings of Christianity at Rome," 103-104).

So Brown concluded: (1) that for both Jews and Christians "the
Jerusalem–Rome axis was strong," (2) "that Roman Christianity came
from Jerusalem, and indeed represented the Jewish/Gentile Christianity associated with such Jerusalem figures as Peter and James," and
(3) that both in the earliest days of the Roman church and at the time
when Paul wrote them, believers at Rome could be characterized as
"Christians who kept up some Jewish observances and remained
faithful to part of the heritage of the Jewish Law and cult, without
insisting on circumcision" (*ibid.*, 104). With such an understanding of
the addressees and their circumstances Joseph Fitzmyer has recently
expressed agreement, though without spelling out the implications of
such a view (*Romans*, 33-34). And it is this understanding that will be
postulated in what follows, believing it to be the position that is best
supported by all of the available data—and believing that it casts
Paul's use of Scripture in Romans in an entirely new light.

Paul's Purpose in Writing
One other preliminary consideration, however, needs also to be
raised—that is, the question regarding Paul's purpose in writing
Romans. For unless one reads the letter in a purely devotional, theological, homiletical, canonical, liberation, or some other "reader
response" manner, how one understands an author's purpose has a
profound effect on how one understands the character and content of
what is written.

This is a matter, of course, that has taken center stage in many
recent scholarly treatments of Romans (cf., e.g., K. P. Donfried's collection of essays in *Romans Debate*, which was first published in 1977
and then revised and expanded in 1991). At the heart of the issue are
the questions: "Was Romans written principally to counteract some
problem or problems within the church at Rome—whether doctrinal
or ethical, and whether arising from outside the body of believers or
from within?," or, "Did the decisive motivation for Paul's writing
spring from within his own ministry—whether to introduce himself to
an unknown audience, to defend himself against possible misunderstanding, to assert his apostolic authority over a group of

believers whom he considered part of his Gentile mission, to set out his understanding of the Christian message as something of a 'last will and testament', or to seek support for his forthcoming mission to the western regions of the Roman empire?" Or to frame the questions in a somewhat different manner: "Was Paul's purpose in writing Romans principally pastoral in nature, being motivated by a desire to correct problems, whether doctrinal or ethical, within the Roman church?" Or, "Was Paul's purpose primarily missionary in nature, being motivated by his own sense of mission, by his own consciousness of being appointed by God as an apostle to the Gentiles, and/or by issues that had arisen previously in his ministry?" (cf. A. J. M. Wedderburn, *The Reasons for Romans* [Edinburgh: T. & T. Clark, 1988], 1-6, 140-42, *passim*; L. A. Jervis, *The Purpose of Romans: A Comparative Letter Structure Investigation* [Sheffield: Sheffield Academic Press, 1991], 11-28).

These two questions, as posed, may not represent mutually exclusive options. Various interpretive possibilities exist within each of them. In fact, scholars have often tried to bring together a number of such possibilities in positing "reasons for Romans," selecting some from the first set and some from the second (so, e.g., Wedderburn, *ibid.*). Yet in asking whether Paul's purpose in writing Romans was motivated principally (1) by conditions within the church at Rome, or (2) by factors arising from within his own consciousness and ministry, we seem to have come to something of a watershed in the matter. And it is probably not too extreme to claim that from this watershed flows almost everything else that one might say about the character, form and content of Romans.

Our thesis regarding Paul's purpose in writing Romans is that it stems principally from his own consciousness and ministry—though also that it may have been occasioned, in part, by the particular circumstances of his addressees. The opening Salutation (1:1-7) and Thanksgiving (1:8-12) and the closing Apostolic Parousia (15:14-32) and Conclusion (15:33–16:23, probably also 16:25-27)—with the first two sections setting out the agenda of the letter and the latter two sections retrospectively referring to that agenda (cf. P. Schubert, *Form and Function of the Pauline Thanksgivings* [Berlin: Töpelmann, 1939]; Jervis, *Purpose of Romans*; J. A. D. Weima, *Neglected Endings: The Significance of the Pauline Letter Closings* [Sheffield: Sheffield Academic Press, 1994])—all highlight Paul's own concerns and his desires for believers at Rome, but provide little data regarding his addressees' situation. And the Body of the letter (1:16–15:13), as well, furnishes little data regarding their situation—unless, of course, one transposes Paul's exposition into polemics, thereby constructing a scenario of doctrinal problems at Rome by analogy to the problems at Galatia and/or ethical problems by analogy to those at Corinth.

A better approach, we suggest, is (1) to identify Paul's purpose(s) for writing Romans by means of a close reading of the agenda that he sets out in the opening sections of the letter and that he retrospectively refers to in the closing sections, especially in the Thanksgiving and Apostolic Parousia sections, but (2) to infer his addressees' circumstances (which must have had some part in occasioning the letter, even though Paul does not refer to them) by reference to the history and experiences of Jews at Rome (which were undoubtedly foundational in many ways for the Roman Christians, and probably analogous) and by reference to the suggestive statements that appear in Ambrosiaster (4th century), Tacitus (2nd century), and Acts (1st century), as referred to above.

With regard to Paul's purpose, it seems clear from the Thanksgiving and Apostolic Parousia that it was at least twofold: (1) to give his readers what he calls a χάρισμα πνευματικόν, or "spiritual gift," so as to strengthen them—a gift that he thought of as being uniquely his, but which he felt obligated to share with all those within the orbit of his Gentile mission (cf. 1:11-15; 15:15-18); and (2) to seek the assistance of the Roman Christians for the extension of his ministry to the western regions of the empire (cf. 1:10b, 13; 15:23-32). It may be, as well, that he wanted to prepare them theologically for his coming, so that they would understand more accurately and appreciate more fully what he was proclaiming in his ministry to Gentiles. And it may be that he wanted to head off doctrinal or ethical divisions among believers at Roman, so that they would be united in their support of his western mission. But these latter purposes, if real, seem to be more related to Paul's own agenda than to his addressees' concerns. And while it may be supposed that Paul had some uncertainties about how his theological views and personal presence would be received at Rome—particularly with believers there having been strongly influenced by Jewish Christianity—such concerns are not easily derived from a mirror-reading of the letter itself.

In characterizing Paul's addressees and their circumstances, therefore, it may be postulated (1) that ethnically they constituted both Jews and Gentiles, though with the latter more dominant, (2) that theologically they looked to the Jerusalem church for inspiration and guidance, reverenced the Mosaic law, and followed some of the Jewish rites, but were not Judaizers like those who troubled the Galatian congregations, and (3) that socially they were not meeting in Jewish synagogues (Claudius's edict having ended such synagogual gatherings) and were without an overarching administrative structure (in common with the situation of the Jews in the city), but were meeting for worship and fellowship in various believers' homes or "house churches" in a somewhat loose association of separate congregations. And if all this be true, one needs to read Paul's letter to the Romans in a different light than is usually done—particularly with respect to his use of Scripture.

3. *The Use of Traditional Materials*

For an understanding of his arguments, methods and procedures in Romans, it is important to have some appreciation of how Paul uses various traditional portions in the letter—particularly, how he uses materials that may be identified as stemming from a Jewish or Jewish Christian milieu. For how Paul uses such materials in Romans parallels to a large extent how he uses Scripture in that letter.

Most significant is Paul's use of early Christian confessional materials (cf. my *New Wine into Fresh Wineskins: Contextualizing the Early Christian Confessions* [Peabody: Hendrickson, 1999], 48-63). A great deal of attention has been directed during the past century to early Christian confessional materials incorporated within the New Testament—whether those materials are in the form of hymns (poetic affirmations), *homologia* (non-poetic statements), "Sayings," or christological titles. Paul's letters, in particular, have been the subject of many such investigations, with confessional materials having been found most readily in Philippians, 1 Corinthians, Galatians, 1 Thessalonians, Colossians and 1 Timothy (largely in that order). Romans, too, has been seen to contain some of these confessional portions— though much of Romans, particularly its large letter body, awaits a proper form-critical mining of what might very well be the "mother lode" of early Christian confessional materials. What have been identified to date as confessional materials within Romans are (1) the christological formulations of 1:3-4, 3:24-26 (or, 3:25-26), 4:25, and 10:9—probably also those of 9:5b and 14:9; (2) the theocentric hymn of 11:33-36; and (3) various confessional fragments brought together in the lyrical and almost defiant statements of 8:33-39. Each of these portions has its own form-critical features, its own history of identification, and its own postulated provenance. It is impossible here to enter into an extended discussion of such matters. Suffice it only to note those portions that have been, to date, identified as early Christian confessional materials used by Paul in Romans, and then to comment briefly on their usage.

Of interest for a structural analysis of Romans is the fact that three of these confessional portions appear as the final items of their respective sections, and so serve to summarize or conclude what was said earlier in those sections. Rom 4:25 ("Who was delivered over to death for our sins, and was raised to life for our justification") seems to function in this manner, summarizing the central statements of 3:21-31 and bringing to a climax the whole presentation of 1:16–4:24. Likewise, the forceful affirmations of 8:33-39, which probably include a number of early confessional statements, summarize and bring to a dramatic conclusion all that is said in chapters 5–8. And while it may be debated whether chapters 9–11 begin with a portion that includes a confessional doxology at 9:5b, certainly the majestic hymn of praise to God in 11:33-36 provides a fitting climax to those three chapters.

What seems to be occurring here is that Paul is using Christian confessional materials to close off each of the three main theological sections of his letter (i.e., 1:16–4:25, 5:1–8:39 and 9:1–11:36). And with addressees for whom he was not their spiritual father, but who looked to the Jerusalem church for their traditions and support (as suggested above), this was undoubtedly a strategic move on his part. For in concluding his three main theological sections with confessional materials that were known and accepted by his addressees—or, at least, with recognizable echoes from such materials—Paul would have "nailed down," as it were, their acceptance of his presentations.

There are also, however, three or four confessional portions used by Paul in the development of his theological arguments and exhortations: (1) 1:3-4, which sets out a two-stage understanding of Christ ("seed of David according to the flesh ... Son of God with power according to the Spirit of holiness by the resurrection from the dead"); (2) 3:24-26, which depicts God's salvific activity through the work of Christ in terms of "justification," "redemption," and "expiation–propitiation" in a manner and with terminology not quite Pauline; (3) 10:9, which incorporates the confession "Jesus is Lord"; and (4) 14:9, which in context has appeared to many to be an early Christian confessional portion: "Christ died and returned to life so that he might be the Lord of both the dead and the living." Perhaps all that need be done by way of highlighting the importance of these confessional portions in the development of Paul's argument is to point out how strategically each of them is located in Romans. For 1:3-4 appears in the salutation of the letter, which Paul uses to highlight a number of themes that he intends subsequently to develop; and 3:24-26 is included in what most commentators take to be a major thesis paragraph of the letter, that is, 3:21-26—though it may be debated whether this paragraph reflects the thesis of the whole letter, the thesis of the first eight chapters, or, more narrowly, the thesis of only the first four chapters. Further, 10:9 appears at the heart of Paul's discussion of the gospel and Israel in chapters 9–11, while 14:9 appears at the heart of his exhortations regarding the weak and the strong.

In addressing Gentile Christians whom he considered within the orbit of his Gentile mission, but whom he also knew did not trace their spiritual heritage back to his preaching—rather, who looked to the Jerusalem church for their traditions and support—Paul uses early Christian confessional materials in at least two ways: (1) to summarize and bring to a climax his presentations in the three main theological sections of his letter (i.e., in 4:25; 8:33-39 and 11:33-36), and (2) to support and focus his arguments (i.e., in 1:3-4; 3:24-26; 10:9 and 14:9). Presumably, these confessional materials were known to his addressees. So Paul builds bridges of commonality with those addressees in his use of these materials.

It could be pointed out, as well, that Paul's letter to a mixed group of believers at Rome—but one in which Gentile Christians were dominant—incorporates a number of features that must have been quite traditional within Jewish Christian circles. For example, there are striking parallels between 1:18-32 and *Wisdom of Solomon* 13:1–14:31 in describing the idolatry and immorality of the Gentile world, but a sharp contrast between 2:1-29 and *Wisdom of Solomon* 15:1-6 with regard to the situation of the Jews. The argument of 1:18–2:29

sounds very much like some of the preaching that must have gone on within Jewish Christian circles, where there was need to counter the propaganda and special pleading of *Wisdom of Solomon* 13–15 (cf. also *Letter of Aristeas* 151–53).

Likewise, in the dialogical context of 2:1-11 the material contained in 2:7-10 may very well stem from a certain facet of Jewish or Jewish Christian ethical teaching (cf. Jas 2:14-26), which Paul quotes and redacts for his own purpose in opposition to some postulated Jewish interlocutor's use of that material. On such a view it may be postulated (1) that the principle that God "will reward each person according to what that person has done" (so v 6, quoting Ps 62:12; Prov 24:12) was being used in a soteriological manner in some Jewish tradition with an emphasis on "doing" and "works" (ἔργα) as being redemptive (so vv 7-10); but (2) that Paul has universalized that tradition by twice adding the statement "first for the Jew, then for the Gentile" (cf. 1:16): "There will be trouble and distress for every human being who does evil—*first for the Jew, then for the Gentile*; but glory, honor and peace for everyone who does good—*first for the Jew, then for the Gentile*" (vv 9-10). The "salvation by works" theology of verses 7-10 is radically opposed to Paul's own theological perspective, particularly as expressed in 3:21–4:25. It is not just un-Pauline, but contra-Pauline. Yet Paul seems to have used just such a tradition as (1) a foil in his diatribe type of argument, allowing him in 2:12-29 to correct the false views of his interlocutor, and (2) an opportunity to highlight the universality and impartiality of God's treatment of human beings. For taken together, 1:16 and 2:9-10 lay stress on the fact that both salvation and judgment are effected by God in an impartial way—as 2:11 states expressly ("God does not show favoritism") and as Paul goes on to elaborate throughout 2:12–3:20.

Mention could also be made of (1) Paul's use of Abraham as the example of faith *par excellence* in 4:1-24, (2) his reference to the "one man" through whom sin and death entered into the world, thereby conditioning all of human life, in 5:12-21, and (3) his development of a remnant theology argument in 9:6–11:32—all of which, it may be postulated, were traditional features within Jewish Christian circles. But these are matters that require close commentary treatment, even full-blown monographs, to be dealt with adequately, and so can only be referred to here.

It may be, of course, that Paul went through "frequent and sudden changes of masks" in Romans in speaking at one time to Jewish believers, at another time to Gentile believers, and at other times to both (as Erasmus claimed, and as many continue to hold). Or that Paul's addressees were principally Jewish Christians, for only such an audience would have been able to appreciate his Jewish-style arguments, content and procedures (as is sometimes asserted). Or, conversely, that they were primarily Gentile Christians, to whom, nonetheless, Paul spoke using the categories and traditions of his own Jewish and Jewish Christian backgrounds—even though his addressees might not have been able to understand all that he said (as many, in essence, have argued). A more cogent explanation of the "dual character" of the letter, however, I believe, is along the lines suggested above: that Paul used materials drawn from the traditions of Jewish Christianity in his letter to a dominantly Gentile group of believers at Rome simply because his addressees, though primarily Gentiles ethnically, were related religiously to the traditions and theology of Jewish Christians at Jerusalem. Thus in Romans Paul (1) speaks of Abraham as "our father" (4:1), even while distinguishing his ancestry from that of his addressees (9:3; 11:14), (2) addresses his readers as "those who know the law" (7:1; cf. 3:19a), while also identifying them as Gentiles (11:13; cf. 1:5-6 and 15:15-16), (3) uses a conciliatory tone and tempered expressions when referring to the Jews, (4) highlights such essentially Jewish and Jewish Christian themes as "the righteousness of God," the validity of the Mosaic law, the nature of redemption, and the election of Israel, and (5) develops his argument in certain sections of the letter in a distinctly Jewish manner.

4. *The Use of Biblical Quotations*

Much of what has been said about Paul's use of traditional materials in Romans can also be said about his use of Scripture in the letter (cf. my *Biblical Exegesis in the Apostolic Period* [Grand Rapids: Eerdmans, 1975; 2nd ed., 1999], 88-116)—that is, that he uses biblical quotations (1) to build bridges of commonality with his addressees, and (2) to support and focus his arguments in ways that his addressees would appreciate and understand. Paul has no doubt that his addressees are believers in Jesus. In fact, he begins the Thanksgiving section by saying: "I thank my God through Jesus Christ for all of you, because your faith is being reported all over the world" (1:8). But though he and his addressees share a common faith and have much in common theologically, Paul wants to add to their understanding of the Christian gospel—in particular, he wants his Roman addressees to understand the gospel as he has proclaimed it in his Gentile mission (cf. "my gospel" in 16:25; see also 2:16). And he wants to give them this "spiritual gift" in order to strengthen them as believers (cf. 1:11-15; 15:15-18) and so that they will then be prepared to receive and assist him in the extension of that gospel to the west (cf. 1:10b, 13; 15:23-32).

His procedure, therefore, is (1) to begin where his addressees are in their Christian lives and thought, arguing for fundamental issues in ways that they will appreciate and understand, but then (2) to move on beyond such commonalities to a proclamation of the Christian faith that he considered to be uniquely his, but which he felt obligated to share with all of those within the orbit of his Gentile mission. Perhaps this can best be seen, in overview, by taking each of the major units of the body of the Romans letter separately.

1:16–4:25 Righteousness and Justification by Faith

Exactly where the first unit of the Body of Romans begins and ends has always been difficult to determine. Some have seen the Thanksgiving as closing at 1:12, with the Body commencing with a disclosure formula ("I do not want you to be ignorant") at 1:13; others view the Thanksgiving as closing at 1:15, with the Body beginning with a thesis statement at 1:16-17; while others close the Thanksgiving at 1:17 and begin the Body at 1:18. Likewise, some close Paul's discussion of "the righteousness of God" and "justification by faith" at 4:25, others at 5:11, and still others at 5:21. The issues are largely epistolary, rhetorical and stylistic in nature, and much too complex to be set out here.

Our view, to come quickly to the bottom line, is that while 1:16-17 could be seen as a transitional portion that functions both to conclude the Thanksgiving and to introduce the Body, and while Paul's discussion of justification by faith could be taken to extend either to 5:11 or to 5:21, (1) the repetition of the axiom "first for the Jew, then for the Gentile" in 1:16 (once) and 2:9-10 (twice) suggests that 1:16–2:11 is a unit and expresses some type of "ring composition," (2) the word chain πιστεύω / πίστις, as well as the dominance of the term δικαιοσύνη, serve to signal the unity of 1:16–4:25, and (3) the illustration of Abraham in 4:1-24 and the confessional portion of 4:25 aptly conclude this section. In addition, 5:1–8:39 holds together as a recognizable unit (as will be argued later).

What needs to be noted here, however, is that this first major theological unit of Paul's letter, that is, 1:16–4:25, is extensively Jewish and/or Jewish Christian in both its content and its type of argument. It begins with a thesis statement in 1:16-17 that speaks of the universality of the gospel ("first for the Jew, then for the Gentile"), highlights the theme of the gospel as being both "the righteousness of God" and "justification by faith," and supports that conjunction of righteousness and faith by the quotation of Hab 2:4. It follows this in 1:18–3:20 with a basically negative presentation that argues that all people—Jews as well as Gentiles—stand without excuse as sinful beings before a God who "shows no favoritism." It makes this negative argument first in 1:18–2:29, by paralleling the presentation of *Wisdom of Solomon* 13–15 regarding the Gentile world (in 1:18-32) and then dramatically turning the self-aggrandizing propaganda of *Wisdom of Solomon* 15:1-6 on its head in speaking to the Jewish world (in 2:1-29); then in 3:1-20, by setting out a series of rhetorical questions (vv 1-9) and a catena of biblical quotations (vv 10-20), all to the effect that "Jews and Gentiles alike are all under sin" (v 9) and that Jewish prerogatives serve to make Jews more accountable before God and not superior to others (vv 19-20).

Positively, however, Paul goes on in the latter half of this opening unit (1) to set out a thesis paragraph on the righteousness of God in 3:21-23, which picks up from his opening thesis statement of 1:16-17 and argues that the righteousness of God, while witnessed to by the Law and the Prophets, is now made known in the gospel apart from the Mosaic law (χωρὶς νόμου), (2) to support that thesis by the use of an early Christian confessional portion in 3:24-26, (3) to elaborate on the "divine impartiality" feature of that thesis in 3:27-31, and (4) to illustrate the factor of faith contained in that thesis by the example of Abraham in 4:1-24. He then concludes in 4:25 with another confessional portion that speaks of the work of Christ in humanity's redemption and justification ("He was delivered over to death for our sins and was raised to life for our justification").

As for biblical quotations, Paul's arguments in 1:16–4:25 are chock-full of Scripture. The first, of course, is the quotation of Hab

2:4 in 1:17b: "The righteous will live by faith." The second appears in
2:24—toward the close of Paul's paralleling of *Wisdom of Solomon*
13–15, where he acknowledges the idolatry and immorality of the
Gentile world but reverses the favorable characterization of
Jews—with a prophetic denunciation against Israel drawn from a
conflation of Isa 52:5b and Ezek 36:22b: "God's name is blasphemed
among the Gentiles because of you." A third biblical passage appears
in 3:4b, quoting Ps 51:4: "So that you may be proved right in your
words and prevail in your judging." Each of these three quotations is
introduced by the formulaic phrase "as it is written" (καθὼς
γέγραπται).

The eight to ten passages strung together in 3:10-18, which are also
introduced by "as it is written," deserve special comment. For this
catena of passages has often been seen to be an early set piece or
testimonia list that Paul used to emphasize the fact that no one is
righteous before God. Its selection of passages is not quite Pauline.
Unpacking all of the possible conflated texts, it quotes Qoheleth once
(Eccl 7:20), Proverbs once (Prov 1:16), Isaiah twice (Isa 59:7, 8), and
the Psalms six times (Pss 14:1-3; 53:1-3; 5:9; 140:3; 10:7; 36:1).
Further, the textforms of the passages evidence a variety of LXX and
MT readings, with the quotations at times being not exactly either.
And its structure, while probably not strophic, evidences great care in
composition, what with its sixfold repetition of the phrase "there is
none" (οὐκ ἔστιν) and its cataloguing of various parts of the body
("throats," "tongues," "lips," "mouths," "feet," and "eyes") to make
the point that all human beings in their totality are sinful.

Paul's argument is that all of these passages refer not just to the
plight of the Gentiles, but more particularly to the condition of the
Jews—for, as he argues, "whatever the law says, it says to those who
are under the law, so that every mouth might be silenced and the
whole world held accountable to God" (3:19). It need not be
supposed, however, that such an application was uniquely his or new
to his addressees. Indeed, he introduces his statement of 3:19 with the
words "Now we know" (οἴδαμεν δέ), which suggests agreement. Perhaps, in fact, this list of passages in 3:10-18 represents a *testimonia*
collection already drawn up by Jewish Christians before him, as the
selection of passages, their textforms, and the structure of the catena
seem to indicate. At any rate, he expects his addressees at
Rome—whom we have posited were plugged into the theology and

traditions of Jerusalem Christianity—to agree with him. And so having begun the negative development of his thesis statement in 1:16-17 with allusions to *Wisdom of Solomon* 13–15, he now closes that portrayal of the universality of sin with what seems to have been a catena of passages drawn up by his Jewish Christian predecessors.

The final group of quotations in Paul's discussion of righteousness and justification by faith is to be found in 4:1-24, where Abraham is presented as the example of faith *par excellence*. Four passages are quoted: (1) Gen 15:6 ("Abraham believed God, and it was credited to him as righteousness") in verses 2 and 22, the first being introduced by the rhetorical question, "For what does the Scripture say?" (τί γὰρ ἡ γραφὴ λέγει) and the second by the inferential conjunction "for this reason" (διό); (2) Ps 32:1-2 ("Blessed are those whose offenses have been forgiven and whose sins have been covered; blessed are those whose sin the Lord will never count against them") in verses 7-8, which is introduced by "David says" (Δαυὶδ λέγει) (3) Gen 17:5 ("I have made you a father of many nations") in verse 17, with an echo in verse 18, which is introduced by "as it is written" (καθὼς γέγραπται); and (4) Gen 15:5 ("So shall your seed be") in v 18b, which is introduced by "according to what was said" (κατὰ τὸ εἰρημένον). Gen 15:5-6 and 17:5 are the main passages that speak of God's blessing and promise to Abraham. To these standard passages is added Ps 32:1-2, which is cited in midrashic fashion to support Gen 15:6 and to highlight God's action in both "crediting righteousness" (ἐλογίσθη εἰς δικαιοσύνην) and "not counting sin" (οὐ μὴ λογίσηται ἁμαρτίαν).

In effect, therefore, Paul begins the first four chapters of his letter to believers at Rome in quite a traditional manner—not only praising his addressees and agreeing with them, but also using materials and methods that they and he held in common. He believes, as he said in the first part of the *propositio* of Gal 2:15-21, that all true believers in Jesus, whether Jewish or Gentile, know that a person is not justified by "the works of the law," but by what Christ has effected and one's faith in him (vv 15-16). So he writes with confidence to his Roman addressees, expressing as he starts his letter what they and he hold in common—before then going on to speak of matters that pertain to the distinctive nature of his proclamation ("my gospel") within the Gentile mission.

5:1–8:39 Relationships "in Adam" and "in Christ"

Though many have taken Paul's discussion of 1:16–4:25 to continue on through 5:11 (e.g., M. Luther [with 5:12-21 being seen as an excursus], P. Melanchthon, T. Zahn, F. Leenhardt, M. Black, J. A. T. Robinson) or on through 5:21 (e.g., J. Calvin, U. Wilckens, O. Kuss, F. F. Bruce, J. D. G. Dunn), most commentators today view 5:1–8:39 as a distinguishable unit of material. (e.g., H. Schlier, A. Nygren, O. Michel, C. H. Dodd, N. Dahl, C. E. B. Cranfield, E. Käsemann, J. A. Fitzmyer, D. Moo). That is not only because the example of Abraham as a "proof from Scripture" is a fitting conclusion to what precedes, but also because 5:1-11 seems to serve as something of a thesis paragraph for what follows—with most of the themes and many of the terms that appear in 5:1-11 reappearing in 8:18-39, thereby setting up an *inclusio* or type of "ring composition." Further, (1) 5:1 seems to function as a literary hinge in first summarizing the argument of 1:16–4:25 ("Since, therefore, we have been justified through faith") and then preparing for what follows in 5:2–8:39 ("we have peace [or, 'let us have peace'] with God through our Lord Jesus Christ"); (2) the word chain shifts from πιστεύω / πίστις and the dominance of the term δικαιοσύνη in 1:16–4:25 to ζάω / ζωή and the dominance of ἁμαρτία and θάνατος in 5:1–8:39 (3) the style shifts from an argumentative tone in 1:16–4:25 to a more "confessional style" that is cast in the first person plural "we" in 5:1–8:39; and (4) there appears throughout the repeated refrain διὰ τοῦ κυρίου (or ἐν τῷ κυρίῳ) ἡμῶν Ἰησοῦ Χριστοῦ, not only as an *inclusio* at 5:1 and 8:39 but also at the end of each of the separate units within this larger section at 5:11, 5:21, 6:23, and 7:25.

Much more, of course, could be said about 5:1–8:39 by way of commentary. What needs to be noted here for our purpose, however, is the difference in the use of Scripture in this portion as compared with 1:16–4:25. For whereas 1:16–4:25 contains some 15–18 biblical quotations located at eight or nine places (see above), biblical quotations in 5:1–8:39 are notoriously lacking. One quotation appears at 7:7 with the citing of the tenth commandment "Do not covet," whether taken from Exod 20:17 or Deut 5:21, or from both—or simply repeated from common Jewish tradition. But the citing of the tenth commandment is only used as an illustration of how a divine prescription, because of human depravity, can be turned into sin and result in death. The only other biblical quotation in chapters 5–8 appears at the end of the section in 8:36, quoting Ps 44:22: "For your sake we face death all the day long; we are consumed as sheep to be slaughtered." It is introduced by the formulaic phrase "as it is written" (καθὼς γέγραπται). But it appears in conjunction with a number of other portions in 8:33-39 that have been seen to be confessional statements drawn from the early church, and so may not be distinctly Paul's own quotation. The only two explicit biblical citations in chapters 5–8, therefore, look very much like traditional materials that Paul used either (1) simply to illustrate in specific fashion a general statement, or (2) because the passage was included in a confessional portion that he quoted. Certainly they do not function as did his biblical quotations in 1:16–4:25—nor do they function, to anticipate a later discussion, as they do in 9:1–11:36.

How does one explain this difference between 1:16–4:25 and 5:1–8:39 in Paul's use of Scripture—the former with an abundant use, evidently to build bridges of commonality with his addressees and to support and focus his arguments; the latter with almost no use at all? Perhaps this difference supports the thesis that chapters 1–11 contain two Pauline sermons: one to a Jewish audience, which was originally made up of materials now in chapters 1–4 and 9–11 but whose parts have somehow become separated; the other to a Gentile audience as represented in chapters 5–8 (so R. Scroggs, "Paul as Rhetorician," 271-98). More likely, however, it can be argued that in chapters 5–8 Paul is presenting what he spoke of in the Thanksgiving section of his letter as his "spiritual gift" to his Roman addressees for their strengthening (1:11)—that is, the form of the gospel that he customarily proclaimed within his Gentile mission, which in the concluding doxology he calls "my gospel" (16:25; see also 2:16).

Approaching the relationship of 1:16–4:25 and 5:1–8:39 from the perspective of this latter thesis, 1:16–4:25 can be seen as the type of proclamation that Paul knew was held in common by all Jewish believers in Jesus—as his opening statement in the *propositio* of Gal 2:15-21 plainly declares: "We who are Jews by birth, and not 'sinners of the Gentiles', know that a person is not justified 'by the works of the law' (ἐξ ἔργων νόμου) but 'by the faith/faithfulness of Jesus Christ' (διὰ πίστεως Ἰησοῦ Χριστοῦ; or, understood as an objective genitive, 'by faith in Jesus Christ'), and so we have put our faith in Christ Jesus" (vv 15-16a). That form of Christian proclamation, it may be posited from Rom 1:16-17 and 3:21-26, laid great stress on such Jewish concepts as "the righteousness of God," "the witness of the Law and the Prophets," "justification by faith," "redemption," and "expiation/propitiation," seeking only to focus attention on Jesus as Israel's Messiah and faith as one's proper response—features that Jewish Christians believed were certainly inherent in Israel's religion. It proclaimed the fulfillment of God's promise to Abraham in Jesus' ministry and the church's message, honored the Mosaic law as the God-ordained "pedagogue" for the nation Israel, cherished the traditions of the Jerusalem church, and supported its proclamation by a christocentric reading of holy Scripture. And with this form of Christian proclamation Paul was thoroughly in agreement, probably often presenting the gospel in this manner himself before strictly Jewish audiences or when occasion might otherwise demand it.

In 5:1–8:39, however, it may be claimed, Paul sets out the features of the gospel as he proclaimed them in his Gentile mission, to those who had no Jewish heritage and no biblical instruction. Prominent among these features, as highlighted in these chapters, are such matters as "peace with God," the experience of divine grace, glory and love, "reconciliation" with God and others, deliverance from sin and death, being "in Christ," being "in the Spirit," and being unable to be separated from "Christ's love," and so from God's love and protection. These are matters that can be based, by analogy, on God's past dealings with Israel as recorded in Scripture. But they were also matters, evidently, that were not directly demonstrable to Gentiles by specific biblical texts. Nor, it seems, would such an approach have been meaningful or appreciated by Gentiles. Rather, Paul's emphases on "peace with God," "reconciliation," being "in Christ," being "in the Spirit," etc. (as in chapters 5–8) appear to have stemmed primarily from his own conversion experience.

Christ's confrontation of Paul on the Damascus Road, with all that went into the apostle's subsequent understanding of it, confirmed for him what the early Jewish believers in Jesus were proclaiming—which, of course, he also proclaimed (so Rom 1:16–4:25). In addition, however, it gave him a new understanding of (1) relationship with God, (2) relationships with others, and (3) the logistics for a Gentile mission (so Galatians 1–2). Therefore in writing to Christians at Rome, who were largely dependent on the theology and traditions of the Jerusalem church, he speaks in the Thanksgiving section of his letter of wanting to give them a "spiritual gift" (1:11) and refers in the concluding Doxology to "my gospel" (16:25; also in 2:16).

The essence of Paul's gospel, it seems, was what he presents in 5:1–8:39. And throughout the history of the Christian church the material of these four chapters has frequently been seen as the apex of his argument in Romans. Augustine, for example, focused most of his exegetical attention on chapters 5 through 9, as witness his *Expositio quarundam propositionum ex epistula ad Romanos* (*PL*, 35.2063-88); and John A. T. Robinson has expressed the attitude of many in comparing the structure of Romans to a canal that crosses an isthmus through a series of locks, with the highest lock being that of chapters 5–8—and with chapter 8 representing "a sustained climax which takes the argument across the watershed" (*Wrestling with Romans* [London: SCM; Philadelphia: Westminster, 1979], 9]). In these chapters can be found both the central issues of human existence (e.g., sin, death, life, relationship with God, relationships with others) and the central proclamation of the Christian gospel (e.g., being "reconciled" to God and with one another, being "in Christ," being "in the Spirit," with an unshakable conviction that nothing can separate a person from "the love of God that is in Christ Jesus our Lord"). And these are matters that (1) Paul found resolved and illuminated by his conversion experience, and (2) he proclaimed in his Gentile mission without any necessary reference to the Jewish Scriptures. So he sets out in 5:1–8:39 what he views as his own distinctive message to the Gentile world—that is, "my gospel," as he calls it in 2:16 and 16:25—to predominantly Gentile believers in Jesus at Rome, after having first set out in 1:16–4:25 the matters on which they and he fully agreed.

9:1–11:36 The Gospel and the Hope of Israel
That 9:1–11:36 comprises a carefully composed unit of material is beyond doubt. It has a clear beginning at 9:1-5—probably including an early Christian confessional portion in v 5b, with its use of Χριστός in the titular sense of "Messiah" (which is the most obvious use of Χριστός as a christological title in Paul's letters). It also has a clear ending in its hymn of praise to God at 11:33-36. And throughout the material contained within this *inclusio* the argument is sustained.

But while the unity of these three chapters is clear, debate continues to rage regarding (1) the relation of chapters 9–11 to chapters 1–4 and 5–8, and (2) the function of chapters 9–11 vis-à-vis the overall argument of the letter. It is impossible here to set out anything approaching the depth and breadth of the discussion that has gone on regarding these two issues. Suffice it only to point out with regard to the first, that is, the relation of chapters 9–11 to the materials of chapters 1–8, that there is a very close connection between 9:1–11:36 and 1:16–4:25, both linguistically and thematically. The word chain πιστεύω / πίστις and the term δικαιοσύνη, which were dominant in 1:16–4:25, reappear in force in 9:1–11:36. More importantly, the axiom "first for the Jew, then for the Gentile" of 1:16, 2:10, together with the extensive denunciation of Jewish self-congratulation in 2:1–3:20, call for a fuller exposition on the state of the Jews, as is found in 9:1–11:36; while the claim that the gospel is supported by "the Law and the Prophets" in 3:21 (also the biblical passages cited throughout 1:16–4:25) and the assertion that Christian faith is illustrated by the faith of Abraham in 4:1-24 call for an answer to the question, "If this be so, why have the Jews rejected it?"

On the other hand, connections between 9:1–11:36 and 5:1–8:39 are more obscure. As Joseph Fitzmyer points out,

> Nowhere in chaps. 9–11 does the "Spirit" appear (save in 9:1 and 11:8, and then in an entirely different sense!), and the whole argument moves in a direction quite different from the thrust of chaps. 5–8. Similarly, the theme of "life" disappears (save in 11:15, which is a problem apart), and *doxa* occurs only in 9:23, a verse that does refer to the predestination of 8:28-30. Moreover, the function of "illustration" [as is sometimes proposed by commentators] does not explain well the bulk of chaps 9–11 (*Romans*, 540).

Still, as noted by Fitzmyer (above), the so-called "golden chain" of 8:28-30—that is, "called ... foreknown ... predestined ... called ... justified ... glorified"—nicely sets up a further exposition of these matters in chapters 9–11. And the expression "the elect of God" (ἐκλεκτοὶ θεοῦ) in 8:33, which is used by Paul with reference to Gentiles who have faith, seems to be the verbal springboard for the ensuing discussion of such topics as "faith," "election," "the remnant," and "relations between believing Gentiles and Jews" in chapters 9–11. So chapters 9–11 must be seen to function as an appropriate conclusion to the materials of chapters 1–8.

Just how chapters 9–11 function as a conclusion to the presentations of chapters 1–8 is beyond the scope of this paper. Various explanations have been offered. Many have seen these chapters to be teaching predestination (e.g., Augustine, Aquinas and Calvin); others, free will (e.g., Origen, Chrysostom and Arminius); and still others, universalism. Some have taken chapters 9–11 to be a theodicy; others, a History of Religions presentation; and still others, a *Heilsgeschichte* ("Salvation History") explanation. For myself, I take a remnant approach, believing that what Paul is doing in these chapters is setting out, in a quite traditional manner, his thesis regarding a remnant of believing Jews, to which he then connects the remnant of believing Gentiles. But all of that must be left for commentary.

What is clear, however, and needs to be highlighted here, is that Paul's discussion in 9:1–11:36 is peppered throughout with biblical citations. Some 30 quotations from the Old Testament, in fact, are set out in 25–26 places in these three chapters, with such standard Pauline introductory formulas appearing as "as it is written" (9:13, 33; 10:15; 11:8, 26), "he [God] says" (9:15, 25; 11:4), "the Scripture says" (9:16; 10:11; 11:2), "Isaiah cries out/says" (9:27, 29; 10:16, 20, 21), "Moses wrote/says" (10:5, 19), and "David says" (11:9). Only in 10:6-8, where Deut 30:12-14 is paraphrastically quoted or alluded to in a proverbial fashion, is there to be found an exception to Paul's usual citation of Scripture. But that passage is introduced by a more general introductory statement, "the righteousness that is by faith says" (v 6). So it probably, as many have argued, represents a traditional proverb based on Scripture that was used among early Jewish believers, and which here Paul used to keep contact with his Roman addressees and to support his argument in a manner that they would appreciate.

Each of the 30 or so quotations in these chapters, of course, needs to be studied separately for any full discussion of Paul's use of Scripture. Generally, however, it can be said that Paul's use of biblical quotations in 9:1–11:36 is very similar to his use of such material in 1:16–4:25, and for the same reasons. For while it might be claimed, on analogy with Galatians, that both of these sections should be read as polemical thrusts against a Judaizing threat (whether lurking or actual; whether arising from within or outside of the various Roman congregations), all that need be seen is that Paul in Romans is (1) addressing a group of Christians (both Gentiles and Jews, though dominantly the former) whose theology and traditions have been extensively formed by Jerusalem Christianity, and (2) speaking to them in ways that they would appreciate and understand, using both their traditions and Scripture in so doing.

12:1–15:13 and 15:14-32 Exhortations and Apostolic Parousia
Likewise, what has been said about 1:16–4:25 and 9:1–11:36 should probably also be said, in the main, about the exhortations of 12:1–15:13 and the Apostolic Parousia of 15:14-32.

The exhortation section may be seen as composed of two units: the first on "Love and Peace" in 12:1–13:14; the second on "Tolerance and Acceptance" in 14:1–15:13—with each unit having its own provenance in Paul's preaching, but now brought together to buttress his purpose in addressing believers at Rome. Further, it might be that such topics as "Love and Peace" and "Tolerance and Acceptance" express some type of polemical thrust, and so the exhortations should be read as Paul's attempts to quiet antagonisms or heal estrangements among certain "strong" and "weak" believers at Rome.

But "mirror-reading" of the supposed polemics does not produce a very clear picture of the postulated situation. More likely, all that need be argued is that Paul is addressing believers whose theology has stemmed largely from the Jerusalem church and speaking to them in ways that they would appreciate and understand. And so he cites some ten biblical passages in his exhortations and one in his Apostolic Parousia.

5. *Conclusion: An Answer to Our Questions*

What, then, can be said in answer to our opening eight questions? To question 1, Why did Paul use so many Old Testament quotations in Romans?, and question 3, Why did he use the Old Testament at all in writing to Christians at Rome?, our answer is: Because he was addressing believers (Gentiles and Jews, but predominantly the former) whose theology and traditions stemmed largely from the Jerusalem church, and so he used Scripture to support and focus his presentation in a manner that would be appreciated and understood by them. To question 2, Why is the distribution of the Old Testament quotations in Romans so uneven?, our answer is: Because in 5:1–8:39, which is the section that is largely devoid of such quotations, Paul's purpose was to present to a dominantly Gentile group of believers the essence of what he customarily proclaimed to Gentiles—

which message he thought of as his unique "spiritual gift" to believers at Rome (1:11), and so he called it "my gospel" (16:25; cf. 2:16). This message, evidently, arose primarily out of his own conversion experience, and so he felt that it did not need to be buttressed by explicit references to Scripture. Answers to questions 1–3, therefore, depend largely on how we have understood "The Addressees and their Circumstances" (mainly as inferred from external data) and "Paul's Purpose in Writing" (mainly from reading the opening and closing sections of the letter).

Our answers to questions 4 and 5 follow along the same lines, being derivative in nature. As for Paul's exegetical procedures (Question 4), we propose that they are those shared by Paul and the traditions from Jerusalem, which were accepted by Gentile believers at Rome. Therefore, there was a commonality of exegetical practice and procedure between Paul and his addressees at Rome, which commonality can be traced back to the practices and procedures of Second Temple Judaism. And as for Paul's use of Scripture in Romans vis-à-vis his use in his other letters, particularly Galatians (Question 5), we believe that the similarities are due not to similar problems being confronted (i.e., the Judaizers and their message) but to the same theological structures and traditions of Jewish Christianity being addressed (i.e., the Jerusalem church)—though with those structures and traditions being differently explicated to Gentile believers in Galatia (who were being asked by Judaizers to understand them wrongly) and to predominantly Gentile believers at Rome (who understood them correctly).

Questions 6-8 (on textforms, scope of treatment, and christocentric interpretation) can be adequately dealt with only by means of a close study of each of the biblical quotations, whether by means of a commentary on Romans generally or separate monographs on the specific subjects. Our purpose in this chapter has only been to set out a prolegomena to such intensive treatments. So we must conclude with the hope that our attempted prolegomena will provide some guidance for future study.

94   *Studies in Paul, Exegetical and Theological*

SELECT BIBLIOGRAPHY

Ambrosiaster. *Commentarium in epistulam beati Pauli ad Romanos* (*PL*, 17.47-197).
——. *Commentarius in epistulas paulinas.* Part I: *In epistulam ad Romanos* (*CSEL*, 81.1)
Augustine, Aurelius. *Expositio quarundam propositionum ex epistola ad Romanos* (*PL*, 35.2063-88).
——. *Epistolae ad Romanos inchoata expositio* (*PL*, 35.2087-2106).
——. *Retractationes* (*CSEL*, 84).
Brown, Raymond E. "Not Jewish Christianity and Gentile Christianity, but Types of Jewish/Gentile Christianity," *CBQ* 45 (1983) 74-79.
——. "The Beginnings of Christianity at Rome" and "The Roman Church near the End of the First Christian Generation (A.D. 58—Paul to the Romans)," in R. E. Brown and J. P. Meier, *Antioch and Rome: New Testament Cradles of Catholic Christianity.* New York: Paulist, 1983, 92-127.
——. "Further Reflections on the Origins of the Church of Rome," in *The Conversation Continues: Studies in Paul and John in Honor of J. L. Martyn,* ed. R. T. Fortna and B. R. Gaventa. Nashville: Abingdon, 1990, 98-115.
Donfried, Karl P., ed. *The Romans Debate.* Minneapolis: Augsburg, 1977; *The Romans Debate: Revised and Expanded Edition,* Peabody: Hendrickson, 1991.
Erasmus, Desiderius. *Desiderii Erasmi Roterodami opera omnia,* 10 vols., ed. J. Leclerc (LB edition). Leiden, 1703–1706. Vol. 7 contains the *Paraphrases.*
Fitzmyer, Joseph A. *Romans. A New Translation with Introduction and Commentary.* AB. New York: Doubleday, 1993.
Jervis, L. Ann. *The Purpose of Romans: A Comparative Letter Structure Investigation.* Sheffield: Sheffield Academic Press, 1991.
Longenecker, Richard N. *Biblical Exegesis in the Apostolic Period.* Grand Rapids: Eerdmans, 1975; 2nd ed., 1999.
——. *New Wine into Fresh Wineskins: Contextualizing the Early Christian Confessions.* Peabody: Hendrickson, 1999.
Robinson, John A. T. *Wrestling with Romans.* London: SCM; Philadelphia: Westminster, 1979.
Schubert, Paul. *Form and Function of the Pauline Thanksgivings.* Berlin: Töpelmann, 1939.
Scroggs, Robin. "Paul as Rhetorician: Two Homilies in Romans 1–11," in *Jews, Greeks, and Christians* (*Festschrift* W. D. Davies), ed. R. Hammerton-Kelly and R. Scroggs. Leiden: Brill, 1976, 271-98.
Wedderburn, Alexander J. M. *The Reasons for Romans.* Edinburgh: T. & T. Clark, 1988.

Weima, Jeffrey A. D. *Neglected Endings: The Significance of the Pauline Letter Closings*. Sheffield: Sheffield Academic Press, 1994.

Wiefel, Wolfgang. "The Jewish Community in Ancient Rome and the Origins of Roman Christianity," in *The Romans Debate. Revised and Expanded Edition*, ed. K. P. Donfried. Peabody: Hendrickson, 1991, 85-101.

5

THE FOCUS OF ROMANS
The Central Role of 5:1–8:39 in the Argument of the Letter

In his highly significant *magnum opus* on "the Holy Spirit in the letters of Paul,"[1] Gordon Fee, in dealing with Rom 1:11, correctly observes (1) that a letter in antiquity (as also today) was meant to serve as "a second-best substitute for a personal visit," (2) that each of the Thanksgiving sections of Paul's letters reveal the apostle's central concerns and purposes in writing, and (3) that in the Thanksgiving section of Romans which begins at 1:8, Paul states his reasons for writing believers at Rome and wanting to be with them. He does this somewhat generally in verse 13b ("in order that I might have fruit also among you") and verse 15 ("so that I might preach the gospel also to you who are in Rome"), but expressly in verse 11: "In order that I might share with you *some spiritual gift* (τι χάρισμα πνευματικόν) so that you might be strengthened." In fact, as Fee rightly asserts, it is the expression "spiritual gift" (χάρισμα πνευματικόν) that Paul uses to characterize what he writes in the letter.

But the question arises: How, then, should Romans be understood in the light of that expression? More specifically, Was Paul referring by that expression to his whole letter generally, or did he have in mind a particular focus or central thrust? Fee points out that the combination of the noun χάρισμα ("gift") and the adjective πνευματικόν ("spiritual") is a "unique collocation" of terms in Paul's letters, which requires both linguistic and contextual explication.[2] Investigating the expression linguistically, he concludes that Paul is not here talking about some "gifting" by the Spirit, as in 1 Cor 12:8-10 and Rom 12:6-8, but about the present letter as a "Spirit gift"

---

[1] G. D. Fee, *God's Empowering Presence: The Holy Spirit in the Letters of Paul* (Peabody: Hendrickson, 1994).

[2] *Ibid.* 486-89.

sent to believers at Rome in lieu of a personal visit in order to strengthen them (v 11)—and so, as more generally stated, to bring about "some fruit" (τινὰ καρπόν) among them as among other Gentiles (v 13) and to fulfill his obligation to proclaim the gospel to them at Rome as he did among other Gentiles throughout the eastern part of the Roman empire (vv 14-15). With approval he cites James Denney: "No doubt, in substance, Paul imparts his spiritual gift through this epistle."[3]

Then referring to the immediate and extended contexts of the expression, Fee suggests:

> In its present context, and especially in light of the letter as a whole, the "Spirit gift" that he most likely wishes to share with them is his understanding of the gospel that in Christ Jesus God has created from among Jews and Gentiles one people for himself, apart from Torah. This is the way they are to be "strengthened" by Paul's coming, and this surely is the "fruit" he wants to have among them when he comes (v. 13). If so, then in effect our present letter functions as his "Spirit gifting" for them. This is what he would impart if he were there in person: this is what he now "shares" since he cannot presently come to Rome.[4]

I am in complete agreement with Fee's general introductory observations and his linguistic analysis of the expression "spiritual gift" in 1:11, and so will not reconsider here the points he has already made. In particular, I am sure Fee is right in understanding χάρισμα πνευματικόν as having reference to the letter itself, either in its entirety or with particular reference to its central thrust. Likewise, I agree that what Paul "most likely wishes to share with them [his addressees] is his understanding of the gospel." I would, however, argue that the focus or central thrust of Romans is not to be found in 1:16–4:25, which can be epitomized by the statement "in Christ Jesus God has created from among Jews and Gentiles one people for himself, apart from Torah," as Fee suggests in the quotation cited above and as has been traditionally understood. Rather, I propose that the focus of the letter—which Paul refers to as "my gospel" in 16:25 of the doxology (see also 2:16)—is to be found in 5:1–8:39, which highlights the themes of "peace" and "reconciliation" with God, the

---

[3] *Ibid.* 488, n. 48.
[4] *Ibid.* 488-89.

antithesis of "death" and "life," and the relationships of being "in Christ" and "in the Spirit."

In support of such a thesis it is necessary to scan Romans contextually. In particular, it is necessary to deal critically with certain features regarding the structures and arguments of the letter. For any complete treatment, of course, the entire letter ought to be taken into account. Here, however, because of space and time limitations, only the structures and arguments of the first eight chapters will be considered and only preliminary comments made regarding these matters. More detailed explication of these chapters, as well as further analyses of the last eight chapters of the letter, will be reserved for a forthcoming commentary.

1. *The Structure and Argument of Rom 1:18–3:20*

A number of perplexing issues arise in any critical reading of Romans. Many of these reflect what has been called the "dual character" of the letter. And most of them come to the fore when comparing the materials set out in 1:18–4:25 with the presentation of 5:1–8:39. It seems best, therefore, especially in a preliminary survey and with limited space available, to deal only with the development of Paul's arguments in the first half of his letter. We will begin by highlighting first the structure and argument of 1:18–3:20, with special attention to chapter 2.

Some Important Issues

The interpretation of 1:18–3:20 has been notoriously difficult for almost every commentator. Problems begin to take form when one attempts to identify exactly who is being talked about or addressed in the passage. Is it Gentiles in 1:18-32, Jews in 2:1-5, Gentiles in 2:6-16, then Jews again in 2:17–3:19, with a conclusion in 3:20? Or is it Gentiles in 1:18-32 and Jews in 2:1–3:19, with a conclusion pertaining to both in 3:20? Or is it humanity generally in 1:18–2:16 and Jews (or a particular type of Jew) in 2:17–3:19, with a conclusion in 3:20? Earlier interpreters such as Origen, Jerome, Augustine and Erasmus wrestled with this issue, and it continues to plague commentators today.

Likewise, problems arise when one tries to evaluate the structures incorporated within 1:18–3:20. In the first part of that section, in 1:18-32, there appears a denunciation of the idolatry and immorality of the

Gentile world that parallels quite closely the denunciation of Gentile idolatry and immorality in *Wisdom of Solomon* 13:1–14:31, with scholars generally agreed that Paul must have drawn on this work for his portrayal in 1:18-32 (perhaps also in 2:1-15) or that he and the writer of *Wisdom* drew from similar traditions. Further, the second part of the section, 2:1–3:8, abounds with characteristic features and stylistic traits that correspond to what was practiced in the Greek diatribal dialogues. And 3:10-18, which is the longest catena of biblical passages in the Pauline corpus, has been seen by many to be a collection of passages that was originally brought together within Judaism and/or Jewish Christianity and then used by Paul in support of his thesis (and theirs?) that "Jews and Gentiles alike are all under sin" (3:9; cf. 3:19, 23,).

More importantly, however, problems of interpretation multiply when one asks: How does what Paul says about Gentiles and Jews in chapter 2 correspond to what he says about humanity generally and Jews in particular in the rest of his letter? For while his conclusions regarding God's impartiality (2:11), Jews and Gentiles being alike under sin (3:9-19, 23), and no one being able to be declared righteous by observing the law (3:20) are clear, there are four texts in Romans 2 that seem to espouse a theology of salvation by works or by obedience to the Mosaic law. And only once in this chapter, in verse 16, does explicit Christian language come to the fore.

The first problem of interpretation appears in 2:7, 10 where it is said that God will give "eternal life"—or, "glory, honor and peace"—to those who persist in doing good works, which seems to conflict with what is said about being justified solely by faith in 1:16-17, 3:21-30, 4:1-25, and throughout 9:1–11:36. The second problem text is 2:13 where it is said that "those who obey the law [are the ones] who will be declared righteous," which seems to be in conflict with (1) Paul's statement that no one is declared righteous by observing the law in 3:20, (2) his references to humans being unable to obey the law in 7:14-25, and (3) his denunciation of Israel for attempting to gain righteousness by means of the Mosaic law in 9:30–11:12. The third is 2:14-15 where there is the parenthetical statement that some Gentiles do by nature "the things of the law" and "show the work of the law written in their hearts," with the inference being that in so doing they are justified before God. But assuming that Paul is using "law" throughout this passage in much the same way, such an inference seems to contradict his earlier picture of the Gentiles in 1:18-32 and his conclusion about the impossibility of righteousness before God being obtained by observing the law in 3:20. And the fourth problem text is 2:25-27, which appears to be built on the assumption that righteousness is associated with the practice of the Mosaic law. But, again, this seems to fly in the face of (1) Paul's express conclusion to this section in 3:19-20, (2) his thesis statement regarding the "righteousness of God" being "apart from the law" in 3:21-23, (3) his use of Abraham as the exemplar of faith in 4:1-24, and (4) his entire depiction of the relation of the gospel to the hope of Israel in 9:1–11:36—as well as, of course, his arguments in Gal 2:15-16; 3:6-14 and exhortations in Gal 4:12–5:12, as repeated here and there in his other letters.

Some Preliminary Observations

What has been made of these seemingly non-Pauline statements in Romans 2? One popular way of reconciling them with Paul's thought elsewhere in Romans and his other letters is to propose that the apostle is here speaking of *Christian* Gentiles, not pagan Gentiles—that is, of Gentiles who obey the Jewish law through faith in Christ and life in the Spirit.[5] Another way is to posit that Romans 2 is speaking primarily about *pre-Christian* Gentiles who had faith in God or about godly Jews *before* the coming of the gospel—or perhaps, in some blended manner, about pre-Christian Gentiles who possessed a God-given faith, faithful Jews who before the coming of Christ expressed their trust in God through the forms of the Mosaic law, *and* Christian believers.[6]

---

[5] Cf., e.g., R. Bultmann, *Theology of the New Testament*, trans. K. Grobel (New York: Scribner's, 1951), 261; K. Barth, *A Shorter Commentary on Romans* (Richmond: John Knox, 1959), 36-39; M. Black, *Romans* (NCB; London: Marshall, Morgan & Scott, 1973), 55-56; C. E. B. Cranfield, *Romans*, 2 vols. (ICC; Edinburgh: T. & T. Clark, 1975), 1.152-62, 173-76; A. Kömig, "Gentiles or Gentile Christians? On the Meaning of Romans 2:12-16," *JTSA* 15 (1976) 53-60; A. Ito, "Romans 2: A Deuteronomist Reading," *JSNT* 59 (1995) 33-34.

[6] E.g., A. Schlatter, *Gottes Gerechtigkeit: Ein Kommentar zum Römerbrief* (Stuttgart: Calwer, 1935), 74-112; *idem, Der Glaube im Neuen Testament*, 5. Aufl. (Stuttgart: Calwer, 1963), 323-28, 380-81; P. P. Bläser, *Das Gesetz bei Paulus* (Münster: Aschendorff, 1941), 195-97; C. K. Barrett, *A Commentary on the Epistle to the Romans* (BNTC / HNTC; London: Black; New York: Harper & Row, 1957), 42-51; J.-M. Cambier, "Le jugement de tous les hommes par Dieu

Still other ways of viewing these statements have been proposed, mostly by means of some combination of the above two approaches.[7] Ernst Käsemann, for example, interprets Romans 2 in terms of "three distinct moments in the chapter":[8] pagan Gentiles in 2:12-16; a "purely fictional" Gentile soteriology in 2:24-27; and the "true Jew" as a Gentile Christian in 2:28-29.[9] Joseph Fitzmyer argues that in 2:7, 10 Paul is referring to Christians "whose conduct (good deeds) is to be understood as the fruit of their faith,"[10] but that in 2:14-15 and 2:26 he is referring to pagan Gentiles and not Christian Gentiles.[11] And James Dunn believes that in 2:7, 10 and 2:26-29 Paul is thinking of Christian Gentiles, whereas in 2:14-15 he is referring to pagan Gentiles.[12]

Quite another approach has been to understand Romans 2 as referring to the *hypothetical* possibility of being justified by good works or obedience to the law, but then to deny that possibility in order to highlight the reality of righteousness before God as being only by faith—that is, arguing that *if* people *could* obey the law they would be justified, but no one can. This is basically an Augustinian approach,

---

seul, selon la vérité, dans Rom 2:1-3:20," *ZNW* 67 (1976) 187-213, esp. 210; K. R. Snodgrass, "Justification by Grace—To the Doers: An Analysis of the Place of Romans 2 in the Theology of Paul," *NTS* 32 (1986) 72-93; G. Theissen, *Psychological Aspects of Pauline Theology* (trans. J. P. Galvin; Edinburgh: T. & T. Clark; Philadelphia: Fortress, 1987), 70-71; and G. N. Davies, *Faith and Obedience in Romans* (Sheffield: JSOT, 1990), 53-71, esp. 55-56 (both OT and NT believers). Snodgrass epitomizes this position in saying: "Those people who have seen Romans 2 as a description of circumstances prior to the coming of the gospel are correct" ("Justification by Grace—To the Doers," 81).

[7] C. E. B. Cranfield cites and evaluates eight such ways (*Romans*, 1.151-53).

[8] To use E. P. Sanders's expression in characterizing Käsemann's understanding, which Sanders calls an example of "tortured exegesis" (*Paul, the Law, and the Jewish People*, 127).

[9] E. Käsemann, *Commentary on Romans* (trans. G. W. Bromiley; Grand Rapids: Eerdmans, 1980), 59, 65, 73.

[10] J. A. Fitzmyer, *Romans* (AB; New York, London, Toronto: Doubleday, 1993), 297, cf. 302.

[11] *Ibid.* 310, 322.

[12] J. D. G. Dunn, *Romans*, 2 vols. (WBC; Dallas: Word, 1988), 1.86, 98, 100, 106-07, 122-25. Cf. also T. R. Schreiner, "Did Paul Believe in Justification by Works? Another Look at Romans 2," *BBR* 3 (1993) 131-55. Somewhat similarly, H. Schlier held that pagan Gentiles are designated in 2:14-15, while in 2:27 Paul passes unconsciously into describing Christian Gentiles (*Der Römerbrief* [HTKNT; Freiberg: Herder, 1977], 77-79, 88).

which was reiterated by Martin Luther in his insistence that "All the Scriptures of God are divided into two parts: commands and promises"—the former being "God's strange work" to bring us down; the latter "God's proper work" to raise us up.[13] Such a view was established in modern critical scholarship by Hans Lietzmann, who argued that Paul is here viewing matters "from a pre-gospel standpoint" and setting out what would have been the case "if (1) there were no gospel, and (2) it were possible to fulfill the Law."[14] Essentially the same position has been espoused by many scholars both before and after Lietzmann.[15] Earlier, in 1964, I also adopted this approach, arguing in my *Paul, Apostle of Liberty*: "The contrast we see between Romans 2:6ff. and 3:21ff. is the same as that between Law and Gospel. In Romans 2:6ff. the Apostle cites the Law, which promises life and would bring life *if* the factors of human sin and inability were not present."[16]

On the other hand, there are scholars today who assert that some or all of the above-listed problem passages of Romans 2 are flatly contradictory to Paul's thought elsewhere in Romans, though they offer diverse explanations for the texts in question. John O'Neill, as might be expected from his treatment of Galatians, sees all of 1:18–2:29 to be contradictory to Paul's teaching and irrelevant to his purpose, and so declares this section to be an interpolation by a later glossator who

[13] M. Luther, "A Treatise on Christian Liberty," in *Works of Martin Luther*, vol. 2 (trans. W. A. Lambert; Philadelphia: Holman, 1916), 317.

[14] H. Lietzmann, *An die Römer* (HNT; 5. Aufl.; Tübingen: Mohr–Siebeck, 1971), 39-40 (my translation). Cf. also 44.

[15] E.g., M. Kahler, "Auglegung von Kap. 2,14-16 in Römerbrief," *TSK* 47 (1974) 274, 277; A. Friedrichsen, "Der wahre Jude und sein Lob: Röm. 2.28f.," *Symbolae Arctoae* I (1922) 43-44; J. Knox, *The Epistle to the Romans* (New York: Abingdon, 1954), 409, 418-19; O. Kuss, *Der Römerbrief* (Regensburg: Pustet, 1957), 1.64-68, 70-71, 90-92; G. Bornkamm, "Gesetz und Natur (Röm. 2,14-15)," in *Studien zu Antike und Urchristentum*, II (Munich: Kaiser, 1959), 110; U. Wilckens, *Der Brief an der Römer* (Neukirchen–Vluyn: Neukirchener Verlag, 1978), 1.132-33, 145; F. F. Bruce, *The Epistle of Paul to the Romans* (TNTC; London: Tyndale; Grand Rapids: Eerdmans, 1985[2]), 90; R. A. Harrisville, *Romans* (ACNT; Minneapolis: Augsburg, 1980), 43-50; B. L. Martin, *Christ and the Law in Paul* (Leiden: Brill, 1989), 40-41, 92-93; F. Thielman, *From Plight to Solution: A Jewish Framework for Understanding Paul's View of the Law in Galatians and Romans* (Leiden: Brill, 1989), 94-96; D. Moo, *The Epistle to the Romans* (NICNT; Grand Rapids: Eerdmans, 1996), 155-57, 171-72.

[16] Longenecker, *Paul, Apostle of Liberty*, 121-22.

drew on material from a hellenistic Jewish missionary tractate.[17] Heikki Räisänen, rejecting an interpolation theory, argues that 2:14-15 and 26-27 are flatly contradictory to Paul's main thesis in 1:18–3:20 that all are under sin, and so evidence quite clearly that "Paul's mind is divided" with respect to humanity's ability to keep the Mosaic law.[18] And E. P. Sanders believes that in 1:18–2:29 "Paul takes over to an unusual degree homiletical material from Diaspora Judaism, that he alters it in only insubstantial ways, and that consequently the treatment of the law in chapter 2 cannot be harmonized with any of the diverse things which Paul says about the law elsewhere."[19]

Most attempts to understand Romans 2, however, other than those of O'Neill, Räisänen and Sanders sketched out above, start on the assumption that everything said in the chapter represents Paul's teaching directly, however derived, and that therefore everything said needs to be reconciled in some way with what is said elsewhere in Romans and Paul's other letters. For most of these scholars it has always seemed incredible that Paul would speak about justification without also having the idea of faith in mind. So they have found it necessary either (1) to clarify the nature of the referents beyond what the apostle himself has done, or (2) to interpret Romans 2 as a hypothetical presentation that functions rhetorically to prepare the way for a later discussion.

Some Proposals

How, then, can the issues that arise in 1:18–3:20 be understood? Personally, while I am prepared to relinquish the designation "hypothetical," I still believe that 1:18–3:20 was written in order to prepare for the discussion of 3:21–4:25—with 1:16-17 being the thesis for the entire section, 3:21-23 the repetition and expansion of that thesis, and 9:1–11:36 the climatic resumption of the issues raised in 2:17–3:20 regarding a Jewish response (or lack of response) to the gospel. But 1:18–3:20 is not properly understood only when seen as containing

---

[17] J. C. O'Neill, *Paul's Letter to the Romans* (PNTC; Harmondsworth: Penguin Books, 1975), 41-42, 49, 53-54, 264-65.

[18] H. Räisänen, *Paul and the Law*, 100-107. For a critique of Räisänen, see C. E. B. Cranfield, "Giving a Dog a Bad Name. A Note on H. Räisänen's *Paul and the Law*," *JSNT* 38 (1990) 77-85.

[19] E. P. Sanders, *Paul, the Law, and the Jewish People*, 123.

declarations about God's impartiality (2:11),[20] Jews and Gentiles be-ing alike under sin (3:9-19, 23), and no one being able to be declared righteous by observing the law (3:20). What also needs to be recog-nized is (1) that 2:1–3:8 is structured along the lines of two diatribal dialogues,[21] and (2) that 2:17–3:8 is entirely, both in the objections raised and the answers given, set out in terms of an intramural Jewish debate.[22]

The first of the diatribal dialogues is introduced at 2:1 by the sudden address to an imaginary interlocutor in the second person singular, "O man!" It follows on the heels of the depiction of humanity's idolatry and immorality presented in 1:18-32—which, as noted above, has often been seen to parallel the depiction of the Gentile world given in *Wisdom of Solomon* 13:1–14:31. It begins in 2:1 with an indicting statement addressed to a censorious person; it continues with a series of questions addressed to that imaginary inter-locutor in 2:2-5; and it concludes in 2:6-11 with a quotation from Ps 62:12 (MT 62:13) and an explication of the significance of that pas-sage—with such quotations from ancient sources being not uncom-mon in Greek diatribal dialogues. Its theme is God's impartiality in dealing with humanity. And its referent is humanity in general, both Gentiles and Jews. For while 1:18-32 seems to have Gentiles primarily in mind, the diatribe of 2:1-11 and the further comments of 2:12-16 broaden out to include both Gentiles and Jews.

A second diatribal dialogue is introduced at 2:17, not by a vocative but by the second person singular pronominal phrase, "You a Jew!"—which is a form of address that was also common in ancient diatribes. It too begins with a number of questions addressed to an imaginary interlocutor in 2:17-23, with an appended quotation from Isa 52:5 in 2:24. As it continues, it poses another set of questions in 3:1-8. And it comes to a close with a conclusion in 3:9-19, which contains what was probably a traditional catena of biblical passages

---

[20] While J. M. Bassler's structural analysis of 1:18–3:20 can be questioned, she is certainly correct is positing that "divine impartiality" is the central axiom of the passage (*Divine Impartiality*, esp. 121-23, 137).

[21] Cf. S. K. Stowers, *The Diatribe and Paul's Letter to the Romans*, esp. 93-98, 110-13; *idem*, "Paul's Dialogue with a Fellow Jew," 707-22; *idem*, *Rereading of Romans*, 83-193.

[22] In addition to S. K. Stowers cited above, see G. P. Carras, "Romans 2,1-29: A Dialogue," 183-207.

(vv 10-18) stitched together by a sixfold repetition of the phrase "there is no one" (οὐκ ἔστιν) and an enumeration of various parts of the body ("throats," "tongues," "lips," "mouths," "feet," and "eyes") to make the point that all human beings in their totality are sinful. The referent throughout this whole latter section of 2:17–3:19 is certainly Jewish—probably, however, not Jews generally or Judaism *per se*, but rather some type of proud and inconsistent Jew who viewed himself as a moral teacher of Gentiles, but who caused the name of God to be dishonored among the Gentiles because he failed to live up to the standards of the Mosaic law.

More important to note with regard to 1:18–3:20, however, is the fact that in both its structures and its arguments the passage is exceedingly Jewish. In fact, as George P. Carras observes (particularly with regard to chapter 2), the entire passage reflects an "inner Jewish debate" and "is best understood as a diatribe whereby two Jewish attitudes on the nature of Jewish religion are being debated."[23] The thesis statement of 1:16, "first for the Jew, then for the Gentile," alerts readers to expect that what follows will deal with relationships between Jews and Gentiles before God. And that is what is spelled out throughout all of 1:18–4:25—first in 1:18–3:20 in depicting God's impartiality in judging all people, both Gentiles and Jews; then in 3:21–4:25 in proclaiming God's impartiality in bestowing his righteousness on all people, whether Jews or Gentiles.

So I propose that here in 1:18–3:20 we see Paul beginning his argument in Romans by agreeing with both Judaism generally and Jewish believers in Jesus in particular about (1) the impartiality of divine judgment (2:11), (2) Jews and Gentiles being alike under sin (3:9-19, 23), and (3) no one able to be declared righteous by observing the law (3:20). Further, I propose that in arguing these points Paul used what he considered to have been rather standard Jewish and Jewish Christian sources and arguments, believing that such materials were used in similar ways in those same circles. And if all this be true, then it cannot be said that the focus of Paul's teaching in Romans—and therefore what he specifically had in mind in speaking about imparting "some spiritual gift" to his addressees in 1:11—is to

---

[23] Carras, *ibid.*, 185 and 206.

be found in 1:18–3:20.[24] Rather, it seems that what he sets out in 1:18–3:20 is something he believed he held in common with his addressees and that he used in preparation for what appears later in his letter.

2. The Structure and Argument of Rom 3:21–4:25

Coupled with 1:18–3:20 is 3:21–4:25, which presents a counter-balance to what has just been depicted. And though this second part of the first section of Romans is similar in tone and language to the first, a critical reading of this latter part highlights certain distinctive issues that need to be observed and evaluated as well.

Some Important Issues
The passage begins in 3:21-23 with what appears to be a thesis paragraph that repeats and expands on the opening thesis statement of 1:17. Immediately readers are faced with an issue of some significance for interpretation. For while the emphatic "but now" (νυνὶ δέ) marks a shift to a new level in Paul's argument, commentators vary as to whether the expression is to be understood as having a purely logical function (i.e., signaling a further aspect of the subject, without necessarily contrasting the two parts of the section) or as having a temporal force (i.e., contrasting the two parts). Likewise, interpreters have varied widely with respect to the meaning of "the righteousness of God," principally as to whether it signifies an attribute of God that determines his actions on behalf of humanity or a quality of existence that he bestows on those who respond to him— and, if the latter, whether it should be viewed in a forensic or an ethical manner. Further, interpreters vary widely in their treatment of the two sets of statements that are used ascriptively with regard to "the righteousness of God," which has been manifested in the gospel: (1) "apart from the law," yet "witnessed to by the Law and the Prophets" (v 21); and (2) "through faith in [or, 'by the faithfulness of'] Jesus Christ" and "to all who believe" (v 22).

A shift in style certainly occurs in 3:21-26, set as it is between the question-and-answer styles of 3:1-8 and 3:27-31. And repeating, as it does, the declarative tone and content of 1:16-17, the passage not only

---

[24] As, e.g., H. P. Liddon, *Explanatory Analysis of St Paul's Epistle to the Romans* (London: Longmans, Green, 1893), 43; C. Gore, *St Paul's Epistle to the Romans*, 2 vols. (London: Murray, 1900), 1.106.

ties together the two parts of the first section of Romans, but also seems to be kerygmatic in nature. For by its emphatic repetition of the phrase "the righteousness of God" in verses 22-23, its ascriptive statements regarding that righteousness in those same verses, its emphasis on divine impartiality in verse 23, and its weighty soteriological affirmations in verses 24-26, the passage highlights the central thrust of what Paul writes at least throughout 1:16–4:25.

The question, however, must be asked: Is 3:21-26 (in conjunction with 1:16-17) the structural center and argumentative focus of all of Romans, which provides "the key to the structure and thought of the letter"[25]—as has traditionally been argued, at least since the Protestant Reformation? Does it, in fact, embody the heart of the Christian gospel in miniature?[26] Or, stated more prosaically, the issue is this: Does 3:21-26 (in conjunction with 1:16-17) set out the controlling thesis of the whole of Romans? Or, alternatively, should 3:21-26, together with 1:16-17, be understood as the thesis of the first eight chapters of the letter—or perhaps, more narrowly, the thesis of only the first four chapters?

Also at issue in any discussion of 3:21–4:25 are questions regarding (1) the provenance of what appears to be early Christian confessional material in 3:24-26 (or, perhaps, 3:25-26a), (2) the nature of the argument about the oneness of God and God's impartial treatment of all people in 3:27-31, (3) the use of Abraham as the exemplar of faith in 4:1-24, and (4) the inclusion of an early Christian confessional portion at the end of this section in 4:25. For 3:24-31 has been seen, particularly of late, to incorporate many fundamentally Jewish ideas about "justification," "justice," "redemption," "repentance," and "atonement"; 4:1-24 to highlight the major Jewish exemplar of relationship with God; and 4:25 to epitomize the essence of the earliest Christian proclamation. Further, the two key terms of the thesis statements of 1:17 and 3:21-23, δικαιοσύνη and πίστις, which appeared also throughout 1:18–3:20, come to dominant expression in 3:24–4:25 as well. And so this "word chain" appears to tie together these two parts of the first section of Romans.

---

[25] Quoting W. S. Campbell, "Romans 3 as the Key to the Structure and Thought of the Letter," *NovT* 23 (1981) esp. 24, 32-35.

[26] So A. Hultgren, *Gospel and Mission: The Outlook from his Letter to the Romans* (Philadelphia: Trinity Press International, 1985), 47, who expresses the view of many.

Some Preliminary Observations

How has this important section of Romans been treated by commentators? The subject is too vast for any brief, comprehensive answer. Suffice it here to say that, since at least the Protestant Reformation, 3:21–4:25 has been seen by most interpreters to be the heart of Paul's teaching in the letter. Reading Romans as a compendium of Christian theology, ignoring Paul's own religious background and possible literary sources, and caricaturing the Judaism of the apostle's day as a religion of "works-righteousness," Christians have felt fairly secure in understanding 3:21–4:25 as the focus of what Paul writes in this letter. So the central thrust of Romans has been seen as (1) a polemic against any form of acceptance before God by human endeavor, and (2) a proclamation of righteousness through faith alone—with these two emphases taken to be the central features of the Christian religion vis-à-vis Judaism and all other religions.

But quite a revolution has taken place among Christian scholars during the past few decades in understanding the Judaism of Paul's day and that of the early (tannaitic) rabbis whose teachings are codified in the Talmud.[27] It may be that scholarship has swung, in pendulum-like fashion, too far in the other direction, exchanging blind condemnation for an almost equally blind approbation, which at times goes beyond the evaluations of the better Jewish teachers themselves. Nonetheless, no longer can the Judaism of Paul's day be simply written off as a legalistic religion of human works-righteousness. And interpreters of Paul have today been alerted to the fact that there is much in the apostle's writings that he took over from Judaism. Though all of his earlier thought and piety were "rebaptized" into Christ, the basic structures of his Jewish thought and the basic ethos of his Jewish piety continued to play a large part in his life as a Christian.

---

[27] Rightly credited, in large part, to E. P. Sanders, *Paul and Palestinian Judaism: A Comparison of Patterns of Religion* (Philadelphia: Fortress, 1977). But just for the record, I quote T. L. Donaldson's comment in his *Paul and the Gentiles. Remapping the Apostle's Convictional World* (Minneapolis: Fortress, 1997), 311: "Aspects of Sanders's analysis, including the use of 'nomism' itself, were anticipated in significant ways by Richard N. Longenecker, *Paul, Apostle of Liberty* (New York: Harper & Row, 1964)." See particularly chapter 3, "The Piety of Hebraic Judaism," in my *Paul, Apostle of Liberty*, 65-85.

Scholars, of late, have demonstrated that much of what Paul says in 3:21–4:25 about "the righteousness of God," "justification," "redemption," "expiation–propitiation," "divine impartiality," and "faith" rests solidly on Jewish foundations, and have argued that much of what he affirms with respect to these matters was voiced by Jewish and Jewish Christian teachers of the day as well.[28] Likewise, scholars have shown that pre-Pauline Christian confessional material is used in 3:24-26 in support of the thesis paragraph in 3:12-23—material which Rudolf Bultmann, Ernest Käsemann, and others have seen as contained in verses 24-26a, starting with the participle δικαιούμενοι ("being justified"), but which Eduard Lohse and others view as contained in verses 25-26a, starting with the relative personal pronoun ὅν ("who").[29] Yet however we evaluate the specific details of the materials in 3:24-26—or, for that matter, the presence and use of traditional structures and language elsewhere in Paul's letters—the suggestion seems irresistible that what Paul writes in 3:21–4:25 was part-and-parcel of the shared faith of his Christian addressees at Rome. And further, it may be claimed that what he writes them was based immediately on the confessions of the earliest Jewish believers in Jesus and ultimately on the fundamental structures and thought of Early Judaism.

A Proposal
What needs here to be noted from our contextual scanning above is that 3:21–4:25 is extensively Jewish and/or Jewish Christian in both

---

[28] Note particularly J. D. G. Dunn, "Paul and Justification by Faith," in *The Road from Damascus: The Impact of Paul's Conversion on his Life, Thought, and Ministry* (MNTS; ed. R. N. Longenecker; Grand Rapids: Eerdmans, 1997), 85-101. Among Dunn's many other writings on the subject, see also his "New Perspective on Paul," 95-122; *idem, Romans*, 2 vols. (WBC; Dallas: Word, 1988), 1.161-241; *idem, The Partings of the Ways between Christianity and Judaism* (London: SCM; Philadelphia: Trinity Press International, 1991), 117-39; *idem*, "How New was Paul's Gospel? The Problem of Continuity and Discontinuity," in *Gospel in Paul: Studies on Corinthians, Galatians and Romans for Richard N. Longenecker*, ed. L. A. Jervis and P. Richardson (Sheffield: Sheffield Academic Press, 1994), 367-88.

[29] For a history of the interpretation of 3:24-26 as a pre-Pauline tradition, see the published dissertation of Herbert Koch, *Römer 3,21-31 in der Paulusinterpretation der letzten 150 Jahre* (Göttingen: Andreas Funke, 1971), 107-34.

its structures and its expressions, as we found also to be true for 1:18–3:20. On the basis of such observations, therefore, I propose that Paul begins his letter to believers at Rome in 1:16–4:25 in quite a traditional manner—not only praising them for their faith in Christ Jesus, but also using materials and arguments that they and he held in common. He believes, as he said in the first part of the *propositio* of Gal 2:15-21, that all true believers in Jesus—particularly Jewish believers, but also, by extension, Gentile believers who had been influenced by Jewish thought in some way—know that a person is not justified "by the works of the law" (ἐξ ἔργων νόμου), but by what Christ has effected (διὰ / ἐκ πίστεως Ἰησοῦ Χριστοῦ, which I understand to be a subject genitive and so to mean "by the faith/faithfulness of Jesus Christ") and one's faith in him (ἐπιστεύσαμεν εἰς Χριστὸν Ἰησοῦν, vv 15-16). So he writes with confidence to Christians at Rome, setting out in the two parts of 1:16–4:25 what he believes that both they and he held in common, before then going on in 5:1–8:39 to speak of matters that pertain to the distinctive nature of his preaching (i.e., "my gospel") within the Gentile mission.

If our proposal be true, then, of course, it cannot be said that the focus of Paul's teaching in Romans—and therefore what he had in mind in speaking about imparting "some spiritual gift" to his addressees in 1:11—is to be found primarily in 3:21–4:25, as has been traditionally held. Rather, it may be argued that what he sets out in his thesis paragraph of 3:21-23, in the early Christian confessional material of 3:24-26, in the highlighting of God's oneness and impartiality in 3:27-31, in the illustration of Abraham as the exemplar of faith in 4:1-24, and in the traditional portion incorporated in 4:25 are matters that he believed he held in common with his addressees and that he used in preparation for what he would write later in his letter, particularly in 5:1–8:39.

3. *The Structure and Argument of Rom 5:1–8:39*

The relation of 5:1–8:39 to 1:16–4:25 has been a perennial problem for interpreters. One common way has been to understand 1:16–4:25 as being about sin in the first part and justification in the second, whereas 5:1–8:39 deals with sanctification. Another way is to view these two sections as setting forth somewhat parallel lines of thought: first by the use of judicial and forensic language in 1:16–4:25; then in language more mystical and participatory in 5:1–8:39. The issues are complex, but they call for some evaluation here.

Some Important Issues

When moving from 1:16–4:25 to 5:1–8:39, the reader is immediately confronted with the problem of how the two forms of "therefore" in 5:1 and 5:12 function to set up the material of these chapters. For 5:1 begins with the statement, "Therefore being justified by faith," with the postpostive transitional conjunction οὖν ("therefore") connecting "being justified by faith" with what was argued in 1:16–4:25; while in 5:12 there appears the prepositional phrase διὰ τοῦτο ("therefore"), which seems not to be a transition from 5:1-11 but to signal some type of logical break and (perhaps) to reach back to 1:16–4:25. Likewise, one must determine whether 5:1a should be read as "let us have (ἔχωμεν, a hortatory subjunctive) peace with God," which is the better-supported reading in the manuscript tradition, or "we have (ἔχομεν, an indicative) peace with God," which most scholars prefer for internal reasons. In effect, what one concludes regarding these seemingly minor linguistic points has a profound effect on how one relates 5:1-11 (also, perhaps, 5:12-21) to the flow of the argument from chapters 1–4 to chapters 5–8—that is, whether it is the conclusion to what precedes in 1:16–4:25, whether it serves as transitional material between 1:16–4:25 and 5:12–8:39, or whether it functions as an introduction to what follows in 5:1–8:39.

There are, of course, a number of similarities between these first and second major sections of Romans, however the sections are precisely delineated—with the similarities often continuing on throughout the rest of the letter as well. For example, the theme of righteousness, which was prominent in 1:16–4:25, appears also in 5:1–8:39 (i.e., in 5:17, 21; 6:13, 16, 18, 19, 20; 8:10) and throughout 9:30–10:21. Likewise, issues concerning the Mosaic law, which were raised in 3:20, 21, 31 and 4:13-15, receive further treatment in 5:13-14, 20; 7:1-6, 7-25; and 8:1-4—with the conclusions reached in these passages underlying the whole presentation of 9:1–11:36. And convictions about Jesus Christ that were implicit in the thesis statement of 1:16-17, interjected almost parenthetically into the discussion at 2:16, and further expressed in the thesis paragraph of 3:21-26, are elaborated in 5:1–8:39—with these convictions then presupposed throughout 9:1–11:36 and the exhortations of 12:1–15:13.

On the other hand, there are a number of striking differences between these two sections. Most obvious is their difference in the use of Scripture.[30] For while there are about 18 quotations of Scripture in eight or nine places in 1:16–4:25—with about 30 quotations in 25–26 places in 9:1–11:36, an additional ten in the exhortations of 12:1–15:13, and one more in the Apostolic Parousia of 15:14-32—only two biblical quotations appear in 5:1–8:39, and then somewhat tangentially: once in 7:7, citing in illustrative fashion the tenth commandment "Do not covet" of Exod 20:17 and Deut 5:21; and once in 8:36, in what appears to be an early Christian confessional portion that makes use of Ps 44:22. Likewise, the word chain shifts from δικαιοσύνη and πίστις / πιστεύω in 1:16–4:25 to ζωή / ζάω and the dominance of ἁμαρτία and θάνατος in 5:1–8:39 (though also, of course, with the appearance of δικαιοσύνη in eight verses of this section, as noted above).

Further, the form of address varies in these two sections. For whereas imaginary interlocutors are addressed in 2:1 ("O man!") and 2:17 ("You a Jew!"), with a rhetorical "we" appearing in 4:1 ("What then shall we say?"), Paul—for the first time since the Salutation of 1:1-7 and the Thanksgiving of 1:8-12—speaks directly to his addressees in 5:1–8:39. He sets up his direct address in this latter section by the pronoun "us" in 4:24, which concludes his illustration of Abraham in chapter 4, and the pronoun "our" in the incorporated traditional portion of 4:25, which closes off the first section. In 5:1–8:39, however, he speaks directly and consistently to his readers by the use of the pronouns and verbal suffixes "we," "you," "yourselves," and "us"—addressing them also as "brothers and sisters" (ἀδελφοί) in 7:1, 4. He uses, as well, a type of rhetorical προσωποποιΐα or "speech-in-character" in 7:7-25 as he expresses in the first person singular "I" the tragic soliloquy of humanity in its attempts to live by its own insights and strength. In addition, the style in these two sections shifts from being argumentative, particularly in the diatribes of 2:2-11 and 2:17–3:8 and the rhetorically structured presentation of God's oneness and impartiality in 3:17-31, to being more "confessional," cast as it is in 5:1–8:39 in the first person plural.

---

[30] Cf. my "Prolegomena to Paul's Use of Scripture in Romans," esp. 146-47, 158-67. See also chap. 4, "Paul and the Old Testament," in my *Biblical Exegesis in the Apostolic Period*, 2nd ed. (1999), 88-116.

Also significant are the differences in content between these two sections of Romans. Two matters, in particular, call for mention here. The first has to do with the differing diagnoses of the "human predicament." For in depicting humanity's situation apart from God, the narrative of 1:18-32 unfolds in terms of humanity's *decline* into idolatry and immorality *during the course of history*—without any reference to Adam's sin; whereas in 5:12-21 (probably also in 7:7-13) the focus is on the disobedience of the "one man" and how his transgression has affected all human beings. The diagnosis of 1:18-32, of course, may be built on *Wisdom of Solomon* 13:1–14:31 and/or similar Jewish traditions (as postulated above), and so conditioned by the materials used. Nonetheless, while the story of Adam's sin in Genesis 2–3 was certainly retained within the Jewish Scriptures, it seems not to be have been widely used as an explanation for humanity's predicament during the time of Early Judaism (except in *4 Ezra* 3:7-8, 21-22; 7:116-26 and *2 Baruch* 23:4; 48:42-43; 54:15; 56:5-6). Certainly it was not used by the tannaitic rabbis whose teachings were codified in the Talmud.

Likewise, 7:7-25 poses numerous problems with respect to both its content and its possible parallels. Commentators have traditionally been concerned with the identity of the speaker and the type of experience described. Questions, however, have also been raised regarding the rhetoric of the passage, with parallels pointed out between 7:14-24 and the tragic soliloquies of the Greek world.[31] In particular, Paul's use of the first person singular and his laments throughout verses 14-24 have been compared to Euripides' Medea, who, driven by rage and thoughts of revenge, determined to murder her own children; and who, in reflecting on such a heinous act, cries out: "I am being overcome by evils. I know that what I am about to do is evil, but passion is stronger than my reasoned reflection; and this is the cause of the worst evils for humans" (*Medea* 1077-80).[32] This "famous Medean saying," as Stanley Stowers points out, was widely known in

---

[31] Cf. H. Hommel, "Das 7. Kapitel des Römerbriefs im Licht antiker Überlieferung," *Theologia viatorum* 8 (1961) 90-116; G. Theissen, *Psychological Aspects of Pauline Theology* (Philadelphia: Fortress, 1987), 211-19; Stowers, *Rereading of Romans*, 260-64.

[32] Among the many parallel Greek texts that could be cited, note also Ovid, *Metamorphoses* vii.19-20: "Desire persuades me one way, reason another. I see the better and approve it, but I follow the worse."

Paul's day, occurring "not only in drama and philosophers' debates, but also in such contexts as letters and public orations."[33]

Some Preliminary Observations

What can be said with respect to such issues? Though many have taken Paul's discussion in 1:16–4:25 to continue on through 5:11,[34] or on through 5:21,[35] most scholars today view 5:1–8:39 as a distinguishable unit of material.[36] That is not only because the example of Abraham as a "proof from Scripture" is a fitting conclusion to what precedes, but also because 5:1-11 appears to serve as something of a thesis section for what follows—with most of the themes and some of the terms of 5:1-11 reappearing in 8:18-39, thereby setting up an *inclusio* or type of "ring composition." Further, as noted above, (1) 5:1 seems to function as a literary hinge, first summarizing the argument of 1:16–4:25—particularly that of 3:21–4:25 ("since, therefore, we have been justified through faith")—and then preparing for what follows in 5:2–8:39 ("we have peace [or, 'let us have peace'] with God through our Lord Jesus Christ"); (2) the word chain shifts from δικαιοσύνη and πίστις / πιστεύω in 1:16–4:25 to ζωή / ζάω and the dominance of ἁμαρτία and θάνατος in 5:1–8:39; (3) the tone shifts from being argumentative in 1:16–4:25 to more confessional in 5:1–8:39; and (4) there appears throughout the section the repeated refrain διὰ τοῦ κυρίου ἡμῶν Ἰησοῦ Χριστοῦ (or, ἐν τῷ κυρίῳ ἡμῶν Ἰησοῦ Χριστῷ) not only as an *inclusio* at 5:1 and 8:39 but also at the end of each separate unit at 5:11, 5:21, 6:23, and 7:25.

Interpreters have usually not been too concerned about the differences identified above between these two sections of Romans, 1:16–4:25 and 5:1–8:39—that is, about differences in their use of Scripture, their respective word chains, their forms of address, or their tones or styles. Usually these matters are viewed as being purely circumstantial in nature, without any inferences drawn as to their significance. On the other hand, where such differences are recognized, they

---

[33] Stowers, *ibid.*, 263.

[34] E.g., M. Luther (with 5:12-21 considered an excursus), P. Melanchthon, T. Zahn, F. Leenhardt, M. Black, and J. A. T. Robinson.

[35] E.g., J. Calvin, U. Wilckens, O. Kuss, F. F. Bruce, and J. D. G. Dunn.

[36] E.g., H. Schlier, A. Nygren, O. Michel, C. H. Dodd, N. Dahl, C. E. B. Cranfield, E. Käsemann, J. A. Fitzmyer, and D. Moo.

have often been seen as evidencing either later interpolations by some undiscerning Paulinist or outright contradictions in Paul's own thought. One scholar has even proposed that Romans 1–11 should be viewed as two distinctly different Pauline sermons: one to a Jewish audience, which is now found in chapters 1–4 and 9–11, but whose parts have somehow become separated; the other to a Gentile audience, which is preserved in chapters 5–8.[37]

Likewise, though the analyses of humanity's condition is set out differently in 1:18-32 and 5:12-21, most interpreters have been content to read 1:18-32 as "the obviously deliberate echo of the Adam narratives,"[38] and so have denied or minimized any difference between them. And though scholars have frequently noted parallels between 7:14-24 and the tragic soliloquies of the Greek world, most have dismissed them as being somewhat trivial in comparison to the seemingly more significant parallels between 7:7-13 (also, of course, 3:21–4:25) and the Jewish world.[39] But it may be doubted whether (1) the differences between 1:16–4:25 and 5:1–8:39 or (2) the parallels between 7:14-24 and the tragic soliloquies of the Greeks can be treated so summarily.

A Proposal

I have not dealt here directly with matters pertaining to the identity and circumstances of Paul's Roman addressees. That is not because I consider such questions unimportant. On the contrary, I consider them to be highly significant. But I have discussed Paul's Roman addressees and Roman Christianity in a recent article,[40] and I have space here only to refer to that article and repeat its conclusions.

My argument, in agreement with Raymond Brown,[41] is that the important question to ask regarding Christians at Rome is not the

[37] So Scroggs, "Paul as Rhetorician," 271-98.

[38] Dunn, *Romans*, 1.53; cf. M. D. Hooker, "Adam in Romans 1," *NTS* 6 (1960) 297-306; *idem*, "A Further Note on Romans 1," *NTS* 13 (1966) 181-83; A. J. M. Wedderburn, "Adam in Paul's Letter to the Romans," in *Studia Biblica* 3, ed. E. A. Livingstone (Sheffield: JSOT, 1980), 413-30; and many others.

[39] Cf. E. Käsemann, *Romans*, 198-211, and many others.

[40] See my "Prolegomena to Paul's Use of Scripture in Romans," 148-52.

[41] Cf. R. E. Brown, "The Beginnings of Christianity at Rome" and "The Roman Church near the End of the First Christian Generation (A.D. 58—Paul to the Romans)," in *Antioch and Rome: New Testament Cradles of Catholic Christianity*, ed. R. E. Brown and J. P. Meier (New York: Paulist, 1983), 92-127;

ethnic question, "Were they Jews or Gentiles, or, if ethnically mixed, dominantly one or the other?"—with the implications being that if Jewish believers, then they should be viewed as non-Pauline in outlook, but if Gentile believers, then adherents to Paul's teaching. Probably the addressees constituted both Jewish and Gentile believers in Jesus. And most likely the Gentiles believers were in the majority, for Paul considered the Roman church to be within the orbit of his Gentile ministry.

Rather than trying to determine the addressees' character on the basis of their ethnicity, "the crucial issue," as Brown points out, "is the theological outlook of this mixed Jewish / Gentile Christianity."[42] In analyzing the factors to be considered for any judgment regarding the theological outlook of the Roman Christians, Brown concludes (1) that for both Jews and Christians "the Jerusalem–Rome axis was strong," (2) "that Roman Christianity came from Jerusalem, and indeed represented the Jewish / Gentile Christianity associated with such Jerusalem figures as Peter and James," and (3) that both in the earliest days of the Roman church and at the time when Paul wrote them, believers at Rome could be characterized as "Christians who kept up some Jewish observances and remained faithful to part of the heritage of the Jewish Law and cult, without insisting on circumcision."[43] And it is this understanding that I bring to the discussion here, believing it to be the position best supported by all the available data—and believing that it casts Paul's argument in Romans in an entirely new light.

My proposal, then, is that in 5:1–8:39 is to be found the focus of what Paul writes in Romans, and so the section that contains, in particular, the "spiritual gift" that he says he wants to give the Christians at Rome in 1:11 and that he speaks about as being "my gospel" in 2:16 and 16:25. This is not to discredit what he writes in

---

idem, "Further Reflections on the Origins of the Church of Rome," in *The Conversation Continues: Studies in Paul and John in Honor of J. L. Martyn,* ed. R. T. Fortna and B. R. Gaventa (Nashville: Abingdon, 1990), 98-115.

[42] Brown, "Beginnings of Christianity at Rome," 109 n. 227.

[43] *Ibid.* 104. For a different attempt to deal with the same data, arguing that the addressees were "a group of Judean Christians" at Rome, see S. Mason, "'For I am not ashamed of the Gospel' (Rom. 1.16): The Gospel and the First Readers of Romans," in *Gospel in Paul: Studies on Corinthians, Galatians and Romans for Richard N. Longenecker,* ed. L. A. Jervis and P. Richardson (Sheffield: Sheffield Academic Press, 1994), 254-87.

1:16–4:25, for that is what he held in common with his addressees. Indeed, it is on the basis of their acceptance of the message of 1:16–4:25 that both they and he originally became believers in Jesus. Undoubtedly he often proclaimed that message, particularly when addressing Jews or those who had been influenced by Jewish thought for the better (as had the Christians at Rome)—or in addressing those who had been influenced by Jewish thought for the worse (as had the Christians in Galatia). But what he also wanted believers at Rome to know was the gospel that he had been preaching to purely Gentile audiences. For believers at Rome, too, were predominantly Gentiles, and he wanted to include them within the orbit of his Gentile proclamation and so to strengthen them. Further, he wanted them to become partners in his Gentile mission as the sending church to the western regions of the Roman empire, just as the church at Antioch of Syria had functioned as the sending church to the eastern regions.

So Paul addresses the recipients of his letter as Gentiles within his Gentile mission (cf. 1:5-6, 13-15,; 11:13; 15:15-18), distinguishing between them and his "own people" (e.g., 11:14). He also, however, speaks of Abraham as "our forefather" (4:1), refers to his addressees as "those who know the law" (7:1), presupposes that they have lived under the law (7:4-6; 8:3-4), and lays stress on the messianic tradition in this letter more than anywhere else in his extant writings (cf. 1:3-4; 9:5; 15:12, quoting Is 11:10). More particularly, in 1:16–4:25 he argues in a thoroughly Jewish and Jewish Christian manner. And he continues that type of argumentation in relating the gospel to the hope of Israel in 9:1–11:36 and in his exhortations of 12:1–15:13.

In 5:1–8:39, however, he sets out the essence of what he proclaims in his Gentile mission—that is, to Gentiles who had not been prepared for the gospel by Jewish or Jewish Christian teaching, and so did not think in Jewish categories. That message, he acknowledges in 5:1a, is based on being "justified by faith." Its thrust, however, consists of (1) a proclamation of "peace" and "reconciliation" with God "through our Lord Jesus Christ," which is unfolded in the theme or thesis section of 5:1-11; (2) the telling of the universal, foundational story of sin, death and condemnation having entered the world by "one man," but grace, life and righteousness brought about "through Jesus Christ our Lord" in 5:12-21; (3) the spelling out of the relations of sin, death and the law, on the one hand, and grace, life and righteousness, on the other, through the use of three rhetorical questions at 6:1, 6:15 and

7:7—with a particularly tragic soliloquy, which had many parallels in the Greek world, coming to voice in 7:14-24; (4) the highlighting of relationships "in Christ" and "in the Spirit" in 8:1-30; and (5) a triumphal declaration, which verges on being a defiant assertion, of God's love and care for his own "in Christ Jesus our Lord" in 8:31-39, with that final portion probably incorporating a number of early Christian confessional statements.

It is in this section that the three basic features of classical rhetoric—that is, *logos* (content or argument), *ethos* (the personal character of the speaker or writer), and *pathos* (the power to stir the emotions)—come most fully to expression in Paul's letter to the Romans. It is in this section that themes most distinctly Pauline are clustered: "peace" and "reconciliation" with God,[44] and the believer being "in Christ" and "in the Spirit." And it is in Romans 8, using John A. T. Robinson's analogy of "a journey by canal across an isthmus" with its "series of locks" rising to and then falling away from "a central ridge," that "the heights of the epistle are reached" and there occurs "a sustained climax which takes the argument across the watershed."[45]

4. *Conclusion*

While different in many respects in its tone and content from the letter that he wrote to Gentile Christians living in the Roman province of Galatia, the approach that Paul takes in Romans has some parallels to the approach he took earlier in Galatians. For in both he begins with matters of agreement and then moves on to those matters having to do with either disagreement or his own distinctive proclamation of the gospel. The *propositio* or proposition statement of Gal 2:15-21, as Hans Dieter Betz has argued and I have agreed, sets out Paul's argument in terms of three movements: first acknowledging matters of agreement with his addressees (vv 15-16), then setting out matters of disagreement (vv 17-20), and finally drawing a conclusion (v 21)[46]—with, then, in the *probatio* or argument section of Galatians the matters of agreement spelled out in 3:1-18, the matters of

---

[44] This is, in particular, the insight of S. Kim, "God Reconciled His Enemy to Himself," 102-24; *idem*, "2 Cor. 5:11-21 and the Origin of Paul's Concept of 'Reconciliation'," 360-84.

[45] J. A. T. Robinson, *Wrestling with Romans* (London: SCM, 1979), 9.

[46] Cf. my *Galatians* (Dallas: Word, 1990), 80-96.

disagreement explicated in 3:19–4:7, and expressions of concern for the believers appended in 4:8-11.[47] Most commentators have taken the central thrust of Galatians to be Paul's argument against "legalism" in 3:1-18. I have argued, however, on the basis of his *propositio* ("proposition") in 2:15-21 and his *probatio* ("arguments") in 3:1–4:11, that (1) Paul's principal arguments in Galatians are against "nomism," which are to be found in 3:19–4:11, and (2) his experiential and biblical arguments in 3:1-18, while valid and meaningful, are primarily given to prepare for his major arguments in 3:19–4:11.[48]

Likewise, in his pastoral counsel set out in 1 Corinthians, Paul often begins with statements that he and his addressees agree on—though, in this case, they seem to have interpreted the statements in one way and he in another. The most obvious of these statements are "Everything is permissible" (6:12; 10:23), "It is good for a man not to have sexual relations with a woman" (7:1), "We all possess knowledge" (8:1), "An idol is nothing at all in the world" (8:4), and "There is no God but one" (8:4). In all of these instances Paul begins by seeking common ground and then moving on to explicate his own understanding.

Something similar, I suggest, is taking place in Paul's letter to believers at Rome, though with the parallels closer to the pattern in Galatians than to that in 1 Corinthians. Thus while the presentations of God's impartiality, Jews and Gentiles being alike under sin, no one being able to be declared righteous by observing the law, and justification by faith in 1:16–4:25 are vitally important, these seem to have been matters of agreement between Paul and his addressees. What Paul wanted to give his readers as a "spiritual gift," which he refers to in 2:16 and 16:25 as "my gospel," is to be found preeminently, I suggest, in 5:1–8:39: a gospel that focuses on "peace" and "reconciliation" with God, that deals with humanity's essential tension of "death" and "life," and that highlights the personal relationships of being "in Christ" and "in the Spirit."

Understanding Romans in this fashion, of course, has rather revolutionary implications for New Testament criticism and for Christian theology. Most of all, however, it has great significance for our living as Christians, our proclamation of the gospel, and our

---

[47] Cf. *ibid.*, 97-183.
[48] *Ibid.* 97-178.

contextualization of the essential Christian message in our own day and culture.

SELECT BIBLIOGRAPHY

Bassler, Jouette M. *Divine Impartiality: Paul and a Theological Axiom.* Chico: Scholars, 1982.

Cranfield, Charles E. B. "Giving a Dog a Bad Name: A Note on H. Räisänen's *Paul and the Law*," *JSNT* 38 (1990) 77-85.

Carras, George P. "Romans 2,1-29: A Dialogue on Jewish Ideals," *Bib* 73 (1992) 183-207.

Dunn, James D. G. "The New Perspective on Paul," *BJRL* 65 (1983) 95-122 (repr. in *Jesus, Paul and the Law: Studies in Mark and Galatians*, London: SPCK; Louisville: Westminster, 1990, 183-214).

——. "Paul and Justification by Faith," in *The Road from Damascus: The Impact of Paul's Conversion on his Life, Thought, and Ministry.* MNTS. Ed. R. N. Longenecker. Grand Rapids: Eerdmans, 1997, 85-101.

Fee, Gordon D. *God's Empowering Presence: The Holy Spirit in the Letters of Paul.* Peabody: Hendrickson, 1994.

Kim, Seyoon. "God Reconciled His Enemy to Himself: The Origin of Paul's Concept of Reconciliation," in *The Road from Damascus. The Impact of Paul's Conversion on his Life, Thought, and Ministry.* MNTS. Ed. R. N. Longenecker. Grand Rapids: Eerdmans, 1997, 102-24.

——. "2 Cor. 5:11-21 and the Origin of Paul's Concept of 'Reconciliation'," *NovT* 39 (1997) 360-84.

Longenecker, Richard N. *Paul, Apostle of Liberty.* New York: Harper & Row, 1964 (repr. Grand Rapids: Baker, 1976; repr. Vancouver: Regent College Publishing, 2003).

——. "Paul and the Old Testament," in *Biblical Exegesis in the Apostolic Period.* Grand Rapids: Eerdmans, 1975; 2nd ed., 1999, 88-116.

——. "Prolegomena to Paul's Use of Scripture in Romans," *BBR* 7 (1997) 145-68, esp. 146-47, 158-67.

O'Neill, John C. *Paul's Letter to the Romans.* Harmondsworth: Penguin Books, 1975, esp. 41-42, 49, 53-54, 264-65.

Räisänen, Heikki. *Paul and the Law.* Tübingen: Mohr, 1983, 1987[2].

Sanders, E. P. *Paul, the Law, and the Jewish People.* Philadelphia: Fortress, 1983.

Schreiner, Thomas R. "Did Paul Believe in Justification by Works? Another Look at Romans 2," *BBR* 3 (1993) 131-55.

Scroggs, Robin. "Paul as Rhetorician: Two Homilies in Romans 1–11," in *Jews, Greeks, and Christians (Festschrift W. D. Davies)*, ed. R. Hammerton-Kelly and R. Scroggs. Leiden: Brill, 1976, 271-98.

Snodgrass, Klyne R. "Justification by Grace—To the Doers: An Analysis of the Place of Romans 2 in the Theology of Paul," *NTS* 32 (1986) 72-93.

Stowers, Stanley K. *The Diatribe and Paul's Letter to the Romans*. Chico: Scholars, 1981, esp. 93-98, 110-13.

———. "Paul's Dialogue with a Fellow Jew in Romans 3:1-9," *CBQ* 46 (1984) 707-22.

———. *A Rereading of Romans*. New Haven: Yale University Press, 1994, 83-193.

PAUL'S VISION OF THE CHURCH AND COMMUNITY FORMATION
IN HIS MAJOR MISSIONARY LETTERS

All thirteen Pauline letters in the New Testament are missionary and pastoral, and all of them represent themselves as speaking with apostolic authority to particular issues or concerns. Nine are addressed to congregations (Romans, 1 and 2 Corinthians, Galatians, Ephesians, Philippians, Colossians, and 1 and 2 Thessalonians, to list them in canonical order), whereas four are addressed to individuals (1 and 2 Timothy, Titus, and Philemon, again in canonical order). None of them, however, is specifically evangelistic, setting forth the nature of the earliest apostolic preaching—though there are reflections and recollections of what was earlier proclaimed. And none of them is of the nature of an ecclesiastical encyclical, setting out for us final truth in unalterable form. For all of them, while working from firm convictions, are "works in progress" that speak to a variety of interests and topics and that seek to contextualize the Christian gospel for particular addressees in their specific circumstances.

Yet every Pauline letter, whether directly or derivatively, presents us with something regarding the apostle's own vision of the church and its formation. That is true not only for the seven generally accepted letters of Paul (Romans, 1 and 2 Corinthians, Galatians, Philippians, 1 Thessalonians, and Philemon), but also for those letters often credited to an immediate follower (Ephesians, Colossians, and 2 Thessalonians) or seen as arising out of a later Pauline school (1 and 2 Timothy and Titus). The latter three letters, the so-called "Pastoral Epistles," deal specifically with issues regarding church order. The special character of these latter letters seems to have been early recognized within the Christian church, for the Muratorian Canon (c. 180–200 CE) speaks of them as not only having been written to individuals (together with Philemon) but also as having to do with "ecclesiastical discipline." In the ten other letters, however, which I will here refer to as Paul's "major missionary letters," matters pertaining to community formation are included, but not as directly as in the Pastoral Epistles. Others have explicated the teachings of the Pastoral Epistles on community formation (see esp. I. H. Marshall, "Congregation and Ministry in the Pastoral Epistles"). Here our concern is with Paul's vision of the church and community formation in his major missionary letters.

1. *Preliminary Observations on Paul's Use of* Ἐκκλησία

The Greek word for "church" (ἐκκλησία) appears more frequently in the Pauline letters than in any of the other writings of the New Testament: sixty-three times in his major missionary letters—nine times in Romans, twenty-two times in 1 Corinthians, nine times in 2 Corinthians, three times in Galatians, nine times in Ephesians, twice in Philippians, four times in Colossians, twice in 1 Thessalonians, twice in 2 Thessalonians, and once in Philemon—though, interestingly, only three times in the Pastoral Epistles; whereas it appears three times in the Gospels (all in Matthew), twenty-one times in Acts, twice in Hebrews, once in James, three times in 3 John, and seventeen times in the Apocalypse. Word counts alone, however, are inadequate for determining meaning. Theology is more than mathematics and significance can only be judged by usage. Yet such a frequency alerts us to the fact that Paul had a great concern for both the church universal and the local churches to which he wrote, and also suggests that it would be profitable to investigate his vision of the church and community formation in his letters.

A number of preliminary observations regarding Paul's ecclesiastical vision can be made based simply on the phenomena of his use of the word ἐκκλησία. One is that he appears to have made little distinction between what we would call the church local and the church universal. Paul seems to have viewed every congregation at whatever time and in whatever locality as an embodiment of the church universal—that is, to have viewed each particular congregation as *the* church of God. A second observation is that there seems to be a development in Paul's ecclesiastical consciousness, which appears to grow from a more localized understanding to one that includes a more universal understanding. This can be seen, for example, by comparing the salutations of his earlier letters with those of his later letters. For in his earlier letters he addresses "the churches in Galatia" (Gal 1:2), "the church of the Thessalonians" (1 Thess 1:1; 2 Thess 1:1), and "the church of God at Corinth" (1 Cor 1:2; 2 Cor 1:1), with the word ἐκκλησία used in a largely localized fashion, whereas in his later letters the addressees are spoken of as "loved by God," "holy ones," and "faithful brothers and sisters," with ἐκκλησία not being used in these salutations (cf. Rom 1:7; Eph 1:1; Phil 1:1; Col 1:2) but left for more developed treatments of the church universal later in those letters.

A third observation regarding Paul's use of ἐκκλησία is the functional way he speaks about the church in his letters. This is true not only when he addresses various doctrinal and ethical issues of the particular churches, but also when he writes about the nature, unity, mission, and activities of the universal church. And fourth, in the Pauline letters the church is "at the same time" both "central and peripheral" (C. K. Barrett, *Church, Ministry, and Sacraments*, 9, who makes this "paradox" the central theme of his book). Paul's essential message had to do with "Christ crucified" (e.g., 1 Cor 1:23; 2:2; Gal 3:1) and being "in Christ" (e.g., Gal 3:26-28), not church order, church politics, or even church sacraments (cf. 1 Cor 1:13-17a). Yet being "in Christ" also meant for him being an integral part of "the body of Christ" (Rom 12:4-5; 1 Cor 12:12-27; Eph 1:22-23; 4:4, 12, 16; 5:23-33; Col 1:18, 24; 2:19). So individual and corporate themes always cohered in his understanding and proclamation (cf. E. Best, *One Body in Christ*).

But all these are only preliminary observations. Further explication requires going beyond merely linguistic considerations to investigate Paul's images of the church, his criteria for community formation, and reflections of church order in his letters.

2. *Images of the Church and Some Implications*

When we ask about church order, we find Paul talking about the nature of the church. And when we ask about the nature of the church, we find him setting out various images of the church—which imagery he evidently meant to signal certain vital features about the church's nature and to suggest certain important implications for its structures and order. Six major images of the church, with their attendant auxiliary images and corollaries, are particularly significant and suggestive in the Pauline letters.

People of God
The identification of Christians as "the people of God" appears a number of times in the New Testament (e.g., Luke 1:17; Acts 15:14; Titus 2:14; Heb 4:9; 8:10; 1 Pet 2:9-10; Rev 18:4; 21:3). The imagery is also used by Paul with special significance in Rom 9:25-26; 11:1-2; 15:10, and 2 Cor 6:16 to set the Christian church in the context of the long story of God's dealings with his chosen people Israel. "People of God" is a covenantal expression that speaks of God choosing and calling a particular people to himself so that he might be in close relationship with them and they with him (Exod 19:5; Deut 7:6; 14:2; Ps 135:4; Heb 8:10; 1 Pet 2:9-10; Rev 21:3). They are God's people not because of their own proclivities or efforts, but because of God's gracious initiative and magnanimous action in creating, calling, saving, judging, and sustaining them. And as God's people, they experience God's presence and working among them.

A whole galaxy of auxiliary images oscillate around the analogy of "the people of God" for Christians and the Christian church. These include in the Pauline letters the following: "God's elect" (Rom 8:33; Eph 1:4; Col 3:12), "Abraham's descendants" (Rom 4:16; Gal 3:29; 4:26-28), "the true circumcision" (Phil 3:3; Col 2:11), and even "the Israel of God" (Gal 6:16). All of these images assert, in one way or another, an enduring solidarity of the people of the church with the people of Israel, whose history provides the church with an authoritative account of the principles and actions of God's past salvific working. It is the task of exegesis and theology to spell out the nature of this relationship.

Certain implications, however, can be drawn from such a solidarity for our purposes here. For we must see not only that Christian theology is rooted in the theology of the Old Testament and Early Judaism, but also that church order has Jewish roots and that the earliest believers in Jesus organized their worship and communal lives in ways congenial to their Jewish experiences. Such implications have important ramifications for any discussion of community formation in the early church and the church today.

Body of Christ
The non-Pauline writings of the New Testament allude a few times to believers either partaking of or being in Christ's "body" (e.g., Mark

14:22 par.; Heb 13:3). But it is only the Pauline letters that use "body of Christ" with direct reference to the church, first by way of illustration and then as an image depicting its nature. In fact, it is in his use of "body of Christ" imagery that it can be said of Paul that "his originality is incontestable and his deeper penetration into the idea of the Church is evident" (R. Schnackenburg, *The Church in the New Testament*, trans. W. J. O'Hara [Freiburg: Herder; Montreal: Palm, 1965], 77). Attention, therefore, has often been directed to the expression "the body of Christ" when dealing with Paul's vision of the church.

Paul's use of "body" (σῶμα), however, is "extremely flexible and elastic" (P. S. Minear, *Images of the Church in the New Testament* [Philadelphia: Westminster, 1960], 173), appearing in a number of ways and therefore not to be treated as simply a "verbalistic monism" (*ibid.*, 197). In Romans, for example, the word is used as a synecdoche for the death of Christ (7:4, "You died to the law through the body of Christ"), as a collective expression to signify the sum total (7:24, "Who will deliver me from the body of this death?"), as a synonym for one's self (12:1, "Present your bodies as a living sacrifice"), and as an illustration of our interdependent relationship in the community of believers with other believers (12:4-5, "As in one body we have many members, and all the members do not have the same function, so we, though many, are one body in Christ, and individually members one of another"). In 1 Corinthians the apostle exhorts his converts not to use their bodies for immorality, and so sin against their own bodies, but to view their bodies as entering into relationship with Christ, with the Holy Spirit, and with God (6:12-20); to understand that as believers "in Christ" they are "one body" who participate in "the body of Christ" (10:16-17); to realize that the Lord's Supper signifies Christ's "body, which is for you" (11:24), and so to celebrate it in a manner that neither profanes "the body and blood of the Lord" (11:27) nor lacks discernment regarding "the body" (11:29); to recognize the interrelational features of being in "the body of Christ" (12:12-27); and to appreciate that the resurrection "body" will be as God ordains it—not just a resuscitated or revivified physical body, but a changed, spiritual body of material substance, which will be in continuity with our earthly bodies (15:35-50). And in Philippians he speaks of awaiting from heaven "a Savior, the Lord Jesus Christ, who will change our lowly body to be like his glorious body, by the power which enables him even to subject all things to himself" (3:21).

Nonetheless, in Rom 12:4-5 and 1 Cor 12:12-27 (cf. 6:15-17; 10:17) Paul uses "the body" as an illustration of the interrelations that believers have with Christ and with one another. This imagery is developed further in Ephesians and Colossians, where "the body of Christ" is specifically identified with the church, Christ is spoken of as "the head" of the church, and the corporate relationship of believers with one another is emphasized (cf. Eph 1:22-23; 4:4, 12, 16; 5:23-33; Col 1:18, 24; 2:19)—though, again, with other uses of the word "body" appearing in these letters as well (cf. Col 1:22; 2:11, 17).

The imagery of the body when applied to the church carries with it a number of implications—not only with respect to believers' relationships with Christ ("the head") and with one another ("the many members"), but also having to do with the order and functioning of the church. Paul himself begins to spell out some of these implications in 1 Cor 12:12-31 when he uses the human body to illustrate both the unity of believers in "the body of Christ" (vv 12-13, 27) and the diversity of functions within the church (vv 14-31). And numerous suggestions can be drawn from Colossians and Ephesians regarding the order and functioning of the church. For in the imagery of "the body of Christ, which is the church," there exists not only the personal theme of being "in Christ" (cf. E. Best, *One Body in Christ*) but also nuances regarding both the unity of believers and the functional diversities of orders and activities within the church.

Household of Faith / God
At two places in the Pauline writings—in one earlier letter and in one later letter—the community of believers in Jesus is called a "household" (οἰκεῖος): "the household of faith" in Gal 6:10; "the household of God" in Eph 2:19. Such a designation undoubtedly stems from the common parlance of the Old Testament and Early Judaism in calling the place where God meets his people a "house" (uniquely the Jerusalem temple) and God's people a "household" (Hebrew: בַּיִת). But it also seems to have arisen from the familial language used by both Jews and Christians, which spoke of God as "Father" (Rom 8:15; Gal 4:6, *passim*; cf. Isa 63:16; *Sirach* 51:10; Matt 6:9 // Luke 11:2; *Shemoneh Esreh*, Benediction 6) and of one

another as "sons [and daughters] of God" (Rom 8:14; 2 Cor 6:18; Gal 4:5-7; cf. Hos 11:1).

Households in antiquity consisted of a number of persons: the immediate family members, who would have included at least three and sometimes four generations; slaves and servants; various business associates or clients; and others who had for one reason or another been drawn into the family circle. Families in antiquity were patriarchal and hierarchical, with the father ruling the household—though, if the father were deceased, at times the mother would become the head of the household. Slaves and servants often had managerial roles as well as menial tasks, and everyone performed his or her assigned duties for the welfare of the household. Thus when the Christian church was referred to as a "household" (whether "of faith" or "of God"), ideas of order, structure, personal relationships, and functional responsibility would inevitably have arisen in the minds of both those who used and those who heard such terminology.

Temple of God

Paul uses the imagery of "the temple of God" (ναὸς θεοῦ) to characterize both believers in Jesus Christ and the church in 1 Cor 3:16-17; 6:19-20; 2 Cor 6:16–7:1, and Eph 2:20-22—with the oscillation of thought between the individual and the corporate evidently only a particularization with respect to the former and a generalization with respect to the latter. He probably took over the imagery of a "new house" or "temple not made with hands" from Jewish apocalypticism and early Christianity (cf. *1 Enoch* 90:28-29; 91:13; *Jubilees* 1:17; *1QS* 8.5-6; Mark 14:58, par.). Through such temple imagery, Paul "depicts the church under its divine aspect as the society of the redeemed, which through sanctification by the Holy Spirit constitutes the inviolable dwelling-place of God" (R. J. McKelvey, *The New Temple: The Church in the New Testament* [London: Oxford University Press, 1969], 92).

The fullest reference to the Christian church as "the temple of the living God" in Paul's letters is to be found in 2 Cor 6:16: "What agreement is there between the temple of God and idols? For we are the temple of the living God. As God has said: 'I will live in them and walk among them, and I will be their God, and they will be my people'" (quoting from Lev 26:12; Jer 32:38; Ezek 37:27). This reference may be Paul's earliest recorded exposition on the subject, for it appears in a portion that many think was part of his "previous letter" to his converts at Corinth (i.e., 2 Cor 6:14–7:1; cf. 1 Cor 5:9).

But Paul also uses temple imagery in characterizing Christians generally. In 1 Cor 3:16-17, when dealing with the problem of divisions within the Corinthian church, he writes: "Don't you know that you are God's temple and that God's Spirit lives in you? If anyone destroys God's temple, God will destroy that person; for God's temple is sacred, and you are that temple." And in 1 Cor 6:19-20, when dealing with issues of sexual immorality in the church, he writes: "Don't you know that your body is a temple of the Holy Spirit, who is in you, whom you have received from God? You are not your own; you were brought at a price. Therefore honor God with your body." Eph 2:20-22 brings all of this temple imagery together: the church is "built on the foundation of the apostles and prophets," with "Christ Jesus himself as the chief cornerstone"; it is "in Christ," being joined together and rising "to become a holy temple in the Lord" (vv 20-21)—with individual believers then spoken of as "in him" being also "built together to become a dwelling in which God lives by his Spirit" (v 22).

Paul's use of temple imagery, however, does not include referring to the church as a place for sacrifice, as in 1 Pet 2:4-10. In Pauline theology (1) Christ is the one "who loved us and gave himself up for us as a fragrant offering and sacrifice to God" (Eph 5:2; Col 1:22), (2) Paul and his associates are those who have offered to God and his people their ministries as a sacrifice (2 Cor 2:15-16; Phil 2:17), and (3) believers in Christ are urged to offer themselves and their service to God and others as sacrifices (Rom 12:1-2; 2 Cor 9:11-15; Phil 4:18)—which, of course, furnishes the basis for the Protestant doctrine of "the priesthood of all believers." Paul's emphases in his use of temple imagery for both believers and the church, therefore, is on (1) the place in the New Covenant where God dwells, (2) the place where God's Spirit is now active, and (3) the holiness and purity that must necessarily characterize God's people, both individually and corporately. For both believers and the church, whether local or universal, have become habitations of God's Spirit.

Community of the Spirit
A further image of the church—one no less important than any of the others, yet one lacking a specific title in the apostle's letters—may be

expressed as "the community of the Spirit." It is an image that underlies much of what Paul writes, particularly in his earlier letters, though often it is more implied than expressed.

In writing to his confused converts in the Roman province of Galatia, Paul lays particular emphasis on the fact that they are a community of the Spirit and so should not be giving heed to the nomistic enticements of the Judaizers. In his *probatio* of 3:1–4:31, where he develops his central arguments, he begins with questions that assume his converts' experience as a community of the Spirit: "Did you receive the Spirit by observing the law, or by believing what you heard?" (3:2); "Does God give you his Spirit and work miracles among you because you observe the law, or because you believe what you heard?" (3:5). And in his *exhortatio* of 5:1-6:10, where he exhorts on the basis of what has been argued in the *probatio*, he urges them to "live by the Spirit," reflect "the fruit of the Spirit" in their lives, and "keep in step with the Spirit" (5:16-26).

Likewise in writing to converts at Thessalonica, Paul alludes to their corporate life as being a community of the Spirit. Almost casually he speaks of the word of God "at work in you who believe" (1 Thess 2:13), affirming that this is so because God "gives you his Holy Spirit" (1 Thess 4:8). It is, in fact, "the sanctifying work of the Spirit," coupled with their "belief in the truth," that makes effective God's salvation in their lives and gives them hope for the future (2 Thess 2:13-14). So they are admonished: "Do not quench ['stifle' or 'suppress'] the Spirit!" (1 Thess 5:19).

Being "the community of the Spirit" means many things for believers in Christ—both doctrinally and ethically; both individually and corporately. It does not, however, mean that one must affirm only the spiritual and renounce everything material or natural; or that one be guided only by the Spirit and oppose everything traditional or ecclesiastical—or, as in our discussion here, that one must espouse a ministry of the Spirit that exists without structures, forms or order. Rather, the church as the community of the Spirit, whose activity necessarily finds expression in local congregations and particular situations, is urged to "keep in step with the Spirit" in whatever circumstances it finds itself, as Paul exhorted his converts in Galatia to do (Gal 5:25). And that holds true, it seems, not only in matters of faith and doctrine, but also with respect to ecclesiastical structures, forms and order.

God's Eschatological Community

"People of God" and "Community of the Spirit" came to have eschatological significance in Early Judaism, and so when used with reference to the church they should be seen as signaling something of eschatological significance for Christians as well. But associated with these two images in Paul's letters are also other expressions that identify the church as a society centered in heaven and striving toward eschatological fulfillment. In Gal 4:26 Paul speaks of the "mother" of believers in Christ as being "the Jerusalem above" (ἡ ἄνω Ιερουσαλήμ), not "the present Jerusalem" (ἡ νῦν Ιερουσαλήμ); in 2 Cor 11:2 he calls the church at Corinth a "pure" or "chaste virgin" whom he wants to present to Christ at his *parousia* for the messianic marriage; and in Phil 3:20 he says that Christians have their citizenship "in heaven," which is their true home and final destiny.

In none of these three verses, however, does the word "church" (ἐκκλησία) appear. Yet all of them speak of corporate existence in the New Covenant and all of them use Old Testament and Early Judaism imagery that suggests eschatological fulfillment. So all three of them, particularly in concert with the expressions "the people of God" and "the community of the Spirit," may be seen as alluding to the church as God's eschatological community. And all of this imagery suggests that the real nature of the church—though presently, and of necessity, embodied in various shapes and forms—cannot be truly grasped simply by a study of any of the church's earthly shapes or historical forms, whether ancient or modern.

3. *Criteria for Church Order*

Protestant studies of church order have all too often pitted the apostolic church, where freedom of the Spirit reigned, against the later church, where hierarchical structures and juridical order are seen to have dominated—frequently setting them out as contradictory and mutually exclusive. But such a scenario is superficial and specious. For while defined orders of church leadership and a definitive constitution for church government cannot be found in the New Testament, the Pauline missionary letters set out certain criteria for community formation and reflect various features of church order within Paul's Gentile churches.

Divine Origin and Control

Basic to Paul's thought about the church—as well as that of all the other .writers of the New Testament—is that the church is fundamentally different from every other humanly constituted community or society. Paul does not credit the founding, growth or building up of the church to his own or any other missionary's abilities or efforts, but only to God, Christ, and the Holy Spirit (cf. 1 Cor 3:5-9; Eph 2:20-22; 4:11-16). Therefore, as Rudolf Schnackenburg has rightly observed, the first matter of importance in any study of church government must be that "all the men [and women] who are entrusted with tasks and services in the Church are simply God's instruments, servants of Christ, organs of the Holy Spirit (1 Cor 4:1; 12:4-6), and so possess an essentially different character from all bearers of office appointed by merely human statute and constitution" (*Church in the New Testament*, 25).

The most unique image of the church in the Pauline letters is, as noted above, that of "the body of Christ"—which suggests that, in Paul's mind at least, the essential nature of the church is not to be viewed simply in terms of some social compact theory. That does not mean that the early Christians did not use the organizational forms of the day to structure their corporate lives. But it does mean that when we discuss Paul's vision of the church and community formation, the first criterion to be highlighted is that the church is fundamentally different from any purely human community or society. For it has God as its founder, Jesus Christ as its chief cornerstone, and the Holy Spirit as the one who directs its affairs.

Importance of Form and Order

The earliest believers in Jesus, as Fenton J. A. Hort long ago pointed out, were neither "enthusiastic cranks" nor "a mere horde of men ruled absolutely by the Apostles," and so without form or organizational structure (*The Christian Ecclesia: A Course of Lectures on the Early History and Early Conceptions of the Ecclesia* [London: Macmillan, 1897], 52). Although they viewed themselves as living in "the last days" of redemptive history and attempted to give free rein to the Spirit, they did not form purely spiritual societies that had no need of structure or order. As the new "people of God" and the new "temple of God," the earliest believers in Jesus were not neophytes in religion, but drew on the long tradition of worship, discipline and organization they had known in their Jewish synagogues and in the Jerusalem temple.

The earliest forms of worship in the Christian church, in fact, reflect in many ways patterns drawn from the Jewish experience of the earliest believers in Jesus—which patterns, undoubtedly through Paul's influence, also continued in large measure in Gentile churches. These inherited features of early Christian worship included (1) praising God in "psalms, hymns, and spiritual songs," as well as through various other means of expressing thankfulness (cf. 1 Cor 14:26; Eph 5:19; Col 3:16); (2) the reading of Scripture (cf. Col 4:16; 1 Thess 5:27; 1 Tim 4:13); (3) prayers (cf. 1 Tim 2:1-2); (4) a sermon, exposition of Scripture, or exhortation (cf. 1 Cor 14:26); (5) the Amen (cf. 1 Cor 14:16); and (6) various confessions of faith (cf. my *New Wine into Fresh Wineskins: Contextualizing the Early Christian Confessions* [Peabody: Hendrickson, 1999], 1-66).

Order was important for Paul. He held, as with Judaism generally, that disorder was a characteristic of Hades (cf. Job 10:22), not of God or his people (cf. 1 Cor 14:33). He recognized a functional order in the hierarchy of God, Christ, man and woman (1 Cor 11:3)—even while going on to highlight a redemptive order "in the Lord" where equality dominates (cf. 1 Cor 11:11-12). He spoke of an order in the resurrection: "Each in his own order: Christ the firstfruits; then at his coming those who belong to Christ" (1 Cor 15:23)—even to the extent of setting out an order of resurrection for first "the dead in Christ" and then "we who are still alive" at the time of the *parousia* (1 Thess 4:15-17). He exhorted his converts at Corinth, whose charismatic and spiritual enthusiasm seemed unbounded, to carrying on their worship in "a fitting and orderly way" (1 Cor 14:40; cf. the whole section of 14:26-40). And he wrote to believers at Colosse about his delight not only in their "firm faith in Christ" but also their "good order" (Col 2:5).

Likewise, form was important for Paul, though not itself a controlling criterion. In his thinking about a future resurrection, for example, he visualized the necessity of embodiment, but was also cognizant of a variety of "bodies" created by God and sure that the precise form of a believer's body at the resurrection would be "as he [God] has determined" (1 Cor 15:35-50). Further, he viewed disembodiment as something repugnant and was not at all interested in any "naked" or "unclothed" soulish resurrection, but looked for a time when both he and all believers in Christ would be "further clothed" (2 Cor 5:1-4).

Creativity and Spontaneity of God's Spirit

No one can read Paul's letters without becoming acutely aware of the creativity and spontaneity of God's Spirit at work in the early churches. "In Christ" and by the work of God's Spirit, nationality, class and sex—the three divisive factors of history—are transcended (cf. Gal 3:28). Women are allowed to pray and prophesy openly in the local church (cf. 1 Cor 11:4-5); "the dividing wall of hostility" between Jews and Gentiles is broken down (cf. Eph 2:11-22); and an unworthy slave is received back as a fellow human being ("in the flesh") and a fellow believer ("in the Lord")—in fact, as a "dear brother" (cf. Philem 8-21). Even traditional forms of worship, as drawn from Early Judaism and reconstituted by early Jewish Christianity, were subject to the creativity and spontaneity of the Spirit's guidance—as witness, for example, Paul's handling of the abuses of the Lord's Supper at Corinth and his directive that its practice be changed, thereby putting an end to those abuses and being better able to signal the true intent of the celebration.

Not all of these instances of the Spirit's creative and spontaneous working may have been fully understood by believers in the churches involved. Nor have they always been seen as significant by Christians during the past centuries or appreciated by everyone within the churches today. But the factor of God's Spirit at work in the church in ways that are both creative and spontaneous must always be held in high regard by Christians in their thinking about their lives, whether individually or corporately. Likewise, it must always be seen as an important principle for church order. For the task of the Holy Spirit is not only to bring to fruition the unity and universality of the church, but also to guide the church and the churches in expressions of such unity and universality in ways that are appropriate for specific times and places—often in ways that are serendipitous, reflecting the Spirit's own creativity and spontaneity.

Unity and Diversity of the Church

That Paul was actively interested in promoting the unity of the church can hardly be contested—though, of course, the unity he advocated was always in terms of the gospel he believed had been entrusted to him, not that of the Judaizers at Galatia, nor that of the party politicians, spiritualists or enthusiasts at Corinth, nor that of the ascetic-mystical gnostics at Colosse. His emphasis on unity is well summarized in the exhortation of Eph 4:3-6:

> Make every effort to keep the unity of the Spirit through the bond of peace. There is one body and one Spirit—just as you were called to one hope when you were called—one Lord, one faith, one baptism; one God and Father of all, who is over all and through all and in all.

And his practice on behalf of church unity is clearly exemplified by his strenuous efforts with regard to the Jerusalem collection, which he organized and eventually joined in taking to "the poor" of the Jerusalem church (cf. Rom 15:25-32; 1 Cor 16:1-3; 2 Cor 8:1–9:15). For though he differed in some respects from believers at Jerusalem, the unity of the church—even amidst its diversity and despite real dangers—was of great importance to him.

Nonetheless, an acceptance of diversity within his own Gentile churches seems also to have been a prominent factor in Paul's thinking, as witness his somewhat differing lists of spiritual gifts in Rom 12:6-8 and 1 Cor 12:4-11 and of ecclesiastical functions in 1 Cor 12:28 and Eph 4:11. It may be difficult to catalogue or classify the apostle's thought regarding ministries within the church. J. B. Lightfoot distinguished between "temporary" and "permanent" ministries (cf. "The Christian Ministry," in *Saint Paul's Epistle to the Philippians* [London: Macmillan, 1868], 181-269 [185-86]); Edwin Hatch between "episcopal-diaconal" and "presbyterial" ministries (*The Organization of the Early Christian Churches* [London: Rivingtons, 1881], Lectures II and III); and Adolf Harnack between "religious" or "charismatic" and "administrative" ministries (*The Constitution and Law of the Church in the First Two Centuries*, trans. F. L. Pogson [London: Williams & Norgate, 1910], 45-60). But however one arranges and identifies the items within Paul's lists of ministries, it appears that they reflect a consciousness of diversity in church order on his part. In fact, they seem to suggest that for Paul the Christian church is to be understood as a unity in diversity and a diversity in unity—that is, a unity that is diversely contextualized and a diversity that expresses various features of an essential unity.

4. *Reflections of Church Order*

But how did Paul's theology of the church and criteria for community formation work out in his own churches? His major "missionary letters" provide very little explicit information on the structures and order of his Gentile churches. They do, however, reflect a few bits of data having to do with such matters. To these we must now turn, asking such questions as: What do Paul's missionary letters suggest regarding church order in the Gentile churches of his day? How are the structures and order of Paul's churches to be related to what can be discerned in the other apostolic churches? and, How normative are the structures and order of Paul's churches for the church today?

Data of the Letters

The ten Pauline letters with which we are here dealing indicate quite clearly that, at least at first, Paul considered himself to be the one to exercise supervision over the affairs of his Gentile churches. He had been called by God to be an apostle to the Gentiles (cf. Gal 1:15-16; 2 Cor 5:18-20); his commission "to preach the gospel to the Gentiles" had been recognized by the "pillar" apostles at Jerusalem (cf. Gal 2:6-9); he had strenuously exerted himself—risking even death—in his mission to bring "the good news" of Christ to the Gentile world (cf. Gal 4:13-16; 2 Cor 1:8-11; 4:8-12; 11:23-33; 2 Thess 3:7-10); he had been to his converts like both "a mother" and "a father" in their Christian birthing (cf. 1 Cor 4:15; Gal 4:19; 1 Thess 2:7-12); and he was responsible before God for all his converts to present them as "pure" or "chaste" virgins to Christ at the *parousia* for the messianic marriage (cf. 2 Cor 11:2). And not only did he feel himself responsible for the welfare of believers in the churches he founded, he also felt responsible for believers in the Gentile churches founded by others (cf. Rom 1:5-6, 13; 15:15-16; Col 1:3-9). For he was pre-eminently the apostle to the Gentiles, who had been given grace by God "to be a minister of Christ Jesus to the Gentiles with the priestly duty of proclaiming the gospel of God, so that the Gentiles might become an offering acceptable to God, sanctified by the Holy Spirit" (Rom 15:15-16).

Paul did not, however, exercise his apostolic mandate to supervise his Gentile churches alone. He also delegated authority to his co-workers to represent him in the administration of his churches, providing them at times with letters of introduction. In particular, we read in his missionary letters of Timothy, who was sent as his delegate to Thessalonica (1 Thess 3:2-6), Philippi (Phil 2:19-23) and Corinth (1 Cor 4:17; 16:10-11; cf. 2 Cor 1:1, 19), and of Titus, who was twice sent to represent him at Corinth (2 Cor 2:13; 7:6-7, 13-16; 8:6, 16-24; 12:18). As Earle Ellis has pointed out, "In the Book of Acts and the canonical literature ascribed to Paul some 100 names, often coupled with a score of assorted titles, are associated with the Apostle" ("Paul and His Co-Workers," 437, see also 438-52; building on W. M. Ramsay, *St Paul the Traveller and the Roman Citizen* [London: Hodder & Stoughton, 1908], 397, and E. B. Redlich, *St Paul and his Companions* [London: 1913], 200-86). The most important of these associates mentioned in his missionary letters are not only Timothy and Titus, but also Barnabas (1 Cor 9:6; Gal 2:1, 9, 13), Silas (2 Cor 1:19; 1 Thess 1:1; 2 Thess 1:1), Apollos (1 Cor 3:4-9; 4:1-13; 16:12), Phoebe (Rom 16:1-2), Epaphras (Col 1:7-8; 4:12; Philem 23), Tychicus (Eph 6:21; Col 4:7), Aristarchus (Col 4:10; Philem 23), Mark (Col 4:10; Philem 24), Demas (Col 4:14; Philem 23), and Luke (Col 4:14; Philem 24).

Further, Paul recognized the presence of many local leaders in his churches. In 1 Thess 5:12-13, for example, he refers to various church leaders at Thessalonica, speaking of them as "those who work hard among you, who are over you in the Lord, and who admonish you," and asks his converts to "respect" them and "hold them in the highest regard in love because of their work." Such leaders were evidently drawn from the Thessalonian congregation itself—probably to fulfill some particular type of service and perhaps on a part-time or rotation basis, which would have allowed them to carry on their normal occupations as well. The fact that Paul does not name these leaders should not be taken to mean that he did not know them or their names, but probably means that he wanted his exhortations to be received as applicable to whoever held such positions of leadership in the congregation. Local leadership at Corinth seems implied in his words to his converts in 1 Cor 5:4-5: "When you are assembled in the name of our Lord Jesus and I am with you in spirit, and the power of our Lord Jesus is present, hand this man over to Satan, so that his sinful nature may be destroyed and his spirit saved on the day of the Lord."

Likewise, the greetings extended to "the overseers" (ἐπίσκοποι) and "those who serve" (διάκονοι) in Phil 1:1 reflect the presence of local leaders in Paul's church at Philippi. Some of these he names: Euodia and Syntyche, two women who had earlier served with him "in the cause of the gospel" at Philippi, but were now at odds with one another (4:2); and Clement, who had also served with the apostle in that city and seems not to have gotten involved in the argument between the two women (4:3). As D. E. H. Whiteley has pointed out with respect to the designations of Phil 1:1: "'Serving' and 'over-seeing' were certainly functions; it is not clear whether in St Paul's day they had hardened into 'offices'" (*The Theology of St Paul* [Oxford: Blackwell, 1964], 203). And although the term "elder" (πρεσβύτερος) is frequently used in Acts and the Pastoral Epistles for a church leader (cf. Acts 11:30; 14:23; 15:2, 4, 6, 22, 23; 16:4; 20:17; 21:18; 1 Tim 5:1, 17, 19; Titus 1:5-6), it does not appear in Paul's major missionary letters—unless, of course, the reference to "pastors and teachers" in Eph 4:11 is a functional way of characterizing the work of "presbyters" or "elders," as Lightfoot held ("Christian Ministry," 194).

Admittedly, there is much that is ambiguous in Paul's missionary letters about church order and leadership in his Gentile churches. We could wish, for example, that we knew more about the "house churches" referred to in Rom 16:3-5 (perhaps also vv 10 and 11); 1 Cor 16:19; Col 4:15, and Philem 2 (see A. J. Malherbe, *Social Aspects of Early Christianity* [Philadelphia: Fortress, 1983[2]], esp. on "House Churches and Their Problems"; V. Branick, *The House Church in the Writings of Paul* [Wilmington: Michael Glazier, 1989]). Likewise, we might wish we knew more about how the Gentile churches chose their delegates to take the money they had collected to Jerusalem for the impoverished Jewish Christians there (cf. 1 Cor 16:1-4; 2 Cor 8:18-19; also Rom 15:25-26). Günther Bornkamm's summation regarding church order generally, however, is apt: "there was no absence of organisation and offices in the Pauline congregations"; and his statement about leaders in the churches is also pertinent: "their authority derives from the ministry accepted and discharged by them, not from their status" ("πρέσβυς, κτλ.," *TDNT*, 6.664).

Even more suggestive regarding church order in Paul's thought is the way he handles certain issues regarding the sacraments or ordinances of the church—that is, regarding baptism and the Lord's Supper. For while he highly values Christian baptism, as his words in

Rom 6:3-7 clearly indicate, he also says in 1 Cor 1:14-17 with respect to the divisions in the church at Corinth:

> I am thankful that I did not baptize any of you except Crispus and Gaius, so no one can say that you were baptized into my name. (Yes, I also baptized the household of Stephanas; but beyond that, I don't remember if I baptized anyone else.) For Christ did not send me to baptize, but to preach the gospel—not with words of human wisdom, lest the cross of Christ be emptied of its power.

Such a disclaimer, coupled with an assertion about his true responsibility, indicates that Paul saw baptism, while vitally important, to be the responsibility of the church and not directly his as an evangelist—except, of course, in the founding of a local church, when he alone would be available to baptize.

And his treatment of the Corinthians' abuses of the Lord's Supper in 1 Cor 11:17-34 is revealing as well. For in the earliest days of the Jerusalem church, believers in Jesus seem to have celebrated two kinds of communal meals: (1) a paschal or sacred meal in their corporate gatherings, which commemorated the death of Jesus and followed the pattern of the Jewish Passover and Jesus' Last Supper with his disciples (cf. Acts 2:42), and (2) a joyful fellowship meal in their homes, which commemorated Jesus' resurrection and continued presence with his followers and was patterned along the lines of a Jewish *Haburah* ("fellowship") meal and Jesus' eating with his disciples during his earthly ministry (cf. Acts 2:46b-47a). These two meals, however, appear to have been combined into one communal feast when the gospel penetrated Gentile regions outside of Jerusalem and when Jewish influence ceased to play a dominant role in the development of Christian worship. But even though a one-meal tradition became something of a fixture among Gentile Christians, Paul in dealing with abuses at Corinth felt free to change matters again by disengaging the Lord's Supper from the more expressly fellowship features of a communal meal (cf. 1 Cor 11:17-34). Evidently he was willing to alter a practice that had become established within his churches rather than to have that practice, when misused, pervert the essential principles of the gospel.

Such a vignette of church life in one of Paul's churches—even though it may reflect the circumstances of only one of his Gentile congregations—speaks volumes as to what Paul saw to be central in the Christian gospel and the extent to which he was prepared to be flexible in his contextualization of that gospel. More important for our purposes here, however, it encapsulates many of the criteria for community formation that are discernible in the Pauline letters, particularly those having to do with the unity and diversity of the church and the creativity and spontaneity of God's Spirit.

Paul's Churches vis-à-vis Other Apostolic Churches

But how do the structures and order of Paul's churches, as reflected in his missionary letters, correspond to the structures and order discernible in other apostolic churches of his day? And how are the differences between them to be understood?

Admittedly, our knowledge of early Christian missionary activity and the founding of Christian churches is limited, being confined largely to the portrayals of the ministries of Peter and Paul in the Acts of the Apostles. Further, Luke has put his own spin on what he relates in Acts, and the vignettes he sets out in his second volume can be variously interpreted. Nonetheless, it does appear that the church at Jerusalem was dominantly monarchical in its organization, with James "the Lord's brother," together with the apostles Peter and John, its overseers (cf. Gal 1:18-20; 2:1-10, 12; also Acts 15:13-21), and that the church of Syrian Antioch was principally oligarchic, with various "prophets and teachers" drawn from the congregation's own ranks taking leadership (cf. Acts 11:22-30; 13:1-3). Yet Paul's churches, however understood, seem not quite the same in their structures and order as the churches of Jerusalem and Antioch.

Some have viewed Paul's whole missionary activity and his founding of churches as "dangerous exceptions" to the established, monarchical structure of the early church. For Antioch was the base and axis of his ministry, not Jerusalem, and the authorization for his ministry came through certain "prophets and teachers" at Antioch, not the apostles at Jerusalem. Others have viewed the churches he founded as being "provisional in nature," asserting that they represented only an initial stage in the growth of the church and that they would later develop more properly into more orderly institutions.

But to characterize what is reflected in Paul's letters about community formation as either "exceptional" or "provisional" is to miss an extremely important point in the interpretation of both the New Testament and church history. For what we have in the pages of the New Testament and the annals of church history are (1) presentations of the essential features of the Christian gospel, (2) representations of the central convictions of those who believed the gospel, and (3) portrayals of how that gospel was contextualized at various times and in differing situations—whether in the apostolic age or later, and whether at Jerusalem, Antioch, Paul's Gentile churches, in our own country, or in lands "overseas."

To understand the New Testament and church history properly, we need to be able to appreciate not only the central features of the apostolic proclamation and how that "good news" has been understood by various people, but also how that gospel message has been variously contextualized from the earliest days of the Christian church to the present day. Paul's missionary letters reflect contextualizations that were appropriate for a particular time, culture, and set of circumstances, which should be appreciated on their own merits. They are recorded to guide us as we attempt to contextualize the Christian gospel for our own particular time, culture, and circumstances.

A Normative Pattern for Today?
How normative, then, is the pattern of church life and order reflected in Paul's major missionary letters—if, indeed, such a pattern can be detected with any degree of certainty—for the ordering of the Christian church today? Many have wanted simply to reproduce the structures and order not only of the New Testament churches generally but also of the Pauline churches. Such a desire has frequently led either to ossification or to heresy, and sometimes to both.

Much could be said about the normativeness of community formation, church polity, and church leadership as reflected in the New Testament generally and Paul's letters in particular. But little can be added to what Fenton J. A. Hort has already said in concluding his Cambridge lectures of 1888–1889 on "The Early History and the Early Conceptions of the Christian Ecclesia" (lectures that he built on J. B. Lightfoot's "The Christian Ministry" of 1868), which were published posthumously in 1897 (five years after Hort's death):

> In this [i.e., the study of early church order] as in so many other things is seen the futility of endeavouring to make the Apostolic history into a set of authoritative precedents, to be rigorously copied without regard to time and place, thus turning the Gospel into a second Levitical Code. The Apostolic age is full of embodiments of purposes and principles of the most instructive kind; but the responsibility of choosing the means was left for ever to the Ecclesia itself, and to each

Ecclesia, guided by ancient precedent on the one hand and adaptation to present and future needs on the other. The lesson-book of the Ecclesia, and of every Ecclesia, is not a law but a history (*Christian Ecclesia*, 232-33).

SELECT BIBLIOGRAPHY

Ascough, Richard S. *What are they Saying about the Formation of Pauline Churches?* New York, Mahwah: Paulist, 1998.

Barrett, C. Kingsley. *Church, Ministry and Sacraments in the New Testament.* Exeter: Paternoster, 1985.

Best, Ernest. *One Body in Christ: A Study in the Relationship of the Church to Christ in the Epistles of the Apostle Paul.* London: SPCK, 1955.

Branick, Vincent. *The House Church in the Writings of Paul.* Wilmington: Michael Glazier, 1989.

Burtchaell, James T. *From Synagogue to Church: Public Services and Offices in the Earliest Christian Communities.* Cambridge: Cambridge University Press, 1992.

Davies, W. D. *A Normative Pattern of Church Life in the New Testament: Fact or Fancy?* London: James Clarke, 1950.

Ellis, E. Earle. "Paul and his Co-Workers," *NTS* 17 (1971) 437-52.

Harnack, Adolf. *The Constitution and Law of the Church in the First Two Centuries*, trans. F. L. Pogson. London: Williams & Norgate, 1910.

Hatch, Edwin. *The Organization of the Early Christian Churches.* London: Rivingtons, 1881.

Holmberg, Bengt. *Paul and Power: The Structure of Authority in the Primitive Church as Reflected in the Pauline Epistles.* Lund: Gleerup, 1978.

Hort, Fenton J. A. *The Christian Ecclesia: A Course of Lectures on the Early History and Early Conceptions of the Ecclesia.* London: Macmillan, 1897.

Lightfoot, Joseph B. "The Christian Ministry," in *Saint Paul's Epistle to the Philippians.* London: Macmillan, 1868, 181-269.

Longenecker, Richard N. *New Wine into Fresh Wineskins: Contextualizing the Early Christian Confessions.* Peabody: Hendrickson, 1999 (esp. "The Pauline Corpus," 48-63, and "Toward an Incarnational and Contextualized Theology," 154-73).

Malherbe, Abraham J. *Social Aspects of Early Christianity.* Philadelphia: Fortress, 1983[2] (esp. "House Churches and their Problems," 60-91).

Marshall, I. Howard. "Congregation and Ministry in the Pastoral Epistles," in *Community Formation in the Early Church and in the Church Today*, ed. R. N. Longenecker. Peabody: Hendrickson, 2002, 105-25

McKelvey, Richard J. *The New Temple: The Church in the New Testament.* London: Oxford University Press, 1969.

Meeks, Wayne A. *The First Urban Christians: The Social World of the Apostle Paul*. New Haven: Yale University Press, 1983 (esp. "The Formation of the Εκκλησια," 74-110).

Minear, Paul S. *Images of the Church in the New Testament*. Philadelphia: Westminster, 1960.

Schnackenburg, Rudolf. *The Church in the New Testament*, trans. W. J. O'Hara. Freiburg: Herder; Montreal: Palm, 1965.

Schweizer, Eduard. *Church Order in the New Testament*, trans. F. Clarke. London: SCM, 1961.

Streeter, B. H. *The Primitive Church, Studied with Special Reference to the Origins of the Christian Ministry*. London: Macmillan, 1929.

The Pauline Concept of Mutuality
as a Basis for Luke's Theme of Witness

In his *magnum opus* on the concept of witness in the New Testament,[1] Allison Trites highlights the importance of the witness theme in the New Testament, which he finds to be "most fully developed in the Johannine and Lukan writings"—particularly in the Fourth Gospel, the Acts of the Apostles, and the Johannine Apocalypse—but "also present in other parts of the New Testament"—that is, in the Synoptic Gospels and the New Testament Epistles.[2] And in explaining how this witness theme came about, he points to the "juridical character" of the language in these writings, sketches out the nature of the opposition against Christianity in the first century, and proposes that Luke, in particular, but also the other New Testament writers, have "taken the original notion of bearing witness before a court of law and adapted it to the conditions of the Messianic Age."[3] Confining here our attention to his treatment of the Lukan writings, Trites's thesis is that "Luke–Acts presents the claims of Christ against a background of hostility, contention and active persecution," using, in large part, "legal terminology" and "ideas drawn from the lawcourt."[4]

Professor Trites has ably demonstrated "a sustained use of juridical metaphor" in the Fourth Gospel[5] and that "the idea of witness" is

[1] A. A. Trites, *The New Testament Concept of Witness* (SBLMS; Cambridge: Cambridge University Press, 1977).

[2] Quoted material taken from *ibid.* 175.

[3] *Ibid.* 133; see 128-35 for Acts.

[4] *Ibid.* 132-33.

[5] *Ibid.* 78-124. For the thesis that "the dominant framework of the narrative of John's Gospel, and its most pervasive motif, is that of a lawsuit or trial on a cosmic scale," see A. T. Lincoln, "Trials, Plots and the Narrative of the Fourth Gospel," *JSNT* 56 (1994) 3-30; *idem, Truth on Trial: The Lawsuit Motif in the Fourth Gospel* (Peabody: Hendrickson, 2000). Quoted summary is taken from

"very much a live metaphor in the Book of Revelation."[6] Discussion of the Johannine writings I must leave to others more qualified. My purpose in this chapter is to build on what Trites has proposed with respect to the Lukan writings—particularly the second of Luke's two volumes, the Acts of the Apostles—and to suggest that, in addition to the testimony terminology of the lawcourts, Luke was also influenced by Paul's understanding of mutuality with respect to the mission of Jesus and the mission of the church. Or, to state matters in a slightly different manner, that while the concept of "interchange" was significant for the church's understanding of the work of Christ and soteriology generally,[7] Paul's concept of "mutuality" was also important for the church's understanding of mission—and that, in particular, it served as an important theological basis for the theme of witness in Acts.

Lincoln's article, "'I Am the Resurrection and the Life': The Resurrection Message of the Fourth Gospel," in *Life in the Face of Death: The Resurrection Message of the New Testament*, ed. R. N. Longenecker (MNTS; Grand Rapids: Eerdmans, 1998), 135.

[6] *Ibid.* 154-74. Cf. G. B. Caird, who was Trites's mentor at Oxford: "The repeated use of the words 'witness' and 'testimony' is one of the many points of resemblance between the Revelation and the Fourth Gospel. In Greek as in English these words could be treated as dead metaphors, without any conscious reference to the lawcourt, which was their primary setting. But both these books use the words in their primary, forensic sense. The author of the Fourth Gospel, perhaps inspired by the example of Second Isaiah, presents his argument in the form of a lawcourt debate, in which one witness after another is summoned, until God's advocate, the Paraclete, has all the evidence he needs to convince the world that Jesus is the Son of God, and so to win his case. In the Revelation the courtroom setting is even more realistic; for Jesus had borne his testimony before Pilate's tribunal [cf. 1:5 and 3:14], and the martyrs must face a Roman judge. What they have to remember as their give their evidence is that that evidence is being heard in a court of more ultimate authority, where judgments which are just and true issue from the great white throne" (*A Commentary on the Revelation of St John the Divine* [BNTC / HNTC; London: Black; New York: Harper & Row, 1966], 17-18).

[7] Cf. M. D. Hooker, "Interchange in Christ," *JTS* 22 (1971) 349-61; *idem*, "Interchange and Atonement," *BJRL* 60 (1976) 462-81; *idem*, "Interchange and Suffering," in *Suffering and Martyrdom in the New Testament*, ed. W. Horbury and B. McNeil (Cambridge: Cambridge University Press, 1981), 70-83; *idem*, "Interchange in Christ and Ethics," *JSNT* 25 (1985) 3-17. Note also K. Berger's expression *ein Tauschgeschäft* in "Abraham in der paulinischen Hauptbriefen," *MTZ* 17 (1966) 52.

1. *A Mutuality of Missions in Luke–Acts*

What immediately strikes the reader of Luke–Acts is the underlying architectural structure of Luke's writings. For not only are the two volumes almost equal in size (the Lukan Gospel being the longest of our New Testament writings, with Acts only about one-tenth shorter) and almost identical in chronological coverage (about thirty-three years for both), they also, more importantly, exhibit, as Charles Talbert puts it, "a remarkable series of correspondences between what Jesus does and says in Luke's Gospel and what the disciples [mainly Peter and Paul] do and say in the Acts."[8] Talbert has set out in quite detailed fashion a large number of parallels of event and expression—even of sequence—that can be found in Luke's two volumes: (1) parallels between Jesus' Galilean ministry (Luke 4:14–9:50) and Jesus' Perean–Judean ministry of the Travel Narrative (Luke 9:51–19:10) in his first volume; (2) parallels between the church's mission to the Jewish world (Acts 2:42–12:24) and the church's mission to the Gentile world (Acts 12:25–28:31) in his second volume; and (3) parallels between the two volumes themselves.[9] In addition, he has argued that the literary genre of Luke–Acts "is similar to the biographies of certain founders of philosophical schools, that contained within themselves not only the life of the founder but also a list or brief narrative of his successors and selected other disciples."[10]

Talbert, of course, has been criticized for overdrawing the redactional parallels that can be found both within and between Luke's Gospel and his Acts, and for identifying too precisely the literary genre of Luke's two-volume work. But his main points have certainly been established: (1) that the architectural structure of

[8] C. H. Talbert, "Discipleship in Luke–Acts," in *Discipleship in the New Testament*, ed. F. F. Segovia (Philadelphia: Fortress, 1985), 63.

[9] C. H. Talbert, *Literary Patterns, Theological Themes, and the Genre of Luke–Acts* (Missoula: Scholars, 1974), 1-65.

[10] Talbert, "Discipleship in Luke–Acts" 63; cf. *idem, Literary Patterns*, 125-40; *idem, What Is a Gospel? The Genre of the Canonical Gospels* (Philadelphia: Fortress, 1977); *idem*, "The Gospel and the Gospels," in *Interpreting the Gospels*, ed. J. L. Mays (Philadelphia: Fortress, 1981), 14-26 (building on a suggestion of H. von Soden, *Geschichte der christlichen Kirche.* I. *Die Entstehung der christlichen Kirche* [Leipzig: Teubner, 1919], 73).

Luke–Acts requires that the two volumes be read together, the first interpreted by the second and the second by the first; and (2) that the ministry of the early church, as depicted in Luke's second volume, be seen as having been shaped by the Jesus tradition, as portrayed in his first. Indeed, in setting out numerous parallels between Jesus' mission and the church's mission, Luke must be seen to be actually proposing the thesis that Jesus' ministry and the church's mission *together* constitute the fullness of God's redemptive activity on behalf of humanity. For though Jesus' mission and the church's mission are not to be taken as being identical, they are, nonetheless, comparable and inseparable. In fact, the very structure of Luke–Acts shouts out to the attentive reader that there exists some sort of mutuality between the mission of Jesus and that of the church—with Jesus' mission being the announcement of God's kingdom and the effecting of human redemption, and that of the church being the proclamation, extension and application of what Jesus has accomplished.

The other canonical Gospels, of course, each in its own way, relate the church's mission to the mission of Jesus—by implication in Mark's Gospel; by direct association of the church with the disciples in Matthew's Gospel; and by the use of the literary device of "two levels" of meaning in John's Gospel. Only Luke, however, juxtaposes the mission of Jesus and the mission of the church, setting out, in parallel fashion, that of Jesus in his Gospel and that of the church in his Acts.

It has often been asked how Luke first came to think of relating the mission of the church to the ministry of Jesus in such a fashion—that is, not just by implication, association or allusion, but by actually juxtaposing the two missions as comparable and inseparable entities. It is the thesis of this chapter that it was probably by association with Paul—or, at least, with those directly involved in the Pauline mission—that Luke would have heard such things as: "And if we are children, we are also heirs: heirs of God and co-heirs with Christ—if indeed we share in his sufferings in order that we may also share in his glory" (as in Rom 8:17); or, "I want to know Christ—the power of his resurrection and participation in his sufferings, becoming like him in his death, and so, somehow, to attain to the resurrection of the dead" (as in Phil 3:10-11); or, "Now I rejoice in what was suffered for you; and I complete in my flesh what is still lacking with respect to

Christ's afflictions, for the sake of his body, which is the church" (as in Col 1:24).

Further, it is our suggestion that such a concept of mutuality between the ministry of Christ and the ministries of those who follow him, once formed in his mind, would have had explosive consequences not only for Luke's understanding of discipleship[11] but also for his understanding of the church's mission. For now the thesis could be made that what was foundational in Jesus' ministry—both in his work and in his teaching; whether expressly evident or only embryonically present—was (and is) to be explicated and more fully expressed in the church's mission.

It is, in fact, just such a concept of mutuality that Luke expresses over and over again throughout the length and breadth of his two volumes, showing how what was basic in Jesus' ministry has been (and should continue to be) the pattern for all of the church's life and ministry. And it is this concept that I want to highlight in what follows by focusing attention on the three Pauline passages cited above.

2. The Concept of Mutuality in Romans 8:17

In many ways, Romans 8 is the high point of Paul's letter to Christians at Rome. Or to use the imagery of John A. T. Robinson, who compared the letter's structure to a series of locks in the Corinthian canal (which, of course, was dug and constructed somewhat after Paul's day): "The heights of the epistle are reached in chapter 8, a sustained climax which takes the argument across the watershed."[12] And one of the most important features of this eighth chapter is the apostle's set of statements in verses 14-17 regarding the "adoption" of Gentile believers into God's family and their resultant status as "sons of God," "children of God," and "heirs of God," as well as "co-heirs with Christ":

> [14] Those who are led by the Spirit of God are the sons of God (υἱοὶ θεοῦ). [15] For you did not receive a spirit that makes you a slave again to fear, but you received the Spirit of adoption (πνεῦμα υἱοθεσίας). It is by him we cry "Abba, Father." [16] The Spirit himself testifies with our spirit that we are God's children (τέκνα θεοῦ). [17] And if we are

[11] See my article, R. N. Longenecker, "Taking Up the Cross Daily: Discipleship in Luke-Acts," in *Patterns of Discipleship in the New Testament*, ed. R. N. Longenecker (MNTS; Grand Rapids: Eerdmans, 1996), 50-76.

[12] J. A. T. Robinson, *Wrestling with Romans* (London: SCM, 1979), 9.

children (τέκνα), we are also heirs (κληρονόμοι): heirs of God (κληρονόμοι θεοῦ) and co-heirs with Christ (συγκληρονόμοι Χριστοῦ)—if indeed (εἴπερ) we share in his sufferings (συμπάσχομεν) in order that (ἵνα) we may also share in his glory (συνδοξασθῶμεν).

There is much in these verses that deserves extended treatment, particularly in any commentary study of the passage. For here we are at the very heart of Paul's gospel! The presence of the Spirit and the Spirit's activity in the believer's life are of vital importance, both in freeing one from slavery and in bringing one into relationship with God. Likewise, the theme of adoption, which is an image used to extend to Gentile Christians the Old Testament concept of God's election of Israel as his chosen people, deserves extensive consideration. And certainly the declarations that believers in Jesus are able, by the Spirit, to address God as "*Abba*, Father" and to think of themselves as "sons of God," "children of God," "heirs of God," and "co-heirs with Christ" are highly significant as statements of fact and revolutionary as bases for a new self-understanding on the part of Gentile Christians.

What is important to note for our purposes, however, is that when Paul talks about believers in Jesus as "sons / children / heirs of God" and "co-heirs with Christ," he adds the further statement—in somewhat parenthetical fashion—about believers also sharing in Christ's sufferings in order that they may also share in his glory. Further, it needs to be noted that in this appended statement of verse 17b he strikes a distinctive note of mutuality by his use of the συν-compound verbs συμπάσχομεν, "we are sharing his [Christ's] sufferings" (present indicative active), and συνδοξασθῶμεν, "we may share his [Christ's] glory" (aorist subjunctive passive).

Scholars have been almost equally divided as to whether the conjunction εἴπερ (a joining of the conditional particle εἴ with the enclitic particle πέρ), which begins this appended statement, should be understood as introducing a statement of fact, and so to be read as "since" or "seeing that" (that is, "*since / seeing that* we share in his sufferings"),[13] or as signaling a condition that exhorts something

---

[13] So, e.g., C. K. Barrett, *A Commentary on the Epistle to the Romans* (BNTC / HNTC; London: Black; New York: Harper & Row, 1957), 164-65; M. Black, *Romans* (NCB; London: Marshall, Morgan & Scott, 1973), 120; C. E. B. Cranfield, *A Critical and Exegetical Commentary on the Epistle to the Romans*, 2

further on the basis of what has just been said, and so to be read as "provided" or "if so be that" (that is, *"provided / if so be that* we share in his sufferings").[14] On basis of the use of εἴπερ elsewhere in Paul's letters, the declarative translation *"since / seeing that* we share in his sufferings" is probably to be preferred.[15]

But whatever reading is accepted, the significant point to be noted here is that in speaking of the status of believers as "sons of God," "children of God," "heirs of God," and "co-heirs with Christ," Paul adds a further statement regarding the lives and mission of those same believers: that they share in Christ's sufferings (or, ought to share in his sufferings) in order that they may share in Christ's glory! For, it seems, when Paul thinks of the status of Christian believers he also thinks of how that status works itself out in their lives and mission. And in so doing, he strikes a note of mutuality in his use of the συν-compound verbs συμπάσχομεν, "we are sharing his sufferings," and συνδοξασθῶμεν, "we may share his glory."

The reference in the expression "we are sharing his sufferings," as C. E. B. Cranfield points out,

> is not to our suffering with Christ in the sense of our having died with Him in God's sight, nor to our having suffered (sacramentally) in baptism. Had either of these "sufferings" been in mind, a past tense

---

vols. (ICC; Edinburgh: T. & T. Clark, 1975, 1979), 1.407-408; see also H. Lietzmann, *An die Römer* (HNT; Tübingen: Mohr–Siebeck, 1906 through 1971[5]), *loc. cit.*; M.-J. Lagrange, *Saint Paul: Epître aux Romains* (EtBib; Paris: Gabalda, 1915 through 1931[4]), *loc. cit.*; O. Michel, *Der Brief an die Römer* (MKEKNT; Göttingen: Vandenhoeck & Ruprecht, 1955 through 1978[14]), *loc. cit.*; H. W. Schmidt, *Der Brief des Paulus an die Römer* (THNT; Berlin: Evangelische Verlag, 1962 through 1972[3]), *loc. cit.*

[14] So, e.g., J. Calvin, *The Epistles of Paul the Apostle to the Romans and to the Thessalonians*, trans. R. Mackenzie, ed. D. W. and T. F. Torrance (Edinburgh: Oliver & Boyd, 1960; Grand Rapids: Eerdmans, 1973), 171; F. Godet, *St Paul's Epistle to the Romans*, 2 vols. (Edinburgh: T. & T. Clark, 1881), 2.85; F. F. Bruce, *The Epistle of Paul to the Romans* (TNTC; Grand Rapids: Eerdmans, 1963), 167; J. D. G. Dunn, *Romans*, 2 vols. (WBC; Dallas: Word, 1988), 1.456; B. Byrne, *Romans* (SP; Collegeville: Liturgical Press, 1996), 253-54.

[15] Cf. Rom 3:30: *"since* there is only one God"; Rom 8:9: *"seeing that* the Spirit of God lives in you"; 1 Cor 8:5: *"even if there are* so-called gods, whether in heaven or on earth, as indeed there are"; 1 Cor 15:15: "but he [God] did not raise him [Christ], *if indeed* [supposedly] the dead are not raised"; 2 Thess 1:6: *"seeing that* God is just"–which, together with that of Rom 8:17, comprise the six uses of εἴπερ in the New Testament.

would have been natural. The reference is rather to that element of suffering which is inseparable from faithfulness to Christ in a world which does not yet know Him as Lord.[16]

Or as Joseph Fitzmyer expresses it (implicitly highlighting the feature of mutuality in their respective missions): "Jesus has suffered before, and Christian suffering is only the overflow of his."[17] And the statement "that we may share his glory" refers, as Cranfield further observes, "not to life after death merely, but to something far more wonderful—the glory of the final consummation."[18]

3. *The Concept of Mutuality in Philippians 3:10-11*

Philippians 3 presents us with "one of the most remarkable personal confessions that the ancient world has bequeathed to us."[19] In it Paul enumerates the privileges of his Jewish descent and his personal achievements in relation to the law (vv 4-6), describes the dramatic reorientation that has taken place in his life because of Christ (vv 7-9), expresses his present desire for his own life and ministry (vv 10-11), and states his ultimate purpose as being to "press on to take hold of that for which Christ Jesus took hold of me ... to win the prize for which God has called me heavenward in Christ Jesus" (vv 12-14).

It is with verses 10-11, however, where Paul expresses—in a somewhat parenthetical fashion (as in Rom 8:17b)—his present desire for his life and ministry, that we are here most concerned:

> [10] [I want] to know Christ (τοῦ γνῶναι αὐτόν)—[that is, to know] the power of his resurrection (τὴν δύναμιν τῆς ἀναστάσεως αὐτοῦ) and participation in his sufferings (κοινωνίαν παθημάτων αὐτοῦ), becoming like him (συμμορφιζόμενος) in his death, [11] and so, somehow (εἴ πως), to attain to the resurrection from the dead (εἰς τὴν ἐξανάστασιν τὴν ἐκ νεκρῶν).

Beginning with an articular infinitive that probably functions to highlight design or purpose (τοῦ γνῶναι), the passage picks up on the

---

[16] Cranfield, *Romans*, 1.408.

[17] J. A. Fitzmyer, *Romans: A New Translation with Introduction and Commentary* (AB; New York: Doubleday, 1993), 502.

[18] Cranfield, *Romans*, 1.408, paraphrasing E. Gaugler, *Der Brief an die Römer*, 2 vols. (Zurich: Zwingli, 1945, 1958), 1.292.

[19] P. Bonnard, *L'épître de saint Paul aux Philippiens et l'épître aux Colossiens* (CNT; Neuchâtel: Delachaux & Niestlé, 1950), 61; translation by P. T. O'Brien, *The Epistle to the Philippians* (NIGTC; Grand Rapids: Eerdmans, 1991), 365.

clause "the surpassing greatness of knowing Christ Jesus my Lord" in verse 8 and explicates more fully what *knowing* Christ means for Paul.

There are a number of exegetical matters in these two verses that demand a more detailed treatment than can be given here. Yet some issues must be dealt with here, even if in a somewhat superficial and tentative fashion, in order to proceed further.

One major issue has to do with the object of Paul's knowing—that is, whether it is threefold ("Christ *and* the power of his resurrection *and* the fellowship of his sufferings"), as commonly expressed in the translations,[20] or unitary, with then a twofold explication of the nature of such knowledge ("Christ—[that is, to know] the power of his resurrection *and* the fellowship of his sufferings"), as often argued by commentators.[21] The first reading views the two occurrences of καί ("and") as simple conjunctions; the second takes the first to be epexegetical and explicative, with only the second functioning as a simple connective. The question cannot be decided on the basis of grammar alone. Also to be considered are the immediate context of the passage and the other references in Paul's letters to the focus of his life. And when such contextual matters are taken into account, it seems best to view the object of the apostle's knowing in verse 10 as being unitary ("Christ"), with then the nature of his knowledge explicated by means of the two clauses that follow.

Another matter concerns the relations between these two explicatory clauses, "the power of his resurrection" and "participation in his sufferings." The better manuscripts (P^{46}, A*, B) omit the articles

---

[20] Cf., e.g., KJV, ASV, RSV/NRSV, NIV—though not always in the more paraphrastic translations of individual translators (such as Moffatt: "I would know him in the power of his resurrection"; see also Williams: "that is, the power of His resurrection").

[21] Cf., e.g., H. A. W. Meyer, *Critical and Exegetical Handbook to the Epistles to the Philippians and Colossians*, trans. J. C. Moore and W. P. Dickson (Edinburgh: T. & T. Clark, 1875), 160; J. B. Lightfoot, *Saint Paul's Epistle to the Philippians* (London: Macmillan, 1881), 150; M. R. Vincent, *The Epistles to the Philippians and to Philemon* (ICC; Edinburgh: T. & T. Clark, 1897), 104; P. Bonnard, *L'épîtres de saint Paul aux Philippiens et l'épître aux Colossiens*, 66; J. Gnilka, *Der Philipperbrief* (HTKNT; Freiburg: Herder, 1968), 195; J.-F. Collange, *L'épître de saint Paul aux Philippiens* (Neuchâtel: Delachaux & Niestlé, 1973), 131; G. F. Hawthorne, *Philippians* (WBC; Dallas: Word, 1983), 143; O'Brien, *Philippians*, 402; G. D. Fee, *Paul's Letter to the Philippians* (NICNT; Grand Rapids: Eerdmans, 1995), 327-28.

before κοινωνίαν ("participation" or "fellowship") and παθημάτων ("sufferings"), leaving only one definite article τήν ("the") before the two clauses. Probably, therefore, these two clauses, being united by a single article, are to be viewed as (in some sense) a single unit. And if that be so, then what Paul is saying is to be understood as follows: "to know him [Christ]" is to experience both "the power of his resurrection and participation in his sufferings."

But what does it mean to know "the power of his resurrection"? Most have assumed that these words have to do with the impact of the risen Jesus on the Christian. Probably, however, they should rather be taken to refer to the power of God himself, which was expressed in the resurrection of Jesus from the dead and is now manifest in the new lives of believers.[22] And what does it mean to know "participation in his sufferings"? Some have restricted these words to the generosity of the Philippians in support of Paul, and so understand the reference being to their financial aid of the gospel. Others have taken them as equivalent to a Christian's faith in the work of Christ, which is epitomized by suffering and death, and so to be interpreted simply as believers having shared Christ's sufferings at their conversion. There may, of course, be some derivative truth in these suggestions. More likely, however, Paul's intended referent when speaking about "participation in his sufferings," as George Caird has expressed it, was "the discharge of his missionary duties"—that is, "the sufferings which come, unsought though not unexpected, in the course of his Christian service," and which "draw him ever closer to his Lord."[23] Or as Ralph Martin says, what is in view here are Paul's own "apostolic

---

[22] Cf. F. W. Beare, *The Epistle to the Philippians* (BNTC / HNTC; London: Black; New York: Harper, 1959), 122; J. A. Fitzmyer, "'To Know Him and the Power of His Resurrection' (Phil 3.10)," in *Mélanges Bibliques en hommage au R. P. Béda Rigaux*, ed. A. Descamps and A. De Halleux (Gembloux: Duculot, 1970), 411-25 (esp. p. 420: "It emanates from the Father, raises Jesus from the dead at his resurrection, endows him with a new vitality, and finally proceeds from him as the life-giving, vitalizing force of the 'new creation' and of the new life that Christians in union with Christ experience and live."); F. F. Bruce, *Philippians* (GNC; San Francisco: Harper & Row, 1983), 90; O'Brien, *Philippians*, 404-05.

[23] G. B. Caird, *Paul's Letters from Prison* (NCB; Oxford: University Press, 1976), 140.

sufferings," which he "regarded as an extension of the 'dying of Jesus' borne in his mortal body (2 Cor. iv.10; cf. Rom. viii.36)."[24]

Accepting, then, that Paul's explication of what it means "to know him [Christ]" has to do with (1) experiencing God's resurrection power in one's life and (2) participating in Christ's sufferings in one's ministry—which may be spoken about as two features in a believer's knowledge of Christ, yet are inseparable factors and so must always be understood and experienced together—there enters here into Paul's autobiographical statements of Philippians 3 the concept of mutuality: that the same divine power that raised Jesus from the dead is also present in Paul's life (and present in every believer's life), which Paul wants to experience more fully, and that the same note of suffering that epitomized Jesus' ministry is also present in Paul's ministry (and present in every believer's ministry), which Paul gladly accepts and is prepared to experience more fully. And this note of mutuality is struck further at the end of verse 10 by the inclusion of the συν-compound participle συμμορφιζόμενος, "becoming like," which is used with respect to "his [Jesus'] death."

In his own life and ministry, therefore, Paul saw the pattern of Jesus' life and ministry being reproduced—a pattern characterized by divine power in one's daily life and by suffering in one's Christian ministry, with that suffering involving even the real prospect of physical death. It was a pattern of mutuality between himself and his Lord. It was also a pattern that caused him to know Christ better. And he longed, as verse 11 has it,[25] to have eventually the pattern of Jesus' resurrection worked out in his life as well.

---

[24] R. P. Martin, *The Epistle of Paul to the Philippians* (TNTC; London: Tyndale, 1959), 149; cf. also "Introduction," pp. 47-50. Martin adds: "There can hardly be any other meaning of these verses which so dramatically set forth the significance which Paul gives to his sufferings for Christ's sake" (*ibid*. 149).

[25] On Paul's use of εἴ πως, "so somehow," M. R. Vincent's judgment still holds: "Much unnecessary difficulty has been made over the apparent uncertainty expressed in these words, and the fancied inconsistency with the certainty elsewhere expressed by Paul, as Rom. viii.38, 39, v.17, 18, 21; 2 Cor. v.1ff.; Phil. i.22,23 … His words here are an expression of humility and self-distrust, not of doubt" (*Epistles to the Philippians and to Philemon*, 106). G. B. Caird's comment is also apropos: "In view of 1.6, 1.21-3, and 3.20-1, and not withstanding 1 Cor. 9.27, it would be absurd to suppose that Paul harboured any serious doubts about his eternal destiny. He puts his passionate longing in this hypothetical form solely

4. *The Concept of Mutuality in Colossians 1:24*

Col 1:24 has been a *crux interpretum* from the earliest days of the church to the present:[26]

> Now I rejoice in what was suffered for you (τοῖς παθήμασιν ὑπὲρ ὑμῶν); and I complete (ἀνταναπληρῶ) in my flesh (ἐν τῇ σαρκί μου) what is still lacking (τὰ ὑστερήματα) with respect to Christ's afflictions (τῶν θλίψεων Χριστοῦ), for the sake of (ὑπέρ) his body (τοῦ σώματος αὐτοῦ), which is the church (ὅ ἐστιν ἡ ἐκκλησία).

The verse, as Peter O'Brien notes, "appears to express ideas that go beyond Paul's statements elsewhere and which seem to have no parallel in the rest of the NT."[27] And, as O'Brien goes on to point out, it raises several significant questions:

> What are Paul's sufferings and how can they be an occasion for rejoicing? In what sense can these sufferings be for the body of Christ (ὑπὲρ τοῦ σώματος αὐτοῦ), or for the Colossians (ὑπὲρ ὑμῶν), a congregation which he had neither evangelized nor visited? Then, what is meant by the phrase "Christ's afflictions"? How can it be meaningfully said that something is "lacking" in these afflictions, and in what way can Paul (or other Christians if it applies to them) fill this deficiency?[28]

Not every matter of importance in this verse can be dealt with here. Three issues, however, are germane to the purposes of this chapter. The first concerns the meaning of "what was suffered for you" (τοῖς παθήμασιν ὑπὲρ ὑμῶν), concerning which Paul says he rejoices. The second concerns the meaning of "I complete (ἀνταναπληρῶ) in my flesh (ἐν τῇ σαρκί μου) what is still lacking (τὰ ὑστερήματα) with respect to Christ's afflictions (τῶν θλίψεων Χριστοῦ)," asking what the apostle means by such expressions as "complete" (or "fill up"), "in my flesh," "what is still lacking," and "Christ's afflictions"—and, further, how he saw such action to be "for the sake

---

because salvation is from start to finish the gift of God and he dare not presume on the divine mercy" (*Paul's Letters from Prison*, 140).

[26] On the history of interpretation, see J. Kremer, *Was an den Leiden Christi noch mangelt: Eine interpretationsgeschichtliche und exegetische Untersuchung zu Kol 1,24b* (Bonn: Hanstein, 1956).

[27] O'Brien, *Colossians, Philemon*, 75.

[28] *Ibid.*

of his body, which is the church." And the third has to do with how these two clauses are to be related.

Almost all commentators have viewed the first statement of the verse, νῦν χαίρω ἐν τοῖς παθήμασιν ὑπὲρ ὑμῶν, as Paul speaking of his own sufferings in the course of his apostolic ministry.[29] The definite article denotes sufferings that have actually been experienced; the first person singular is used in saying "I rejoice" (following on from v 23b); and the statement appears at the head of the section of the letter in which the apostle's own pastoral concerns are clearly expressed (1:24–2:5). It seems reasonable, therefore, to conclude that the article τοῖς denotes possession, and so should be read as signaling Paul's sufferings. The inclusion of the pronoun "my" (μου) in a corrected version of the fourth-century Codex Sinaiticus (א[3]), in a seventh-century Syriac translation (sy[h]), and in an eleventh-century minuscule Greek manuscript (81) clearly indicates that at least some scribes read the statement in this way—though most commentators have concluded that "the meaning is plain enough without this explanatory addition."[30]

Further, almost all commentators have treated the two clauses as having the same referent and understood the first clause as being more fully explicated by the second. So having established—or, more frequently, simply accepting as fact—that the writer is speaking about his own sufferings in verse 24a, they have focused their attention on the fuller exegetical data of verse 24b. Eduard Lohse, for example, says of verse 24a: "This phrase [τοῖς παθήμασιν ὑπὲρ ὑμῶν] is more closely explained in the clarifying clause which follows the

---

[29] Cf., e.g., J. B. Lightfoot, *Saint Paul's Epistles to the Colossians and to Philemon* (London: Macmillan, 1882[6]), 164; E. F. Scott, *The Epistles of Paul to the Colossians, to Philemon and to the Ephesians* (MNTC; London: Hodder & Stoughton, 1930); G. H. P. Thompson, *The Letters of Paul to the Ephesians, to the Colossians, and to Philemon* (CBC; Cambridge: Cambridge University Press, 1967), 138-39; E. Lohse, *Colossians and Philemon* (Hermeia; Philadelphia: Fortress, 1971; trans. from 1968 German edition), 68; R. P. Martin, *Colossians: The Church's Lord and the Christian's Liberty* (Exeter: Paternoster; Grand Rapids: Zondervan, 1972), 62; P. T. O'Brien, *Colossians, Philemon* (WBC; Dallas: Word, 1982), 75-77; M. J. Harris, *Colossians and Philemon* (EGGNT; Grand Rapids: Eerdmans, 1991), 65; W. T. Wilson, *The Hope of Glory: Education and Exhortation in the Epistle to the Colossians* (NovTSup; Leiden: Brill, 1997), 238-41.

[30] O'Brien, *Colossians, Philemon*, 76.

'and' (καί): 'and in my flesh I complete what is lacking in Christ's afflictions for the sake of his body, that is, the church."[31] And Jacob Kremer's history of the interpretation of Col 1:24 does likewise in its almost exclusive focus on the second part of the verse, as its title suggests.[32]

A better understanding of these clauses and their relationship, I suggest, is provided when one takes the definite article τοῖς to be referring *not* to Paul's sufferings, but to the sufferings of Christ spoken about just a few verses earlier—that is, to the sufferings of Christ referred to at the end of the confessional portion of 1:15-20 in verse 20b ("making peace *through his blood, shed on the cross*") and highlighted in the writer's comment on this portion in verse 22 ("But now he has reconciled you *by the body of his flesh through death*, to present you holy in his sight, without blemish and free from accusation").

The article, indeed, points to sufferings that have actually been experienced. But rather than understand it as denoting possession with Paul as its referent, and so to be more fully explicated by the second clause of verse 24, I suggest it is better understood as denoting possession with Christ as its referent, and so to be picking up from the earlier references to *peace* having been brought about "through his [Christ's] blood, shed on the cross" (v 20b) and *reconciliation* effected "by the body of his [Christ's] flesh through death" (v 22a).

On such an understanding, the "now" (νῦν) of verse 24 is not to be seen as having in mind the time of Paul's imprisonment (as often assumed by commentators), which is not referred to until 4:3, but should be taken as the first word of a sudden outburst of thanksgiving ("Now I rejoice!") for God's great redemption, which has been provided in the work of Jesus Christ. The expression "I rejoice" (χαίρω) has as its object what God has effected by means of the suffering of Christ—that is, "through his blood, shed on the cross" and "by the body of his flesh through death." It probably also signals something of the difference between Paul and the "hollow and deceptive philosophy" (τῆς φιλοσοφίας καὶ κενῆς ἀπάτης) that someone (τις) was promulgating among believers at Colosse (cf. 2:8). For whereas the errorist and others at Colosse may have been embarrassed—even repelled—by references to Christ's "physical

---

[31] Lohse, *Colossians and Philemon*, 69.

[32] Cf. Kremer, *Leiden Christi … Untersuchung zu Kol 1,24b*.

body," "blood," "cross," "sufferings" and "death" in effecting human redemption, Paul's attitude was just the reverse: he rejoiced in the sufferings of Christ!

On such a reading, therefore, τοῖς παθήμασιν ὑπὲρ ὑμῶν refers to Christ's sufferings on behalf of believers at Colosse—as well as, of course, on behalf of all believers "in Christ"—and so should be translated either "that which was suffered for you" or "what was suffered for you." And on such a reading, this first part of the verse (1) picks up on the theme of Christ's physical sufferings highlighted in verses 20 and 22, (2) restates in dramatic fashion Paul's attitude toward those sufferings ("I rejoice in what was suffered for you," probably in contradistinction to the attitude of the errorist and some Christians at Colosse who started to believe him), (3) ties together what Paul said earlier about Christ's sufferings and what he says in what follows about sufferings in his own ministry, and (4) furnishes a platform for the presentation of his own ministry, which he designates as his service (διάκονος) on behalf of the gospel (τὸ εὐαγγέλιον) in 1:23b and describes more fully in 1:24b–2:5.

The second part of verse 24, "and I complete in my flesh what is still lacking in regard to Christ's afflictions, for the sake of his body, which is the church," clearly has the apostle's own sufferings in view. And this is in line with the fact that while the expression τὰ παθήματα τοῦ Χριστοῦ / αὐτοῦ ("the sufferings of Christ" or "his sufferings") is used elsewhere in Paul's letters for both Christ's sufferings and Paul's sufferings (cf. 1 Cor 1:4-7; Phil 3:10), neither the noun θλῖψις ("oppression," "affliction," "tribulation") nor the phrase αἱ θλίψεις τοῦ Χριστοῦ ("Christ's afflictions") appear in the apostle's other writings with reference to Christ's sufferings, but are always used in a derivative fashion of the apostle's own sufferings (cf. Rom 5:3; 8:35; 2 Cor 1:4, 8; 4:17; 6:4; 7:4; Eph 3:13; Phil 1:17; 4:14; 1 Thess 3:3, 7) or those of other believers (cf. Rom 12:12; 2 Cor 1:4; 8:2, 13; 1 Thess 1:6; 2 Thess 1:4, 6) on behalf of Christ.[33]

How, then, should "Christ's afflictions" (τῶν θλίψεων Χριστοῦ) in this second part of verse 24 be understood? Further, what are the things that are "still lacking" (τὰ ὑστερήματα)? And what did Paul have in mind when he said "I complete (ἀνταναπληρῶ) in my flesh

---

[33] The only place in the Pauline letters where αἱ θλίψεις τοῦ Χριστοῦ could be taken to refer to Christ's own sufferings is in Col 1:24b, but that, we argue here, is not the case (*contra* BAG, 363a).

(ἐν τῇ σαρκί μου) what is still lacking with respect to Christ's afflictions"?

Some have supposed that Paul believed that there was something lacking in the vicarious sufferings of Christ and that he needed to complete Christ's redemptive work in his own ministry.[34] But, as Eduard Lohse points out, "Paul and all other witnesses in the New Testament unanimously agree that the reconciliation was truly and validly accomplished in the death of Christ, and that no need exists for any supplementation."[35] Others have proposed some type of mystical union with Christ's passion that calls for the "his body, which is the church," to so enter into the experience of Christ's sufferings that believers individually and the church corporately will be able to complete experientially what Christ began objectively.[36] The majority of interpreters today, however, view the statement "I complete in my flesh what is still lacking with respect to Christ's afflictions" in an apocalyptic context—a sentiment that parallels the Jewish expectation of an increase of "Messianic travail," or woes of the Messiah, which must come about before the final culmination of human history—and so see Paul speaking about the messianic afflictions that he must accomplish in his ministry on behalf of the church before the end of time.[37]

---

[34] Cf. H. Windisch, *Paulus und Christus: Ein biblisch-religionsgeschichtlicher Vergleich* (Leipzig: Heinrich,1934), 236-50. In Windisch's view, Col 1:24 is to be interpreted as Paul bearing the sufferings "that Christ could not carry away completely" (*ibid.*, 244).

[35] Lohse, *Colossians and Philemon*, 69; citing his *Märtyrer und Gottesknecht*, 200-203.

[36] Cf. A. Deissmann, *Paul: A Study in Social and Religious History*, trans. W. E. Wilson (London: Hodder & Stoughton, 1926), 162-63, 181-82, 202; O. Schmitz, *Die Christus-Gemeinschaft des Paulus im Lichte seines Genetiv-gebrauchs* (Gütersloh: 1924), 190-96; J. Schneider, *Die Passionsmystik des Paulus: Ihr Wesen, ihr Hintergrund und ihre Nachwirkungen* (Leipzig: 1929).

[37] Cf., e.g., E. Lohse, *Colossians and Philemon*, 69-72. See also O'Brien, *Colossians, Philemon*, 79-80: "The apostle, through the suffering which he endures in his own flesh ..., contributes to the sum total of these eschatological afflictions. By helping to fill up this predetermined measure Paul brings the end, the dawning of the future glory, so much closer" (*ibid.* 80); Caird, *Paul's Letters from Prison*, 184: "*Christ's afflictions* will not be complete until the final victory over evil is won. Someone must carry the burden, and the strong may take over the share of the weak (Gal. 6.2). Paul is glad that he has been able to do enough of the heavy lifting to spare his churches some of their load. It is almost as if he is

My suggestion, however, is that what is presented in Col 1:24 is a juxtaposition of (1) what Christ accomplished in his physical sufferings (the τοῖς παθήμασιν ὑπὲρ ὑμῶν of the first clause), which vicariously effected redemption for all believers, and (2) what Paul experienced in his ministry on behalf of the church generally and Christians at Colosse in particular (the τῶν θλίψεων Χριστοῦ ... ὑπὲρ τοῦ σώματος αὐτοῦ, ὅ ἐστιν ἡ ἐκκλησία of the second clause), which he saw as completing that redemption by extending it to all people. It was Christ's mission to *effect* redemption; it is the church's mission—and particularly Paul's mission—to be involved in the *extension* of what Christ effected.

On such an interpretation, the feature of mutuality between the mission of Christ and the mission of Paul is highlighted. For what Christ effected once-and-for-all by his vicarious sufferings on behalf of humanity yet needs to be extended through the apostle's sufferings on behalf of the church. Nonetheless, even if both clauses of verse 24 are understood to refer to Paul's own suffering—and so not seen as setting up a parallel between what Christ effected and what Paul was doing by way of extension—such a note of mutuality is still present in the juxtaposition of the person and work of Christ in 1:15-23 and the ministry of Paul in 1:24–2:5. For as N. T. Wright points out with respect to "the whole paragraph" of 1:24–2:5 (with also allusions to 2 Cor 1:3-7 and 4:7-12): Paul "applies to himself the same pattern, of suffering on behalf of others, that was worked out on the cross."[38]

5. Conclusion: Mutuality as a Theological Basis for Witness

The concept of "interchange" was significant for Paul's and the early church's understanding of the work of Christ, as Morna Hooker has frequently point out.[39] Concomitant with the idea of interchange was the concept of "mutuality," particularly with respect to understanding relations between Christ's mission and the church's mission. Other factors of a political and sociological nature were undoubtedly at work in the motivation, conditioning, and expression of the church's mission, as Professor Trites has ably demonstrated. At the heart of the

---

thinking of a fixed quota of suffering to be endured, so that the more he can attract to himself the less will remain for others."

[38] N. T. Wright, *Colossians and Philemon* (TNTC; Grand Rapids: Eerdmans, 1986), 89.

[39] See note 7 above.

early church's understanding of mission, however, was the theological concept of mutuality.

Such a concept seems to have been particularly lively in Paul's own self-understanding and his rationale for a mission to Gentiles, as his highly personal statements of Rom 8:17, Phil 3:10-11 and Col 1:24 suggest. It would also have continued to be an important concept among his immediate followers, which may be argued if Colossians was written by a later follower of the apostle. In all likelihood, therefore, it was from such a concept of mutuality that Luke derived the theological basis for his theme of witness. And it is in the concept of mutuality that the individual believer and the church corporately find theological grounding for their witness today.

SELECT BIBLIOGRAPHY

Barrett, C. Kingsley. *A Commentary on the Epistle to the Romans.* BNTC / HNTC. London: Black; New York: Harper & Row, 1957.

Bruce, Frederick F. *The Epistle of Paul to the Romans.* TNTC. London: Tyndale; Grand Rapids: Eerdmans, 1963.

Caird, George B. *Paul's Letters from Prison. Ephesians, Philippians, Colossians, Philemon.* NCB. Oxford: University Press, 1976).

Cranfield, Charles E. B. *A Critical and Exegetical Commentary on the Epistle to the Romans.* ICC. 2 vols. Edinburgh: T. & T. Clark, 1975, 1979.

Dunn, James D. G. *Romans.* WBC. 2 vols. Dallas: Word, 1988.

Fee, Gordon D. *Paul's Letter to the Philippians.* NICNT. Grand Rapids: Eerdmans, 1995.

Fitzmyer, Joseph A. "'To Know Him and the Power of His Resurrection' (Phil 3.10)," in *Mélanges bibliques en hommage au R. P. Béda Rigaux*, ed. A. Descamps and A. de Halleux. Gembloux: Duculot, 1970. 411-25.

——. *Romans: A New Translation with Introduction and Commentary.* AB. New York: Doubleday, 1993.

Godet, Frédéric L. *Commentary on St Paul's Epistle to the Romans*, 2 vols., trans. A. Cusin. Edinburgh: T. & T. Clark, 1880, 1881; New York: Funk & Wagnalls, 1883; repr. Grand Rapids: Kregel, 1977.

Harris, Murray J. *Colossians and Philemon.* EGGNT. Grand Rapids: Eerdmans, 1991.

Hawthorne, Gerald F. *Philippians.* WBC. Dallas: Word, 1983.

Kremer, Jacob. *Was an den Leiden Christi noch mangelt: Eine interpretationsgeschichtliche und exegetische Untersuchung zu Kol 1,24b.* Bonn: Hanstein, 1956.

Lightfoot, Joseph B. *Saint Paul's Epistle to the Philippians.* London: Macmillan, 1881.

——. *Saint Paul's Epistles to the Colossians and to Philemon.* London: Macmillan, 1882[6].

Lohse, Eduard. *Die Briefe an die Kolosser und an Philemon.* Göttingen: Vandenhoeck & Ruprecht, 1968; English translation: *Colossians and Philemon.* Hermeneia. Philadelphia: Fortress, 1971.

Martin, Ralph P. *The Epistle of Paul to the Philippians.* TNTC. London: Tyndale, 1959.

O'Brien, Peter T. *Colossians, Philemon.* WBC. Dallas: Word, 1982.

——. *The Epistle to the Philippians.* NIGTC. Grand Rapids: Eerdmans, 1991.

Trites, Allison A. *The New Testament Concept of Witness.* SBLMS. Cambridge: Cambridge University Press, 1977.

Wright, N. Thomas. *Colossians and Philemon.* TNTC. Grand Rapids: Eerdmans, 1986.

"WHAT DOES IT MATTER?"
Priorities and the *Adiaphora* in Paul's Dealing with Opponents during
his Mission

One of the seemingly strange things about Paul is that while he argued single-mindedly and vigorously, even vehemently and defiantly, for "the truth of the gospel," he also responded diversely to those who opposed him—sometimes castigating them in caustic and virulent language; at other times pleading with them in a self-deprecating and humble manner; and at still other times taking a rather relaxed attitude toward them and their preaching. Three situations reflected in his letters come immediately to mind. The first is his response to certain Jewish believers from Jerusalem who followed him throughout Galatia and were confusing his converts; the second, his response to some believers at Corinth who opposed him; the third, his response to some Christian leaders at Philippi who were jealous of him and sought to make trouble for him.

But while Paul's reactions in certain conflict situations have often been viewed as a bit strange—even, perhaps, somewhat contra-dictory—his differing responses in the three cases cited above should more likely be understood as (1) springing from an inner consistency of thought and action in his own life and ministry, and (2) setting a paradigm for the thought, actions, and ministries of Christians today. For the apostle's responses in these situations reflect both the central priorities and the *adiaphora* of his mission—that is, both matters of great importance and matters of relative indifference, at least as he saw them. And even though it is often confusing to sort out issues that belong to the one category or the other, a study of Paul's responses in such conflict situations has much to teach us with regard to our own priorities, reactions and activities today.

1. *The Situation of Galatians and Paul's Response*

Galatians is a letter that has been variously dated, variously interpreted, and variously applied. Most of the issues regarding provenance and interpretation, however, need not detain us here (for a treatment of these matters, see my *Galatians* commentary). All I want to do in this chapter is to sketch out the situation that Paul faced when writing to his Galatian converts and highlight certain features of his response.

The Situation

Paul's opponents in the Roman province of Galatia were, it seems, Jewish believers in Jesus who came from the Jerusalem church to Paul's churches with a message that called for Gentile believers to be circumcised and to keep the rudiments of the Jewish calendar. Undoubtedly they presented their message as being biblically and theologically based. Further, they evidently claimed to be interested only in Gentile Christians being fully integrated into the chosen people of Israel, and so full recipients of the blessings of the Abrahamic covenant. Probably they asserted that they represented the concerns of James, Peter, and the Jerusalem church regarding Jewish–Gentile relations in Christian communities outside of Palestine. And probably, as well, they portrayed themselves as not being in opposition to Paul but only seeking to complete his message, thereby bringing the Galatian believers to perfection.

Paul, however, accuses these "Judaizers" of wanting Gentile Christians to be circumcised primarily in order "to avoid being persecuted for the cross of Christ" and so "that they may boast about your flesh" (Gal 6:12-13). Such an evaluation of their motives suggests that in the rising tide of Jewish nationalism—which existed during the decades prior to the nation's final conflict with Rome in 66– 70 CE, with antagonism from Jewish Zealots being directed against any Israelite who had Gentile sympathies or who associated with Gentile sympathizers—these Jewish believers from Jerusalem wanted Gentile Christians to be circumcised so that they might be able to demonstrate to their Jewish compatriots that belief in Jesus actually brought Gentiles into the fold of Judaism, and so thwart any Jewish purification campaign against the church at Jerusalem.

Paul's Response

Paul's response to these Judaizers is direct, forceful and condemnatory—even, in fact, caustic and crude. Immediately after the letter's salutation, he denounces the Judaizers' message as being "no gospel at all"—not a supplement to the Christian gospel (i.e., an ἄλλο εὐαγγέλιον), as they evidently claimed, but a different kind of message altogether (i.e., a ἕτερον εὐαγγέλιον)—and declares that their teaching causes people to depart from "the one [i.e., God] who called" them and confuses and perverts "the gospel of Christ" (1:6-7). He twice pronounces an anathema (ἀνάθεμα ἔστω) on them and their preaching (1:8-9), with the word "anathema" meaning "delivered over to divine wrath for destruction" and so "accursed" (RSV, NRSV) or "eternally condemned" by God (NIV). And, in what is surely the crudest of all his extant statements, Paul says that his wish for his opponents who wanted to circumcise his Gentile converts is that "they would go the whole way and emasculate themselves!" (5:12).

Yet while stern in its warnings and admonitions, Paul's response to the Gentile Christians of Galatia—who had evidently begun to observe the Jewish cultic calendar (cf. 4:10), but not yet submitted to the rite of circumcision (cf. 4:9; 4:21)—is not anywhere as vitriolic as it is toward those who were troubling and confusing them. He addresses the Christians of Galatia as ἀδελφοί ("brothers and sisters") at a number of places in his letter (1:11; 3:15; 4:12, 31; 5:11, 13; 6:1, 18), thereby reminding them of his and their family relationship, even though they were beginning to forget it. Likewise, he speaks of his fears and perplexities about them (4:11, 20), reminds them of their former concerns for him (4:13-15), pleads with them for a present positive response (4:12), and expresses his confidence in them as to their final commitments (5:10).

Nonetheless, he cannot bring himself to include an opening thanksgiving section in his Galatian letter, as he does in all of his other extant letters. Rather, he (1) expresses astonishment over his converts' proposed acceptance of "another gospel" (1:6), (2) calls them "foolish" or "undiscerning" for not appreciating the work of the Spirit and the importance of faith in their lives (3:1-9), (3) warns them quite sternly of the disastrous results of following the Judaizers' program (3:10-12; 4:8-9; 5:2-4), (4) exhorts them to live in love and by the direction of the Spirit (5:13-25), and (5) asks them to help one another in their Christian lives (6:1-10).

The central priority of Paul's missionary activity was what he calls "the truth of the gospel" (2:5 and 14; cf. 2 Cor 11:10, "the truth of Christ"; Col 1:5, "the word of the truth of the gospel"). He defines this gospel in terms of the grace of God (1:3, 6, 15, *passim*), the work of

Christ (1:4; 2:16-17; 3:13-14a; 4:5; 6:14; *passim*), the ministry of the Holy Spirit (3:3-5; 5:16, 22-25; *passim*), and the faith of believers (2:16-17; 3:2, 5, 6-9, 14b; 3:26; *passim*). Thus he closes his Galatian letter with the statement: "May I never boast except in the cross of our Lord Jesus Christ, through which the world has been crucified to me, and I to the world" (6:14). And he contextualizes this central focus of the Christian gospel for his Galatian converts in their situation as follows: "Neither circumcision nor uncircumcision means anything; what counts is a new creation" (6:15).

So when Paul speaks about those who were detracting from the truth of the gospel and confusing his converts with "another" teaching that contradicted it, he speaks in language that is both denunciatory and condemnatory. His opponents may have presented themselves as pious and devout believers in Jesus, used carefully formulated biblical and theological arguments, and expressed outrage at any suggestion that their message was motivated by anything other than the best of intentions. Paul, however, views their actions and teachings as perverting the gospel of Christ, undermining his ministry to Gentiles, and being under the condemnation of God. It is therefore, as Paul saw it, to be directly, openly and fervently opposed—just as at Syrian Antioch, in a situation somewhat similar, he had previously opposed Peter and other Jewish believers because "he was clearly wrong" and "they were not acting in line with the truth of the gospel" (2:11-14).

2. *The Situation of 2 Corinthians and Paul's Response*

2 Corinthians is a difficult writing to analyze, chiefly because of uncertainties regarding its compositional character. There is no external manuscript evidence for any of the partition theories proposed for the letter. Nonetheless, there are a number of internal features that suggest the work should probably be seen as a composite of various Pauline letters (or, portions of letters) to Christians at Corinth, which have been somehow brought together to form what we now have as 2 Corinthians. These internal matters have to do with (1) changes of tone and rhetorical style in the writing, most obviously between chapters 1–7 (or, 1–9) and 10–13, (2) the seemingly disparate character of some portions of the writing, chiefly that of 6:14–7:1, (3) the separate treatments of Titus and the brothers in chapter 8 and of the collection in chapter 9, and (4) references to events in Paul's life and allusions to relations with his Corinthian converts that seem to suggest

various times of writing—principally his statement "this is the third time I am coming to you" of 13:1; his reference to having written the Corinthians a letter "out of great distress and anguish of heart and with many tears" after a "painful visit" with them in 2:1-4; and various allusions in chapters 10–13 to strained relations between the Corinthian Christians and Paul.

A number of competent scholars have argued for the unity of 2 Corinthians, most often positing some type of "compositional hiatus" between chapters 1–7 (or, 1–9) and 10–13. The major problem with such a view has always been: Why, then, did Paul retain that earlier conciliatory section of chapters 1–7, which speaks of his joy over his Corinthian converts' repentance, in a letter that he then concludes in chapters 10–13 in such a severe, harsh and even sarcastic manner? Most scholars today, therefore, have invoked some type of "partition theory" and postulated some such order for Paul's Corinthian correspondence as follows: (1) a "previous letter," which is referred to in 1 Cor 5:9 and is either no longer extant or represented (to some extent) by 2 Cor 6:14–7:1; (2) our present 1 Corinthians, which is a unified letter; (3) an "intermediate letter," which is possibly referred to in 2 Cor 2:3-4; (4) a "severe letter," which now appears as 2 Corinthians 10–13; and (5) a "conciliatory letter," which now appears as 2 Corinthians 1–7 and was written about 57–58 CE—with, perhaps, chapters 8 and 9 appended to that final letter.

We need not get bogged down here in the current critical debates regarding the composition of 2 Corinthians. The integrity of what is written—that is, that Paul is the author of all that we have in 2 Corinthians—is not in question. Nor is it questioned that what Paul wrote in 2 Corinthians has conditions at Corinth in view. It is, in reality, only the historical order of the "conciliatory letter" (chapters 1–7) and the "severe letter" (chapters 10–13) that is of any importance for a discussion of Paul's responses to his detractors at Corinth. But even that issue is not of overwhelming significance for dealing with the fact of opposition to Paul among certain Christians at Corinth and highlighting how he responds to them.

The Situation
However we relate the various portions of 2 Corinthians to one another, it seems obvious that Paul's relations with his Corinthian converts were often strained and that he had his detractors among the

Christians of that city. It is clear from chapters 10–13 that there was a breakdown of relations between them. For evidently they were claiming that Paul was timid and unimpressive and that he lacked eloquence when with them in person, but that he wrote bold and forceful letters when away from them (10:1-11), that his ministry, when compared with those of others, was not very significant (10:12-18), and that he was somehow inferior to the more imposing "apostles" of their acquaintance (11:1–12:21). And in chapters 1–7, even amidst a certain conciliatory tone within these chapters, there still reverberates a refrain of difficulty and distrust between Paul and his converts—as witness, for example, his reference to a former "painful visit" (2:1), his statements about the distress caused by that visit (2:2-4), his allusions to grief caused by someone in some particular situation at Corinth (2:5-11), and various hints that he was aware of a growing unhappiness among his converts regarding his ministry (e.g., 3:1-3, *passim*).

Paul's converts at Corinth seem to have wanted an apostle who was forceful and eloquent in his preaching and teaching (probably more of a "trained speaker" than he appeared to be); who was a bold leader about whom they could "boast" (not one who exhibited weaknesses in his leadership); and who compared well with the other "apostles" of their acquaintance (not one who was inferior to them in his person). They seem to have thought of themselves as commendable people who needed an apostle who was also commendable; a strong people who needed strong leadership. And in their debates about how to rank their leaders, their apostles, and their "super-apostles," they seem to have entered into "quarreling, jealousy, outbursts of anger, factions, slander, gossip, arrogance and disorder" and to have considered matters of "impurity, sexual sins, and debauchery" to be rather incidental—not only countenancing such matters but also indulging in them (cf. 12:20-21).

Paul's Response

Paul's response to his Corinthian converts in 2 Corinthians is twofold. With respect to "the truth of Christ" (11:10), his converts' "sincere and pure devotion to Christ" (11:3), and their lives of holiness (13:2-7), he has a "godly jealousy" for them (11:2) and admonishes them quite sternly—comparable in many ways to his admonitions to his converts in Galatia (cf. esp. the wording of such passages as 10:11;

11:4; 12:20). Thus, for example, his opening words in chapters 10–13 are words of passion and rebuke:

> I beg you that when I come I may not have to be as bold as I expect to be toward some people who think that we live by the standards of this world (10:2).

> What we are in our letters when we are absent we will be in our actions when we are present (10:11).

> I am jealous for you with a godly jealousy. I promised you to one husband, to Christ, so that I might present you as a pure virgin to him. But I am afraid that just as Eve was deceived by the serpent's cunning, your minds may somehow be led astray from your sincere and pure devotion to Christ" (11:2-3).

And his concluding words of these chapters comprise a series of severe warnings and admonitions:

> This will be my third visit to you. "Every matter must be established by the testimony of two or three witnesses" [quoting Deut 19:15]. I already gave you a warning when I was with you the second time, and I now repeat it while absent: on my return I will not spare those who sinned earlier or any of the others (13:1-2).

> Examine yourselves to see whether you are in the faith; test yourselves. Do you not realize that Christ Jesus is in you—unless, of course, you fail the test? (13:5).

> This is why I write these thing when I am absent, that when I come I may not have to be harsh in my use of authority—the authority that the Lord gave me for building you up, not for tearing you down (13:10).

With respect to his detractors' accusations against him personally, however, Paul is somewhat self-deprecating and responds more humbly. He speaks of a traumatic personal experience that took place in the province of Asia at some time when he was away from Corinth—probably shortly before writing what he wrote in chapters 1–7—and interprets that experience as something brought about by God for his converts' "comfort and salvation" (1:4-7). It was a time when he was "under great pressure, far beyond our ability to endure, so that we despaired even of life"—a time, in fact, when he "felt the sentence of death" and experienced "deadly peril" (1:8-11). And he continues to allude to that experience elsewhere in chapters 1–7, principally in 1:3-7 and 4:7-12.

In chapters 10–13 he couches his response in terms of his love for his detractors (e.g., 11:11; 12:15) and his desire for their perfection (e.g., 10:8-9; 13:11). And in responding to their accusations, he "boasts" about certain features of his ministry and certain incidents in his life that he believes ought to indicate that their assertions against him are invalid. But he does this, it needs to be noted, in a somewhat self-deprecatory and humble fashion.

One such feature of his ministry was his willingness not to be a financial burden to believers at Corinth, but to proclaim "the gospel of God" to them "free of charge" (11:7-12). Another was the whole set of circumstances related to his Jewish heritage and apostolic experiences, which should authenticate to anyone his claim to be a "servant of Christ" (11:22-33). Another was his experience of having been "caught up" in a vision "to the third heaven"—that is, "to Paradise"—and hearing "inexpressible things, things that a person is not permitted to tell" (12:1-6). Another, of being given by God "a thorn in my flesh, a messenger of Satan, to torment me," but also of being assured by God: "My grace is sufficient for you, for my power is made perfect in weakness" (12:7-9). And still another was the complex of "signs, wonders and miracles" expressed in his ministry among the Corinthians themselves, which marked him out as an apostle and should have settled the matter of his authority among them (12:11-13).

In the repetition of these features and incidents from his life and ministry, Paul speaks somewhat sarcastically, rebuking the self-serving pride and blatant impertinence of those who leveled accusations against him. But he also, it needs to be noted, responds to his detractors with self-depreciation and humility, saying that he has been forced by them to make such boasts—or, as he says in 12:11: "I have made a fool of myself, but you drove me to it."

3. *The Situation of Philippians and Paul's Response*

Scholars have often taken Philippians to be a composite of two or three letters—for example, a letter of thanks for a monetary gift in 4:10-23; another letter regarding Paul's ministry at Philippi in 1:1–3:1 and 4:4-7; and another letter on certain disturbances within the Philippian church in 3:2–4:3 and 4:8-9. On such a view, one must first determine the respective situations and relative chronologies of the various parts of the writing before dealing with any of its themes. But partition theories for Philippians are usually seen today as being, in the words of Werner G. Kümmel, "totally unconvincing" (*Introduction to the New Testament*, trans. H. C. Kee [Nashville: Abingdon, rev. ed., 1975], 333; see also 332-35)—and deservedly so.

More serious is the question of the letter's provenance and date. For while 1:12-26 indicates quite clearly that it was written from prison, the question remains: Was it written from Ephesian imprisonment (sometime during 53–57 CE), from Caesarean imprisonment (about 58–59 CE), or from Roman imprisonment (about 60–62 CE)? Issues regarding provenance usually have to do with (1) the number and nature of the journeys between Philippi and Rome as reflected in the letter, and (2) the kinship of the contents and rhetoric of the letter to Paul's other letters, particularly to material found in Galatians and 2 Corinthians. Cogent arguments can be mounted in support of each of these postulated situations and times. I personally favor the view, for reasons set out long ago by C. H. Dodd (cf. his "The Mind of Paul: Change and Development," *BJRL* 18 [1934] 5-26; repr. as "The Mind of Paul: II," in *New Testament Studies* [Manchester: Manchester University Press, 1953], 85-106), that Philippians was written from Roman imprisonment, and so after Galatians and 2 Corinthians.

Obviously, whatever is accepted with respect to the provenance and date of Philippians has a profound effect on how one relates its themes, rhetoric and language to the other Pauline letters. Yet on this matter of Paul's responses to those who opposed him, the data from Galatians, 2 Corinthians and Philippians bear striking resemblances of tone and content, as well as distinguishable differences of response, and so can be treated together, whatever the exact provenances and dates of the letters themselves and/or of the pertinent sections within those letters.

The Situation

The exact nature of the situation addressed in Philippians is difficult to determine. What can be inferred with confidence from the letter itself, however, whether viewed as a single letter or a collection of two or three letters, is (1) that Christians at Philippi were experiencing some kind of hostility, which Paul believed called for instruction on his part as to how they should live under such conditions, and (2) that certain Christian teachers were opposing Paul in some manner, which motivated Paul to speak about those teachers and to instruct his converts regarding how to respond to them. These two matters—hostility against Paul's converts and opposition to Paul himself—seem to have been related in some way, for intertwined throughout Philippians are ethical teachings for Christians who find themselves in a hostile environment (cf. 1:27–2:18; 3:12–4:9) *and* statements about those who opposed Paul (cf. 1:15-18; probably also 3:2-11).

Paul's Response

The exact nature of the situation at Philippi may be difficult to ascertain. But it is clear that when Paul deals with the issues faced by his addressees—whether external hostility or internal division—he does so by using the Christ-hymn of 2:6-11 as the basis for his pastoral instructions and the paradigm for how his converts should think and act.

So in dealing with how his converts should live in the face of hostility, Paul holds up the example of Christ as lauded in 2:6-11. For though Christ possessed equality with God, he willingly humbled himself in the incarnation and became obedient throughout his earthly ministry, even to the extent of death (vv 6-8)—with that attitude and action being approved by God, who then exalted him to the highest of positions (vv 9-11).

In the exhortations that immediately precede and follow this Christ-hymn, Paul urges the Philippian Christians, who were facing some type of external hostility, to adopt Christ's attitude of humility, steadfast obedience, and concern for others. Thus on the basis of the Christ-hymn of 2:6-11 he exhorts his converts: "Do nothing out of selfish ambition or vain conceit" (2:3a); be humble and "consider others better than yourselves" (2:3b); "look not only to your own interests, but also to the interests of others" (2:4); continue in a life of obedience (2:12a); "continue to work out your own salvation with fear and trembling" (2:12b); "do everything without complaining or arguing" (2:14); "hold on to the word of life" (2:16a), and "be glad and rejoice with me" (2:18). He also implies on the basis of this confessional portion that God will vindicate them for their steadfast adherence to the gospel in the midst of hostility, for God has set the precedent for such action in his vindication of Christ.

Then Paul goes on to show how this pattern of humility, obedience and concern for others was being exemplified in the ministries of two of his co-workers, who were well known to his addressees: (1) in the ministry of Timothy, whom he characterizes as one who "takes a genuine interest in your welfare" and "has served with me in the work of the gospel" (2:19-24), and (2) in the ministry of Epaphroditus (2:25-30), whom he describes as the one "you sent to take care of my needs," who "almost died for the work of Christ" (2:25-30). Further, he declares his desire to have the pattern of Christ's life reflected in his own life (3:10-11). Then he presents certain features and motivations of his ministry, which he believes reflect the paradigm given by Christ, as a further example for his converts to follow (3:12-21). And he concludes his letter by reminding the Philippians of how this pattern of humility, obedience and concern was expressed in their repeated financial support of him, for which he thanks them and assures them of God's blessing for their actions (4:10-19).

Likewise, when Paul speaks of the Christian teachers at Philippi who opposed him, he also makes use of the main themes of the Christ-hymn of 2:6-11. For when compared with the attitudes and actions of Christ, the selfish ambitions and feigned sincerity of those teachers (1:15-18)—together with their activities (whether actual or possible) as "mutilators of the flesh" (3:2-3)—come off quite badly. Implied throughout the Philippian letter, in fact, are requests (1) for the opposing teachers to measure themselves by the attitudes and actions of Christ, not by their envious reactions to Paul, and (2) for the Philippian believers to judge those teachers in terms of how they model Christ's pattern of humility and obedience, not by their pretensions or claims.

It is most significant for our purposes, however, to note that when Paul deals with issues at Philippi his response is twofold, just as it was when responding to conflict situations in his churches in the province of Galatia and at Corinth. For when dealing with "Judaizing" perversions of the gospel—whether those perversions were then being actively promulgated at Philippi, or viewed by Paul as a live possibility in the future, or only remembered from his past experience with Judaizers in Galatia—he speaks quite sternly and in denunciatory fashion: "Watch out for those dogs, those men who do evil, those mutilators of the flesh! For it is we who are the circumcision; we who worship by the Spirit of God, who glory in Christ Jesus and put no confidence in the flesh!" (3:2-3). Yet when he refers to a situation where the gospel was being truly proclaimed, but where the motivations of some of those who proclaimed it were suspect ("some preach Christ out of envy and rivalry, but others out of good will—the latter do so in love, knowing that I am put here for the defense of the gospel; the former preach Christ out of selfish ambition, not sincerely, supposing that they can stir up trouble for me while I am in chains," 1:15-17), he responds: "What does it matter? The important thing is that in every way, whether from false motives or true, Christ is preached. And because of this I rejoice" (1:18).

4. *An Excursus on Martin Luther*

This ability to distinguish between central priorities and the *adiaphora* should also be seen as having characterized, in large measure, Martin Luther, the great Protestant Reformer of the first half of the sixteenth century. Admittedly, many of Luther's "protestant" convictions were developed over a span of time during his earlier days, and much of what he later said and wrote was not particularly unique or highly important. Luther himself, on both counts, acknowledged that to be true. Further, Luther was a man of his day, with frequent use of rather earthy (though not obscene) expressions, coarse (though not bawdy or lascivious) language, and polemical invective. Such language is amply attested in his "Table Talk," which was transcribed by some of his friends from his conversations at dinner in the former Augustinian Black Cloister at Wittenberg, where he lived from the time of his marriage to Katherine von Bora in 1525 until his death in 1546. By today's standards, Luther could hardly be called "politically correct" in many of his ideas or much of his speech. Nonetheless, Luther was a genius at being able to discern between the central priorities of the Christian gospel and many other matters of relative indifference. And that ability should be credited as going a long way toward the establishment of the Protestant Reformation.

For example, in Part II of his 1539 tractate "On the Councils and the Church," where he discusses the historical significance of the apostolic council at Jerusalem (Acts 15) and the first four ecumenical councils of Nicea (325), Constantinople (381), Ephesus (431) and Chalcedon (451), Luther makes a number of distinctions between the central priorities of the gospel and the *adiaphora* of those days. One such issue has to do with the date of Easter, which had split Christendom into warring parties—with the Eastern Church, Anabaptists, and various other sectarians (the so-called *Rotten*) being on one side of the debate, whereas western Christendom was generally on the other. For while Luther believed that the Eastern Church, Anabaptists, and many of the *Rotten* were on this matter essentially right, and western Christendom wrong, he also viewed this issue as part of the *adiaphora*, and so insisted:

> Therefore I advise that one let Easter come as it now comes, and keep it as it is kept now, and let the old garment be patched and torn (as was said); and let Easter wobble back and forth until the Last Day, or until the monarchs, in view of these facts [i.e., astronomical calculations] unanimously and simultaneously change it. For this is not going to kill us, nor will St. Peter's bark suffer distress because of it, since it is neither heresy nor sin ... but only an error or solecism in astronomy, which serves temporal government rather than the church (trans. C. M. Jabobs, *Works of Martin Luther*, vol. 5 [Philadelphia: Holman, 1916], 186; also *Luther's Works*, vol. 41 [Philadelphia: Fortress, 1966], 66).

Or again on Acts 15, Luther argues that central to a proper interpretation of the Jerusalem council is the distinction that must be made between the central doctrinal issue that drew the council together—that is, the necessity of circumcision for the acceptance of Gentile believers—and certain peripheral issues that the council also discussed—such as are dealt with in the so-called Jerusalem Decree. The former Luther saw as binding on the Christian conscience, but the latter he understood as having to do with matters of concern for that day (cf. *Luther's Works*, 41.68-79). And in his treatment of the first four ecumenical councils, Luther also distinguishes between the central matter of doctrine that brought each of the councils together and was decided at each of these councils—that is, the divinity of Christ against Arius at the Council of Nicea, the divinity of the Holy Spirit against Macedonius at the Council of Constantinople, the one person of Christ against Nestorius at the Council of Ephesus, and the two natures of Christ against Eutyches at the Council of Chalcedon, where the councils sought to protect the church from error—and the *adiaphora*, where no new articles of faith were created but only matters relative to that day were considered (cf. *ibid.* 67-68 and 79-142).

It is in his "Table Talk," however, which has sometimes been something of an embarrassment to modern admirers of Luther, that such distinctions between the central priorities of the gospel and the *adiaphora* particularly appear. So, for example, when speaking about baptism and its administration—that is, whether cold or warm water should be used, as was "hotly" debated in that day—Luther is quoted as saying in December, 1532:

> I don't care about the element, whatever one may have. Indeed, it's enough to speak the words. Let the children be committed to our Lord God. The baptism itself is of no concern to me [i.e., it's God's business, not mine]. Besides, the Word is the principal part of baptism. If in an emergency there's no water at hand, it doesn't matter whether water or beer is used (words recorded by Veit Dietrich, "Table Talk" No. 394 in *Luther's Works*, vol. 54, trans. T. G. Tappert [Philadelphia: Fortress, 1967], 61).

And when in the spring of 1533 Ignatius Perknowsky, who is referred to in the text as "our Bohemian," interrupted Luther to say that he still had doubts about baptism, Luther is reported by have replied "gently":

> When you first came here you were not at the stage which you have now attained. Continue to be patient. Give our Lord God time. Let the trees bloom before they bring forth fruit! (words recorded by Veit Dietrich, "Table Talk" No. 515 in *Luther's Works*, vol. 54, 92—with a marginal note appended by a later editor reading: "Observe with what moderation he [Luther] bore this weakness" *ibid.*, note 328).

5. *Some Observations and Conclusions*

The genius of Paul, as well as that of Luther, was that they were able to make distinctions between priorities and the *adiaphora*, and to make them for the benefit of the Christian gospel and the good of God's people. Such an ability, of course, does not provide a full explanation for the measure of success that the first-century apostle or the sixteenth-century reformer enjoyed, for many other factors, both human and divine, were also at work in their respective missions. Nor does it guarantee that proper distinctions were always made or always expressed, or will always be made and worked out. Human finitude and fallibility must also always be taken into account with respect to even the best and noblest of people. But the ability of Paul and Luther to make such distinctions needs to be recognized as at least one important feature in the mental outlook and activity of them both.

Not all of Paul's associates seem to have shared this ability, at least to the same extent as he did. In the "Antioch episode" of Gal 2:11-14, for example, Paul recalls how he rebuked Peter for being "terribly wrong" in not seeing how eating separately with Jewish believers undercut a vitally important principle of the Christian gospel (vv 11-13)—and he bemoans the fact that "even Barnabas was led astray" by the "hypocrisy" of Peter and his friends (v 14). And many of Luther's associates, whether of the sixteenth century or today, have been, at times, perplexed about the flexibility of their hero in the context of his reforming zeal. But an important point with regard to both Paul and Luther is that they were able to distinguish between the central features of the Christian gospel, which must be proclaimed forthrightly and defended stoutly, and the *adiaphora* or matters of relative indifference, which are not to be confused with the central priorities and about which one can be flexible, even though one may have one's own preferences.

"What does it matter?," though posed somewhat rhetorically by Paul in Phil 1:18 (and echoed by Luther in his statement "It doesn't matter!"), is a question of importance for the proclamation of the Christian gospel and the course of the Christian mission. For Paul and for Luther, some things mattered dearly, for they stemmed from and expressed the heart of the Christian message. Other matters, however, could be considered *adiaphora*—that is, matters of concern for the day on which one needed to make decisions appropriate for the day, but not matters of eternal significance or abiding importance. And it needs to be the prayer of the church collectively and Christians individually today to ask God for such a gift of discernment: "Lord, teach us to be able to discern between the central priorities of the gospel and the *adiaphora* of our day—to be forthright in the former and conciliatory in the latter!"

SELECT BIBLIOGRAPHY

Barrett, C. Kingsley. *A Commentary on the Second Epistle to the Corinthians.* BNTC / HNTC. London: Black; New York: Harper, 1973.

Betz, Hans Dieter. *Galatians: A Commentary on Paul's Letter to the Churches in Galatia.* Hermeneia. Philadelphia: Fortress, 1979.

Bruce, Frederic F. *The Epistle to the Galatians: A Commentary on the Greek Text.* NIGTC. Grand Rapids: Eerdmans, 1982.

Burton, Ernest deWitt. *A Critical and Exegetical Commentary on the Epistle to the Galatians.* ICC. Edinburgh: T. & T. Clark, 1921.

Caird, George B. *Paul's Letters from Prison: Ephesians, Philippians, Colossians, Philemon.* NCB. Oxford: University Press, 1976.

Dunn, James D. G. *The Theology of Paul's Letter to the Galatians*. Cambridge: Cambridge University Press, 1993.

Fee, Gordon D. *Paul's Letter to the Philippians*. NICNT. Grand Rapids: Eerdmans, 1995.

Furnish, Victor Paul. *2 Corinthians*. AB. New York: Doubleday, 1984.

Harris, Murray J. *2 Corinthians*. EBC. Grand Rapids: Zondervan, 1976.

Hawthorne, Gerald F. *Philippians*. WBC. Dallas: Word, 1983.

Héring, Jean. *The Second Epistle of Saint Paul to the Corinthians*, trans. A. W. Heathcote and P. J. Allcock. London: Epworth, 1967.

Lightfoot, Joseph B. *Saint Paul's Epistle to the Galatians*. London: Macmillan, 1865; 10th. ed. 1890.

——. *Saint Paul's Epistle to the Philippians*. London: Macmillan, 1881.

Longenecker, Richard N. *Galatians*. WBC. Dallas: Word, 1990.

Martin, Ralph P. *The Epistle of Paul to the Philippians*. TNTC. London: Tyndale, 1959.

——. *2 Corinthians*. WBC. Dallas: Word, 1986.

Matera, Frank J. *Galatians*. SP. Collegeville: Liturgical Press, 1992.

Mussner, Franz. *Der Galaterbrief*. Freiburg: Herder, 1974.

O'Brien, Peter T. *The Epistle to the Philippians*. NIGTC. Grand Rapids: Eerdmans, 1991.

Thrall, Margaret E. *A Critical and Exegetical Commentary on the Second Epistle to the Corintians*. ICC. 2 vols. Edinburgh: T. & T. Clark, 1994, 1998.

9

THE NATURE OF PAUL'S EARLY ESCHATOLOGY

It is fairly common today to explain the development of New Testament thought along the lines of an early fixation on the future and progressive shifts brought about by the parousia's delay.[1] On such a view, it was apocalyptic eschatology that dominated Paul's outlook in his early days, while soteriology, christology, ecclesiology and ethics came to assume importance only later. Few scholars, of course, lay out Paul's thought quite so explicitly as that. Yet it is something like that which has become fairly fixed in the minds of many.

In what follows it is not our purpose to deny that eschatology was a major factor in Paul's thought—either in a temporal sense or as signifying more a depth dimension; either in his pre-Christian or his Christian understanding; either in his earlier or his later Christian theology. Nor are we desirous to mount an attack against the concept of development in Paul, so as to deny that his earlier eschatological expressions were more influenced by apocalyptic imagery than they were later, or that his earlier eschatological expectations were more dominated by an imminent (in the sense of immediate) parousia than they were later, or that his earlier teaching on the subject was more elemental than it was later—though, admittedly, such development views are not as popular today as they once were. Both "eschatology" and "development" are, I believe, so basic to an understanding of Paul that I want to state clearly at the outset of this chapter that my purpose has nothing whatsoever to do with setting them aside. Elsewhere I have dealt in a preliminary fashion with the concept of development in

---

[1] E.g., E. Käsemann: "Ever since the eschatological understanding of the New Testament replaced the idealistic interpretation, we can and must determine the various phrases of earliest Christian history by means of the original imminent expectation of the parousia, its modifications and its final extinction" (*New Testament Questions*, 236-37).

Pauline thought.[2] Here all that I want to do is to consider the nature of Paul's early eschatology, principally in order to clarify the essence of his earliest Christian convictions and to identify more precisely the starting point for his Christian theology.

1. *A Brief History of Discussion*

Johannes Weiss in 1892 first proposed the importance of eschatology for the New Testament,[3] and his discovery has been built on in many ways since. Albert Schweitzer capitalized on it to argue his thesis of "Thoroughgoing Eschatology" (or, "Consistent Eschatology") in which Jewish apocalypticism is seen as the major ideological background for Jesus and his earliest followers, to the exclusion of almost all other features in the mosaic of Judaism in that day.[4] Thus for Schweitzer, Jesus was "simply the culminating manifestation of Jewish apocalyptic thought";[5] and Paul—though eventually brought to positions more soteriological, christological, ecclesiological and ethical in nature—was similarly influenced, so that Jewish apocalypticism must be seen as the matrix not only for his earliest Christian convictions but also for all later developments in his thought.[6]

Rudolph Bultmann also built on the foundations laid by Weiss and rooted Jesus' message in "the historical context of Jewish expectations about the end of the world and God's new future," particularly in those expectations of sectarian Judaism as "primarily documented by the *apocalyptic* literature"[7]—though, contra Schweitzer, with "signifi-

---

[2] Cf. R. N. Longenecker, "On the Concept of Development in Pauline Thought," in *Perspectives on Evangelical Theology*, ed. K. S. Kantzer and S. N. Gundry (Grand Rapids: Baker, 1979), 195-207.

[3] J. Weiss, *Die Predigt Jesu vom Reiche Gottes* (Göttingen: Vandenhoeck & Ruprecht, 1892; 2nd ed. 1902); ET *Jesus' Proclamation of the Kingdom of God*, trans. R. H. Hiers and D. L. Holland (Philadelphia: Fortress, 1971).

[4] A. Schweitzer, *The Quest of the Historical Jesus*, trans. W. Montgomery (London: Black, 1910), 222-401. See also *idem, The Mystery of the Kingdom of God*; *idem, The Mysticism of Paul the Apostle*; *idem, Psychiatric Study of Jesus*, trans. C. R. Joy (Boston: Beacon, 1948); *idem, The Kingdom of God and Primitive Christianity*, trans. L. A. Garrard (London: Black, 1968).

[5] Cf. Schweitzer, *Quest of the Historical Jesus*, 365ff.

[6] Schweitzer, *Mysticism of Paul the Apostle*, 52ff.

[7] R. Bultmann, *Theology of the New Testament*, 2 vols., trans. K. Grobel (New York: Scribner, 1951, 1955), 1.4 (italics his). See also *idem, Primitive Christianity*

cant reduction of detail" and "not in its nationalistic form."[8] As for Paul, he argued that Paul's theology must be distinguished from Jesus' preaching and so seen as "a new structure."[9] Nonetheless, Bultmann pointed to a similar combination of monotheism and eschatology in Paul's earliest thought (citing Acts 17:31 and 1 Thess 1:9-10) and interpreted Paul *de facto* in terms of what has been called "Proleptic Eschatology."[10] Likewise, Ernst Käsemann, to mention only one prominent Bultmannian, lays heavy emphasis on the eschatological in Paul and views much else that follows as not only later developments but also later deviations—that is, as the product of "Early Catholicism,"[11] which is a term used by Roman Catholics with approval but by Käsemann and many Protestants pejoratively.

C. H. Dodd, too, contributed to the rise of this attitude we are describing, for—though in many ways opposed to both Schweitzer and Bultmann—Dodd's "Realized Eschatology," particularly in its distinctions between an early futuristically oriented Paul and a later "realized" Paul, parallels in large measure the pattern of development set out by Schweitzer and assumed by Bultmann.[12] Thus, though (contra Schweitzer) "Paul's thought was indeed never wholly eschatological nor did it ever become purely mystical,"[13] it began, Dodd insisted, within the apocalyptic categories of Second Temple Judaism—as represented particularly by *1 Enoch, 4 Ezra* and *2 Baruch*—and only after an eschatological adjustment brought about by a serious illness at Troas was it transformed into the more mature theology of 2 Corinthians 1–9, Romans, and the Prison Epistles.[14]

---

in its Contemporary Setting, 86-93; *idem, History and Eschatology* (Edinburgh: University Press, 1957), 29-37.

[8] Bultmann, *Theology*, 1.5-11; *idem, Primitive Christianity*, 87-88.

[9] Bultmann, *Theology*, 1.189.

[10] *Ibid.*, 1.74-79; *idem, History and Eschatology*, 38-55.

[11] Cf. Käsemann, *New Testament Questions*, 108-37, 236-51; *idem, Perspectives on Paul*, 123-24.

[12] Cf. C. H. Dodd, "The Mind of Paul: Change and Development," *BJRL* 18 (1934) 3-44; repr. *idem, New Testament Studies* (Manchester: Manchester University Press, 1953), 83-128.

[13] Dodd, "Mind of Paul: Change and Development," 31; repr. *idem, New Testament Studies*, 113.

[14] Dodd, "Mind of Paul: Change and Development," 27ff.; repr. *idem, New Testament Studies*, 109ff.

Similarly, Charles Buck and Greer Taylor, explicating a stance attributable basically to John Knox, laid out a developmental understanding of Paul, which began with an "extremely simple" eschatology that was "completely consistent with current Jewish apocalyptic," and then went on to depict how "Paul departed further and further from this position as the years passed."[15] And John C. Hurd has committed himself to the task of spelling out the nature of this early "fervent apocalypticism" in Paul's thought—by means of a reconstruction of what must have been the content of Paul's "previous letter" (cf. 1 Cor 5:9) and analyses of the Thessalonian correspondence (particularly 2 Thessalonians)—and detailing the stages of his departure from it,[16] thereby combining in explicit fashion the development interests of Charles Buck and Greer Taylor (his professors) and the chronology of John Knox (the professor of Buck and Taylor).

The extent to which such an eschatological view of Paul has become ingrained in contemporary New Testament scholarship is illustrated by E. P. Sanders's phrase "Participationist Eschatology" as capturing the essence of Paul's Christian thought.[17] In opposition to any view that would see Paul's basic Christian conviction and the beginning feature of his theology as being the Messiahship of Jesus, Sanders insists that Paul's "dominating conviction" and the "starting point" was "that the end is at hand, that Christ is Lord and that only those who belong to the Lord will be saved on the Day of the Lord"—directly countering, thereby, W. D. Davies' view that "Fulfilled Messianism" was central to Paul and should be seen as having characterized his thought.[18] Indeed, Sanders recognizes soteriological and christological themes in Paul's letters as well (as the adjective "participationist" is meant to signal), and he even suggests that there are elements in those letters that would later give rise to "a new form

---

[15] C. Buck and G. Taylor, *Saint Paul: A Study of the Development of his Thought* (New York: Scribner's Sons, 1969), 12-13.

[16] J. C. Hurd, *The Origin of I Corinthians* (New York: Seabury, 1965); see also *idem*, "Pauline Chronology and Pauline Theology," in *Christian History and Interpretation: Studies Presented to John Knox*, ed. W. R. Farmer, C. F. D. Moule, and R. R. Niebuhr (Cambridge: Cambridge University Press, 1967), 225-48.

[17] Cf. Sanders, *Paul and Palestinian Judaism*, 431-556; esp. 552. See also Beker, *Paul the Apostle*; *idem, Paul's Apocalyptic Gospel*.

[18] Sanders, *ibid.*, 514-15.

of covenantal nomism" in the church.[19] But the stress in Sanders's understanding of Paul is on eschatology as the substructure for all of the Christian apostle's thinking, whatever other features may have become incorporated into his theology from his own experience, from Christian tradition, and from an all-pervading hellenistic environment.

2. *An Analysis of the Eschatology of the Thessalonian Letters*

It is in the Thessalonian letters that we have the earliest explicit evidence as to the nature of Paul's early eschatology, and therefore it is with those letters that we must here be principally concerned. John Hurd's attempt to show that the "previous letter" to Corinth that is referred to in 1 Cor 5:9, the basic content of which he believes can be recovered by his own type of "reader response" to what Paul says in 1 Corinthians, contained the same type of eschatology as the Thessalonian letters (particularly so-called 2 Thessalonians) is inter-esting, informative and suggestive.[20] But it remains unproven. And even if so, the Thessalonian correspondence antedates that "previous letter" to Corinth and so must take precedence over whatever may be circumstantially inferred from the Corinthian correspondence regard-ing some earlier position held by the apostle—and which, somewhat unwittingly, the apostle argues against. Likewise, a "South Galatian" view of the provenance of Galatians, which would allow for Galatians to be seen as the earliest extant Pauline letter, need not be invoked here. Even if Galatians is earlier than the Thessalonian letters, as I believe (see my *Galatians* commentary [Dallas: Word, 1990], lxi-lxxxviii), its few allusions to eschatology (cf. Gal 1:4; 6:10) cannot be taken as a basis for the treatment of the theme in the Thessalonian letters or as detailing in any adequate fashion the nature of Paul's early eschatological thought. At best, Galatians on this matter can only be considered supplementary to the Thessalonian letters.

It is, therefore, to the Thessalonian letters that we must turn when asking about Paul's early eschatology. And in those letters, three matters are especially significant and need to be highlighted—parti-cularly since they are frequently overlooked.

The Place of Eschatology in the Structure of the Thessalonian Letters

[19] Sanders, *ibid.*, 513.
[20] Cf. Hurd, *Origin of I Corinthians.*

It is frequently taken for granted that eschatology is the dominant theme of Paul's Thessalonian letters and was the apostle's major concern when writing. For example, William Neil says of 1 Thess 4:13-18: "This important passage ... gives the epistle its characteristic note."[21] Certainly 2 Thess 2:1-12 comprises the main discussion of that letter. Further, the assumption of the dominance of eschatology in the Thessalonian letters is strengthened by reversing the canonical order of the letters, with the first letter (our present 2 Thessalonians) seen as presenting a cruder apocalypticism and the second letter (our 1 Thessalonians) a more mature apocalypticism. Likewise, the fact that Paul refers directly in 2 Thess 2:5 to having taught his new converts about eschatology when he was first with them ("Don't you remember that when I was with you I used to tell you these things?") and alludes in 1 Thess 5:1-2 to such instruction ("Now, brothers and sisters, about times and dates we do not need to write you, for you know very well that the day of the Lord will come like a thief in the night") suggests that this topic was of importance to him and that he viewed it as of importance for them as well.

Nonetheless, though parousia references rest easily on Paul's lips in praising his converts and in praying for them (cf. 1 Thess 2:19; 3:13; 5:23), an analysis of 1 Thessalonians indicates that eschatology was not the focus of Paul's concern when writing and does not represent the main purpose of the letter. It may be somewhat extreme to call 1 Thess 4:13–5:11 "simply one paraenetic section among others," as A. L. Moore does.[22] But Moore is certainly correct to point out that the passage "is not the high peak" of the letter.[23] What concerned Paul principally in writing 1 Thessalonians was what he speaks of in chapters two and three: a defense of his and his companions' conduct while at Thessalonica, against certain charges made against them, and a message of encouragement to his converts who were facing some type of persecution. His discussions of ethics in 4:1-12 and of

---

[21] W. Neil, *Commentary on I and II Thessalonians* (London: Hodder & Stoughton, 1950), 89; though note also Neil's shorter *St Paul's Epistles to the Thessalonians* (London: SCM, 1957), 83ff., where a similar statement ("the same question gives the Thessalonian correspondence a characteristically eschatological flavour") is appropriately tempered.

[22] A. L. Moore, *The Parousia in the New Testament* (Leiden: Brill, 1966), 108; though Moore also insists, "It is not, however, unimportant" (*ibid.*).

[23] *Ibid.*

eschatology in 4:13–5:11 seem almost tacked on as afterthoughts, written in view of further concerns for those at Thessalonica.

And while some have argued that the canonical order should be reversed (e.g., Hugo Grotius in the seventeenth century; Johannes Weiss, T. W. Manson, and John C. Hurd spanning the twentieth century), most have concluded that 1 Thessalonians can be satisfactorily interpreted apart from any reliance on 2 Thessalonians and that 2 Thessalonians is best understood as having been written to clear up some misunderstanding about "the day of the Lord" that had arisen among the Thessalonian Christians after Paul's first letter to them—a misunderstanding that arose, as Paul states it, because of "some prophecy, report or letter supposed to have come from us, saying that the day of the Lord has already come" (2 Thess 2:2). The present order of the letters is, of course, no guarantee of their original order, since Paul's letters seem to have been arranged in the New Testament according to length, comparable to the arrangement of the sixty-three tractates of the Mishnah in their respective six Sedarim. Yet most scholars today, on the basis of internal phenomena that they believe cannot be explained otherwise, are convinced that the canonical order in this case is the correct historical order as well.[24]

Probably serving to signal the place of ethics and eschatology in the hierarchy of Paul's concerns at the time when he wrote 1 Thessalonians is the colloquial expression λοιπὸν οὖν, "finally then," that begins the paraenesis section of 4:1–5:22. In late Greek, as George Milligan has pointed out, λοιπόν served to do "little more than mark the transition to a new subject" and was "practically equivalent to an emphatic οὖν"—and "in modern Greek λοιπόν has displaced οὖν altogether."[25] Paul, however, appears to have used λοιπόν in the structure of his letters with slightly more significance than that. In 2 Thess 3:1, to cite a closely related example, he uses it (τὸ λοιπόν ... ἀδελφοί) to introduce a further series of exhortations that appear after his main discussion. In 2 Cor 13:11 he begins his final greetings (whether they are the final greetings of the "severe letter" of chapters 10–13 or the final greetings of the whole of 2 Corinthians) with the use of the expression (λοιπὸν ἀδελφοί). And in Phil 3:1 he introduces his exhortation to "rejoice in the Lord" by the same expression (τὸ λοιπόν, ἀδελφοί μου), then gets "carried away

---

[24] Cf., e.g., E. Best, *First and Second Epistles to the Thessalonians*, 42-45.
[25] G. Milligan, *Epistles to the Thessalonians*, 46.

by a word" (i.e., ὑμῖν δὲ ἀσφαλές, "it is a safeguard for you") into a denunciation of the Judaizers, a recounting of his own attitudes in contradistinction to theirs, and some further exhortations—and, then, *finally* (if we may be permitted to use the word ourselves) he comes back to his conclusion by the use in Phil 4:8 of the expression again (τὸ λοιπόν, ἀδελφοί). With such parallels, we agree with Alfred Plummer on the use of λοιπόν in 1 Thess 4:1: it "implies that a good deal has been said, but that the end has not been quite reached; and it seems to show that what follows was not the main purpose of the letter."[26]

The Basis for Eschatological Hope in the Thessalonian Letters

Contrary to the popular notion that christological thought was one of those compensatory features that arose among Christians as a result of eschatological disillusionment brought about by the parousia's delay, Paul's argument in the Thessalonian letters for the resurrection of believers, his exhortations to preparedness for Christ's coming, and even much of his imagery in describing that event rest firmly on a christological base. Rather than christology being derived from eschatology, the Thessalonian letters indicate that eschatological hope among the early Christians was based on a functional christology.

In 1 Thess 4:14 Paul states: "For if we believe that Jesus died and rose again, even so will God bring with him those who have fallen asleep through Jesus." Paul is here probably quoting an early confessional statement of the church (i.e., "Jesus died and rose again"), and drawing from that an implication of great importance for his Thessalonian converts.[27] The verb ἀνίστημι ("raise up," "erect") suggests that we should see here some type of early Christian confessional material, for Paul usually uses its synonym ἐγείρειν ("raise up," "erect"; about forty times and normally in the passive) when speaking himself about Christ's resurrection and the resurrection of Christians. The exceptions to this Pauline pattern are to be found where the apostle is quoting—that is, in Rom 15:12, citing Isa 11:10; 1 Cor 10:7, citing Exod 32:6; Eph 5:14, using Isa 26:19 and 60:1 in a proverbial manner; and later in this same section of 1 Thessalonians in 4:16, citing (as we will argue below) a "word of the Lord." Likewise,

---

[26] A. Plummer, *First Epistle to the Thessalonians*, 57.

[27] Cf. E. Best, *First and Second Epistles to the Thessalonians*, 186-88; see also my *New Wine into Fresh Wineskins*, 19, 58-60.

Paul's use of the single name "Jesus" supports the view that he is here quoting an early Christian confession, for usually he speaks of "Christ," "Christ Jesus" or "Jesus Christ"; only rarely of "Jesus" alone—in Rom 8:11; 2 Cor 4:14; 1 Thess 1:10 (which may be part of early Christian confessional material as well); and in the latter part of our verse here, in 1 Thess 4:14b, whose phraseology has probably been conditioned by the statement of 4:14a. Further, Paul's use of ὅτι ("that") lends support to the confessional nature of the statement as well (cf. the four confessional statements of 1 Cor 15:3-5a, each of which is so introduced).

But however the statement "Jesus died and rose again" received its present form, its content was certainly at the heart of all early Christian conviction and proclamation. And the point to be noted here is that the fact of Christ's resurrection is used by Paul in 1 Thessalonians 4 as the basis for confidence regarding the future of departed loved ones. Eschatological hope in one of Paul's earliest letters, therefore, is founded on a christological basis—not, of course, on a developed christology of an ontological variety, but on what may be called a functional christology that had to do with the fact of Christ's resurrection and Christians' firm belief in the same.

In 1 Thess 4:15 Paul says: "For this we tell you by the word of the Lord (ἐν λόγῳ κυρίου), that we who are alive, who remain till the coming of the Lord, will not precede those who have fallen asleep." Then he goes on in 4:16-17 to support his statement by what appears to be a quotation that in some way stems from Jesus. There is little question by his use of "Lord" elsewhere in 1 Thessalonians (e.g., 1:1, 3, 6, 8; 2:15, 19; 3:8, 11-13; 4:1) and in the latter half of 4:15 here that Paul means by "the word of the Lord" a word from Jesus. Our problems with this expression have to do, rather, with (1) identifying from whence Paul derived this "word" or logion, (2) delineating its extent in the verses here, and (3) reconstructing its original form.

Joachim Jeremias has been the most prominent advocate of the view that "the word of the Lord" in this verse refers to an *agraphon*—that is, a word of the historical Jesus that was known in the church's tradition but not included in any of the Gospels, either canonical or sectarian.[28] Others have argued that it arose from a saying of Jesus now incorporated into Matt 24:30-31 or John 6:39-40, or that

---

[28] Cf. J. Jeremias, "Isolated Sayings of the Lord," 1.87-88; *idem, Unknown Sayings of Jesus*, 80-83.

it was an inference Paul made from Jesus' words now recorded in Matt 22:32 ("He [God] is not the God of the dead but of the living"), or that Paul was quoting from an early form of the Olivet Discourse. Of late, many have seen this as a revelatory word of the exalted Jesus, given to the church through one of its prophets—perhaps even by Paul himself.[29]

Because of the allusions to the teachings of the historical Jesus in 1 Thess 5:1-11 and 2 Thess 2:1-12 (which I will refer to below), I tend to side with Jeremias on the question of provenance and to believe that Paul was doing something similar here as he was there—that is, reaching back to the words of Jesus preserved in the church's tradition, many of which would be later incorporated into our canonical Gospels, though evidently not this one. On the more debated questions regarding the extent of the "word" or logion in Paul's letter here and its original form, I take it that it is probably contained in 1 Thess 4:16-17 and originally existed much as we have it now in those verses—except, perhaps, for the phrase "that the Lord himself' (ὅτι αὐτὸς ὁ κύριος), and certainly for the evident Pauline insertions of "in Christ" (ἐν Χριστῷ) and "we" (ἡμεῖς).

But whatever answers may be given to questions of provenance, extent and original form, the extremely important point to note for our purposes is that when Paul ventures beyond the mere fact of the resurrection and begins to speak more particularly of events and relationships, he does so on the basis of a "word" of Jesus. In 1 Thess 4:15-17, therefore, as in 4:14, eschatological hope is based on what one thinks of Christ Jesus, and not vice versa.

Further, in the exhortations to preparedness of 1 Thess 5:1-11, Paul seems to have various eschatological teachings of Jesus in mind, as later incorporated into the canonical Synoptic Gospels and Acts. His words of 5:1, "about times and dates, brothers and sisters, you have no need that we write to you," may well be an allusion to Jesus' words of Mark 13:32 ("No one knows about that day or hour, not even the angels in heaven, nor the Son, but only the Father") and those of Acts 1:7 ("It is not for you to know the times or dates the Father has set by his own authority"). His words of 5:2, "for you know very well that the day of the Lord will come like a thief in the night," recalls Jesus' imagery of Matt 24:43-44 ("But understand this: If the owner of the

---

[29] Cf. J. G. Davies, "The Genesis of Belief in an Imminent Parousia," *JTS* 14 (1963) 104-06; E. Best, *First and Second Epistles to the Thessalonians*, 189-93.

house had known at what time of night the thief was coming, he would have kept watch and would not have let his house be broken into. So you also must be ready, because the Son of Man will come at an hour when you do not expect him"). And his figure of birth pangs in 5:3, "as labor pains on a pregnant woman," may reflect Jesus imagery of Matt 24:8—which, of course, was in line with the Jewish doctrine of "Messianic Travail" in the final eschatological days.

Even 2 Thess 2:1-4 seems to reflect Jesus' apocalyptic teaching in the Olivet Discourse—particularly its discussion of "the apostasy" (ἡ ἀποστασία) and "the man of lawlessness" (ὁ ἄνθρωπος τῆς ἀνομίας) in verses 3-4, which appears to be Paul's interpretive elaboration of Daniel's "the abomination that causes desolation" (τὸ βδέλυγμα τῆς ἐρημώσεως) referred to by Jesus in Mark 13:14 and Matt 24:15 (cf. Dan 9:27; 11:31; 12:11). Paul's claim that "when I was with you I used to tell you these things" (2 Thess 2:5) suggests that such an eschatological presentation was part of his evangelistic preaching at Thessalonica—even to Gentiles who had no knowledge of Daniel's prophecy—and it is not too difficult to believe that his preaching at this point had Jesus' Olivet Discourse in mind. Indeed, so related are Paul's words of 2 Thessalonians 2 to Jesus' Olivet Discourse, that not only can they be taken as an interpretive elaboration of Jesus' teaching, but also, as H. A. A. Kennedy long ago insisted, " It is no exaggeration to say that Matt. xxiv is the most instructive commentary on the chapter before us."[30]

In sum, therefore, however we spell out the specifics of the case, there is a fairly clear indication in the Thessalonian letters that when Paul spoke about the fact of the Christian's resurrection hope, about events and relationships having to do with that hope, and when he exhorted his converts to preparedness, he did so on the basis of Jesus' resurrection and teachings. So it may be claimed that eschatology for Paul in this early stage of his ministry was rooted in what may be called a functional christology.

---

[30] H. A. A. Kennedy, *St Paul's Conceptions of the Last Things* (London: Hodder & Stoughton, 1904), 56.

The Purpose of the Eschatological Presentations in the Thessalonian Letters

To hear some scholars speak about the eschatology of the Thessalonian letters, one would think that Paul's purpose was mainly didactic—that is, to teach and reinforce apocalyptic doctrines about the future. But Paul's purpose was not so much to enunciate doctrine as to encourage and comfort distraught converts about the fate of their deceased Christian relatives and friends. He writes as a pastor rather than a theologian—though, of course, as a good pastor he gives theological reasons for his words of consolation and encouragement.

In 1 Thessalonians Paul deals with the question, Will Christians who have died before Christ returns be at a disadvantage compared to those who are still alive? And then he exhorts his addressees to preparedness. In concluding both the answer to the question and the exhortation that follows, Paul says: "Therefore encourage one another" (ὥστε / διὸ παρακαλεῖτε ἀλλήλους, 4:18; 5:11). In 2 Thessalonians he deals with the false notion, which was evidently circulating among believers at Thessalonica as an interpretation of Paul's teaching and was disturbing many, that "the day of the Lord has already come" (2 Thess 2:2). And his conclusion to that discussion highlights his pastoral concern there as well: "May our Lord Jesus Christ himself and God our Father, who loved us and by his grace gave us eternal encouragement (παράκλησιν αἰωνίαν) and good hope, encourage your hearts (παρακαλέσαι ὑμῶν τὰς καρδίας) and strengthen you in every good deed and word" (2 Thess 2:16-17).

The form of Paul's eschatological teaching, without a doubt, is apocalyptic. But the content is pastoral in its message of encouragement and is prophetic in urging Christians to be active here and now for God. While 1 Thess 4:13-18 lays out the rudiments of Christian eschatology in an apocalyptic fashion, its purpose is not to teach a system of speculative eschatology but to comfort alarmed believers who were worried about their deceased relatives and friends missing out at Christ's return. And while 2 Thess 2:1-12 is even more apocalyptic than 1 Thess 4:13-18 in some of its expressions, its argument is essentially negative: that (1) if "the day of the Lord" had already come, the Christians at Thessalonica would be able by hindsight to identify "the apostasy" and "the man of lawlessness" (2:3-4) spoken about in Christian tradition and by Paul in his earlier preaching among them (2:5), but (2) since they can't, it hasn't! This is not the kind of presentation one finds in the apocalyptic writings of Second Temple Judaism. Rather, here is a Christian pastor and prophet speaking in the forms of the day, but for whom apocalyptic speculation, while accepted as legitimate, was not kerygmatically foundational but pastorally supportive.[31]

3. *Conclusion*

What, then, can be said about the nature of Paul's early eschatology from a study of the Thessalonian letters? Admittedly, much more could and should be considered in any full treatment of the subject. I have here attempted only to highlight three significant matters that are frequently overlooked. But if I have been anywhere close to the mark in my treatment of these matters, I believe we must say, in opposition to many presentations to the contrary, that Paul's basic Christian conviction and the starting point for all this Christian theology was not apocalypticism but functional christology—that is, that his commitment was not first of all to a program or some timetable of events but to a person: Jesus the Messiah.[32]

Commitment to Jesus as God's Messiah, of course, would have had profound eschatological ramifications for any Jew. Certainly it did for Saul of Tarsus. And the evidence from Paul's letters suggests that reflection on God's working in Jesus' ministry, death and resurrection continued to have profound effects on Paul's understanding of eschatology through his life, as did that developing eschatology on his christological perspectives. Christology and eschatology, therefore, must be seen as having been always reciprocally related in Paul's thinking—with both being dominantly functional in nature at first and both being developed more fully during the course of the apostle's Christian life and ministry. But rather than thinking of Paul's early

[31] Cf. G. E. Ladd, "Why Not Prophetic-Apocalyptic?," 192-200.

[32] Cf. W. C. van Unnik: "Has the delay of the *parousia* really wrought that havoc that it is sometimes supposed to have done, or did the early Christians react differently from the way modern scholars would have done? In the light of the history of early Christianity this effect of the *Parousieverzögerung* is highly overrated. The faith of the early Christians did not rest on a date but on the work of Christ" ("Luke–Acts, a Storm Center in Contemporary Scholarship," in *Studies in Luke–Acts*, ed. L. E. Keck and J. L. Martyn [Nashville: Abingdon, 1966], 28).

thought as essentially an enthusiastic eschatology, which underwent a series of compensatory shifts due to the delay of the parousia and various factors confronted in his missionary travels, the Thessalonian letters indicate that his early eschatology was rooted in a functional christology wherein what Jesus did and said were the controlling factors. Thus it must be insisted that the expression "Fulfilled Messianism"—with full recognition of the importance of the eschatological adjective, yet with an emphasis on the christological noun[33]—captures the essence of Paul's thought better than any other.

SELECT BIBLIOGRAPHY

Beker, J. Christiaan. *Paul the Apostle: The Triumph of God in Life and Thought.* Philadelphia: Fortress, 1980.
——. *Paul's Apocalyptic Gospel: The Coming Triumph of God.* Philadelphia: Fortress, 1982.
Best, Ernest. *A Commentary on the First and Second Epistles to the Thessalonians.* BNTC / HNTC. London: Black; New York: Harper, 1972.
Bultmann, Rudolf. *Primitive Christianity in its Contemporary Setting*, trans. R. H. Fuller. London: Thames & Hudson, 1956.
Davies, W. D. *Paul and Rabbinic Judaism. Some Rabbinic Elements in Pauline Theology.* London: SPCK, 1948, 1955[2], 1970[3]; Philadelphia: Fortress, 1980[4]; see esp. "Preface to the Fourth Edition," xxi-xxxviii.
Donfried, Karl P. and I. Howard Marshall. *The Theology of the Shorter Pauline Letters* [Donfried on 1 & 2 Thessalonians; Marshall on Philippians and Philemon]. Cambridge: Cambridge University Press, 1993.
Jeremias, Joachim. "Isolated Sayings of the Lord," in *New Testament Apocrypha*, 2 vols. Ed. E. Hennecke, W. Schneemelcher; trans. R. McL. Wilson. London: Lutterworth, 1963, 1.87-88.
——. *Unknown Sayings of Jesus*, trans. R. H. Fuller. London: SPCK, 1964. 80-83.
Käsemann, Ernst. *New Testament Questions of Today*, trans. W. J. Montague. London: SCM, 1969.
——. *Perspectives on Paul*, trans. M. Kohl. London: SCM, 1971.
Ladd, George Eldon. "Why Not Prophetic-Apocalyptic?" *JBL* 76 (1957) 192-200.
Longenecker, Richard N. *New Wine into Fresh Wineskins: Contextualizing the Early Christian Confessions.* Peabody: Hendrickson, 1999.
Marshall, I. Howard. *1 & 2 Thessalonians.* NCBC. Grand Rapids: Eerdmans, 1983.

---

[33] Cf. W. D. Davies, *Paul and Rabbinic Judaism, passim* and "Conclusion." See also his "Preface to the Fourth Edition" (1980[4]), esp. xxix-xxxviii.

Milligan, George. *St Paul's Epistles to the Thessalonians*. London: Macmillan, 1908.

Moore, Arthur L. *The Parousia in the New Testament*. Leiden: Brill, 1966.

Morris, Leon. *The Epistles of Paul to the Thessalonians: An Introduction and Commentary*. NICNT. Grand Rapids: Eerdmans, 1984, rev. ed. 1991.

Plummer, Alfred. *A Commentary on St Paul's First Epistle to the Thessalonians*. London: Robert Scott, 1918.

Sanders, E. P. *Paul and Palestinian Judaism: A Comparison of Patterns of Religion*. Philadelphia: Fortress, 1977.

Schweitzer, Albert. *The Mystery of the Kingdom of God*, trans. W. Lowrie. London: Black, 1914.

———. *The Mysticism of Paul the Apostle*, trans. W. Montgomery. London: Black, 1931.

Wanamaker, Charles A. *The Epistles to the Thessalonians: A Commentary on the Greek Text*. NIGTC. Grand Rapids: Eerdmans, 1990.

"GOOD LUCK ON YOUR RESURRECTION"
Beth She'arim and Paul on the Resurrection of the Dead

That there existed a wide diversity of opinion within Second Temple Judaism regarding the fate of the dead—particularly on matters pertaining to the two main conceptual axes of "immortality" and "resurrection"—is today axiomatic. Oscar Cullmann, while laudable in his explication of Paul, considerably oversimplified the first-century situation when he argued that Greeks held to "the immortality of the soul" whereas Jews believed in "the resurrection of the dead."[1] Rather, views regarding the state of the dead were in flux, with implications and significances being variously spelled out. Nonetheless, there did develop during the first and second centuries CE certain distinctive doctrines regarding the resurrection of the dead. These I would like to highlight, citing in particular data from the tombs at Beth She'arim and the letters of Paul.

1. A Summation of Diverse Treatments

Immortality doctrines within Second Temple Judaism were rampant, with some clothed in resurrection language, others in astral imagery, others in phraseology that paralleled ideas about reincarnation and the transmigration of souls, and still others in distinctly Grecian anthropological forms of expression. Yet convictions regarding "the resurrection of the dead" came into greater focus and arose more and more into prominence during this time as well. It is impossible to deal in brief compass with all of the issues and statements of pertinence from this period, but at least the following data needs to be noted.

On the Immortality of the Soul
In "The Apocalypse of Weeks" of *1 Enoch* 91–93 and "The Epistle of Enoch" of *1 Enoch* 94–104 (both written in pre-Maccabean times) there appears, for example, an amalgam of terms and ideas that have

---

[1] O. Cullmann, "Immortality of the Soul or Resurrection of the Dead" (1955/56), 5-36; *idem, Immortality of the Soul or Resurrection of the Dead* (1958).

to do with "sleep" as a locution for death, "souls" or "spirits" as disembodied personal beings, resurrection language, and astral imagery (e.g., *1 Enoch* 91:10, "Then the righteous one shall arise from his sleep, and the wise one shall arise"; see also 92:3-4; 100:5; 103:3-4; 104:1-4)—with such a mixture evidently drawn from a blending of Dan 12:2-3 and Greek anthropology. *Jubilees* 23:30-31 speaks of the "healing" of God's "servants," who will "rise up and see great peace" (a national restoration?) and to whom it is promised that "their bones shall rest in the earth, but their spirits shall have much joy." And in the Qumran *Psalms of Thanksgiving* we read not only of "souls" existing in the "perfidy of the flesh" (e.g., *1QH* 1.20-21; 2.20; 5.29-30, 34-39) but also of "souls" or "spirits" existing in the afterlife (e.g., *1QH* 6.29-35; 11.10-14).

Josephus speaks of the Pharisees as holding to a doctrine of resurrection, but describes their belief in terms of the immortality of the soul tinged with a distinctly reincarnation flavoring:

> Every soul, they maintain, is imperishable, but the soul of the good alone passes into another body, while the souls of the wicked suffer eternal punishment (*War* 2.163; written about 75-79 CE).

> They believe that souls have power to survive death and that there are rewards and punishments under the earth for those who have led lives of virtue or vice: eternal imprisonment is the lot of evil souls, while the good souls receive an easy passage to a new life (*Antiq.* 18.14; written about 93–94 CE).

Perhaps, as often argued, Josephus was here slanting his words so as to be understood by his Roman and Greek audiences, using their concepts more than his own or those of the Pharisees. Yet since in *War* 3.362-82 he speaks about differences between the soul and the body in qualitative terms (they are "fond companions," with the body being "mortal, composed of perishable matter, but the soul lives for ever, immortal: it is a portion of the Deity housed in our bodies") and reasserts an immortality doctrine for the righteous at death ("Their souls, remaining spotless and obedient, are allotted the most holy place in heaven, whence, in the revolution of the ages, they return to find in chaste bodies a new habitation"), it is more likely that such statements reflect, in fact, Josephus's own early Essene apocalyptic understanding, and that he retained such views throughout his life.[2]

---

[2] Cf. S. Mason, *Flavius Josephus on the Pharisees*; *idem*, *Josephus and the New Testament*, esp. 36-40, 132-35, 142-43.

Even more distinctly Grecian are the first five chapters of the *Wisdom of Solomon* (probably written some time during the mid-first century BCE, though perhaps as late as 10 CE), which depict the *summum bonum* of a righteous life as being the immortality of the disembodied soul immediately after death, without any reference to a resurrection.[3] For example, in contrasting the situations of the wicked and the righteous at death, 2:22-24 states that although the wicked were created for immortality, they have lost eternal life and now face only death; but of the righteous, 3:1-4 states:

> But the souls of the righteous are in the hand of God, and no torment will ever touch them. In the eyes of the foolish they seemed to have died, and their departure was thought to be an affliction, and their going from us to be their destruction. But they are at peace. For though in the sight of men they were punished, their hope is full of immortality.

The death of the righteous, therefore, marks the beginning of a better, non-physical existence "in the hand of God" and "at peace"—an existence where the hope of immortality will be realized, whether that immortality was understood as an inherent, pre-existent quality of the soul or as a reward from God for righteousness, or both.

Likewise in *4 Maccabees*, which is a philosophical treatise on "Inspired Reason" (probably written at the close of the first century or during the first two decades of the second century CE), a doctrine of the immortality of the soul dominates, with no reference to a resurrection either spiritual or physical. Even the Maccabean martyrs, who are cited as examples of enthusiastic devotion to their faith, are not portrayed as looking forward toward a future resurrection (as in *2 Macc* 7:1-41; 14:37-46; cf. 12:43-45), but depicted as passing immediately at death into the bliss of eternal life (cf. 10:15; 13:17; 17:4, 18; 18:23)—with the wicked punished immediately at death with eternal torment (cf. 9:8, 32; 10:11, 15; 12:19; 13:15; 18:5, 22). And such a view of death as release for the righteous to the immortality of eternal life appears in such later Jewish apocalyptic

---

[3] Recension B of *Wisdom of Solomon* 7:16 reads: "You will be taken up into the heavens, while your body remains on earth until seven thousand ages are fulfilled; for then all flesh will be raised." Recension B, however, is widely regarded as the less reliable recension, and so this resurrection reference should probably be seen as a later addition that attempted to bring the eschatology of *Wisdom of Solomon* into the orbit of later orthodox Jewish thought.

passages as *2 Enoch* 22:8-10 (cf. 42:3-5; 65:7-8), *Apocalypse of Moses* (or, *The Life of Adam and Eve*) 32:4, and at various places in *The Testaments of the Twelve Patriarchs*, *The Testament of Abraham*, and *The Testament of Job*.

On the Resurrection of the Dead

On the other hand, *1 Enoch* 22, which is the major pre-Maccabean passage on Sheol, contains allusions to "the spirits/souls of the righteous" who will experience a resurrection (v 9) and to "sinners" who lived prosperously and without punishment during their lives being raised so as to receive the judgment that they escaped in life (vv 10-11)—with it being said directly that thoroughly wicked and despicable people (i.e., "sinners and perfect criminals") will not rise (v 13). And while the resurrection of "the righteous" in 22:9 may be seen in purely spiritual terms and that of "sinners" in 22:10-11 is described as a "retribution of their spirits," the fact that elsewhere in "The Book of the Watchers" (*1 Enoch* 6–36) the righteous are said to be destined to eat of the tree of life (25:4-6) and to enjoy abundant life in the messianic kingdom on a purified earth (10:16-22), with Jerusalem and the Temple as its center (25:5), seems to suggest that a physical resurrection of some type is in view.

Likewise, "The Dream Visions" of *1 Enoch* 83–90 (probably written sometime around 165–161 BCE) come to a climax in 90:28-42 in a vision of "all those sheep [i.e., the righteous within Israel] that have been destroyed and dispersed, and all the beasts of the field and the birds of the sky," being "gathered together" at the end of history into a "new house" (90:33)—with, then, "a snow-white cow" born and all the righteous "transformed" into "snow-white cows" (90:37-38). The vision suggests a resurrection and gathering of righteous Jews into an earthly messianic kingdom, with some type of transformation of the righteous then taking place. And it implies that Gentiles who have survived the judgment will be brought in and transformed as well (cf. 89:10-27, 42-43, 49, 55-58, 65-68; 90:2-19). Although the vision of 90:28-42 is powerful in its imagery and dramatic in its hope, its content is exceedingly difficult to unpack.

Explicit statements regarding the resurrection of the dead are to be found in *2 Maccabees*, which was written in the last decade of the second century BCE (perhaps about 106 BCE): in 7:1-41 (the martyrdom of the seven brothers and their mother); in 12:43-45 (the action of Judas Maccabeus on behalf of certain of his fallen soldiers, which he did "bearing in mind the resurrection"); and in 14:37-46 (the martyrdom of Razis, an elder and esteemed patriot of Jerusalem). And a recently published text from Qumran on "The Messiah of Heaven and Earth," which is catalogued as *4Q521*, also includes an explicit reference to belief in the resurrection of the dead among the Dead Sea covenanters: "[T]hen he [the Messiah] will heal the sick, resurrect the dead."[4]

Resurrection statements are also to be found in the "Parables" or "Similitudes of Enoch," which most today view as a Jewish composition written sometime during the middle or late first century CE. *First Enoch* 51:1-5, for example, begins: "In those days, the earth will give back all that has been entrusted to it,[5] and Sheol will return all the deposits which she had received, and hell will give back all that which it owes"; while 61:5 speaks of "those who have been destroyed in the desert, those who have been devoured by the wild beasts, and those who have been eaten by the fish of the sea" as those who will "all return and find hope in the day of the Elect One—for there is no one who perishes before the Lord of Spirits, and no one who should perish." And 62:14-16 says of "the righteous and elect ones":

> The Lord of the Spirits will abide over them; they shall eat and rest and rise with that Son of Man forever and ever. The righteous and elect ones shall rise from the earth and shall cease being of downcast face. They shall wear the garments of glory. These garments of yours shall become the garments of life from the Lord of the Spirits. Neither shall your garments wear out, nor your glory come to an end before the Lord of the Spirits.

Likewise, reference must be made to *4 Ezra* (i.e., *2 Esdras* 3–14), which was most likely written about 100 CE. For although an immortality doctrine appears at various places in 3:1–9:25—particularly in the depiction in 7:75-101 of disembodied souls awaiting final rewards or punishments in Sheol/Hades—the ultimate hope of the author is in God's resurrection of the dead, as set out in 7:32-38: "The earth will give up those who are asleep in it, and the chambers [i.e., Sheol/Hades] will give up the souls which have been committed

---

[4] Cf. M. Wise, M. Abegg, and E. Cook, *Dead Sea Scrolls*, 421.

[5] This opening line is present in manuscripts B and C, and so has been included by R. H. Charles (*APOT*, 2.218) and M. Black (*Book of Enoch*, 51). It is omitted, however, by E. Isaac (in J. H. Charlesworth, *OTP*, 1.36).

to them"(7:32); "the Most High will be revealed upon the seat of judgment" and judgment of both the righteous and the wicked will take place (7:33-36); and "the nations that have been raised from the dead" will be similarly judged (7:37-38). Thus the author's final words to the people in 14:35 are fitting: "After death the judgment will come, when we will live again; and then the names of the righteous will become manifest, and the deeds of the ungodly will be disclosed."

In *2 Baruch* (probably written during the first or second decade of the second century CE) there is a much more focused depiction of the resurrection of the dead than is found in *4 Ezra*, particularly with respect to the nature of the resurrection body. For while in the earlier portions of *2 Baruch* there are numerous statements of a somewhat general nature regarding the final fate of both the righteous and the wicked, with these statements often including *allusions* to the resurrection of the dead (e.g., 14:12-13 and 30:1-4 of the righteous; 30:5 and 36:11 of the wicked), in 50:1–51:16 those resurrections are spelled out in quite *explicit* detail in answer to the question posed in 49:1-3:

> I ask you, O Mighty One; and I shall ask grace from him who created all things: In what shape will the living live in your day? Or how will remain their splendor which will be after that? Will they, perhaps, take again this present form, and will they put on the chained members which are in evil and by which evils are accomplished? Or will you perhaps change these things which have been in the world, as also the world itself?

Thus in 50:1-4 resurrection is set forth in terms of the revivification or reanimation of dead persons, as seen earlier in *2 Macc* 7:1-41. The purpose of this "not changing anything in their form" is stated as being so as "to show those who live that the dead are living again, and that those who went away have come back" (50:3)—or, in other words, so that the living and the dead might be able to recognize one another (50:4). Yet in 51:1-16 there is also an emphasis on the transformation of both the righteous and the wicked dead, with the righteous taking on "the splendor of angels" and becoming "equal to the stars" (51:5, 10,) and the wicked changed into "horrible shapes" (51:5). The reason given for such transformations is so that resurrected bodies might be suited to their places of final destination: the righteous "so that they may acquire and receive the undying world which is promised to them" (51:3) and the wicked so that they will "waste away even more" (51:5).

Book 4 of the *Sibylline Oracles* (whose Jewish authorship is fairly well established, whose provenance is presently located in Syria or Palestine, and whose date is usually assigned to the latter part of the first century CE) presupposes a similar doctrine of the resurrection of the dead as found in *4 Ezra* 7:32-38 and *2 Baruch* 50:1–51:16. This is most clearly evidenced in lines 175-91, with the following statements being most significant for our purposes here:

> God himself will again fashion the bones and ashes of men,
>> and he will raise up mortals again as they were before (lines 181-82).

> But as many as are pious, they will live on earth again,
>> when God gives spirit and life and favor to these pious ones.
> Then they will all see themselves beholding the delightful and pleasant light of the sun.
> O most blessed, whatever man will live to that time (lines 187-91).[6]

2. The Tombs at Beth She'arim

The excavations at Beth She'arim in 1936–1940 and 1953–1958 have been declared "one of the most important archaeological projects undertaken by the Israel Exploration Society."[7] The catacombs and "outer tombs," in particular, have yielded significant data for understanding Jewish views regarding the fate of the dead at the end of the Second Temple period.

The Site and its History

Beth She'arim is located on a hill called Shekh 'Abreq, which juts out from the southern extensions of the Galilean highlands, overlooks the Jezreel Valley to the southeast, and views the Carmel range to the west. It was never on a major transportation route, and is situated today south of the Haifa–Nazareth highway.

Excavations have shown that the site was first inhabited in the ninth century BCE and continuously occupied until the middle of the fourth century CE, when it was destroyed by the Roman general Gallus in

---

[6] Lines 190 and 191 have textual problems, with 191 missing in some manuscripts.

[7] N. Avigad, "Preface," in *Beth She'arim: Report on the Excavations during 1953–1958. III: Catacombs 12–23.*

352. It may have been rebuilt as a poor and sparse village later in the fourth century. But it was finally abandoned some time in the sixth century and thereafter forgotten. Earlier the town seems to have been established by Simeon (143–134 BCE) or Alexander Jannaeus (103–76 BCE) as the central city of the Hasmonean royal estates in the Jezreel Valley. Later it probably was taken over by Herod (37–4 BCE) and so became a Herodian domain. It is first mentioned in any extant historical source by Josephus, who, in describing his efforts to protect Galilee from squadrons of the Tenth Roman Legion, speaks of Βησάρα (the Greek name for Beth She'arim) as a large town at the center of the estates of Queen Berenice, daughter of King Agrippa I, and a place for storing grain from the neighboring villages (*Life* 118–19 [24]).

Most of our historical knowledge about Beth She'arim, however, is derived from talmudic writings where it is called by its Hebrew name Beth She'arim (בית שערים) as well as Beth Sharei (בית שריי) and Beth Sharein (בית שריין), which are forms resulting from the Galilean Aramaic dialect. It was the hometown of a prominent third generation Tannaitic teacher of about 120–140 CE, Rabbi Johanan ben Nuri, who had been a pupil of Rabban Gamaliel II and who is frequently mentioned in talmudic literature. During the Bar Kochba revolt of 132–135 CE, however, Beth She'arim began to experience a decisive change. For when Roman forces invaded Israel, a large number of Jews left Jerusalem and their Judean villages and moved to Galilee for refuge—with Beth She'arim, in particular, becoming one of the most important Galilean cities of refuge.

Beth She'arim also became a city of refuge for talmudic scholars, with Rabbi Judah ha-Nassi ("the Prince")—a fifth generation Tannaitic teacher, who was a highly esteemed member of the Hillelian dynasty and president of the Sanhedrin—establishing the seat of the Sanhedrin there.[8] Rabbi Judah was a friend of Marcus Aurelius Antoninus, who reigned as emperor at Rome during 161–180. And it was probably through Antoninus that the ownership of Beth She'arim,

---

[8] Cf. *b. Rosh Hashanah* 30a-b and *Genesis Rabbah* 97: "The Sanhedrin was transferred … from Jerusalem to Jabneh and from Jabneh to Usha … and from Usha to Shafar'am and from Shafar'am to Beth She'arim and from Beth She'arim to Sepphoris, and from Sepphoris to Tiberias"; see also *b. Sanhedrin* 32b: "It [the Sanhedrin] went … after Rabbi to Beth She'arim."

together with its neighboring villages, was transferred from the estates of Queen Berenice to the Jewish Nassi-hood.

Illness, however, overtook Rabbi Judah, and for the last seventeen years of his life he lived at Sepphoris, a Jewish aristocratic city in the heart of fertile Galilee where the air was thought to be healthier.[9] At his death in about 220 CE he was brought back to Beth She'arim for burial. For after the Bar Kochba rebellion and Rome's subsequent prohibition of Jews being buried on the Mount of Olives, the town of Beth She'arim became the central Jewish necropolis. And Rabbi Judah had earlier prepared there a burial vault for himself and his family.

The Golden Age of Beth She'arim came to an end with the transfer of the Jewish Sanhedrin to Sepphoris and Rabbi Judah's death. Nevertheless, the city continued to be an important necropolis until its destruction in the middle of the fourth century. Jews who wanted to be buried in a holy place in the Holy Land came from all over Israel and the Diaspora to this little town in the Galilean foothills in order to spend their last days there and be buried there, just as it had been customary for them to come to Jerusalem to be buried there. So Beth She'arim became an "international" center of Jewry from the mid-second through the mid-fourth centuries CE, just as Jerusalem had been earlier.

The Excavations

On the summit of Shekh 'Abreq, where the city center of Beth She'arim was located, the remains of large public buildings and a synagogue were found, together with some private homes. Excavations in this area have provided important insights and materials for a reconstruction of the city's history. But it is the catacombs and "outer tombs" of Beth She'arim—all of which have been broken into and plundered—that have proven to be most significant. For their dimensions go far beyond the needs of the town itself, and the materials, ornamentations, inscriptions and graffiti found in connection with the burials have been most revealing.

Catacombs 1–11, which are located on both sides of a valley to the west of the central town area, were excavated by Benjamin Mazar

---

[9] Cf. *b. Ketuboth* 103b: "Rabbi was at Beth She'arim, but since he became ill, they brought him to Sepphoris, which was a high place with fragrant air."

during four seasons of excavation in 1936–1940.[10] Catacombs 12–23 and several "outer tombs," located closely together on the northern slope of the town's central hill, were excavated by Nahman Avigad during four seasons in 1953–1958[11]—with Benjamin Mazar returning to conduct another season of excavation during the summer of 1956 when Avigad was away on sabbatical leave.

Catacombs 14 and 20 are the most important catacombs at Beth She'arim. They are the largest of the catacombs excavated, with extensive courtyards, magnificently arcaded facades, and large rooms— all of which suggests that here were interred people of wealth and status who were highly esteemed by the community. Catacomb 14, while not as large as Catacomb 20, is a fine example of a family burial vault. It had an open-air assembly area above it for gatherings of people to commemorate those buried beneath. The excavators, in fact, believe that the double tomb at the end of Room II in Catacomb 14 was probably the tomb of Rabbi Judah ha-Nassi and his wife, for it is distinguishable from all the others by its location, size, large stones used and space given to it, and unique though modest construction. Further, they believe that around this tomb were located the tombs of Rabbi Judah's family members and close associates—such as the three tombs simply inscribed with the designations:

"Rabbi Shim'on" (רבי שמעון);

"This is [the tomb of] Rabbi Gamaliel" (זו שלרבי גמליאל); and,

"This is [the tomb of] Rabbi Aniana" (זו שלרבי אניאנא).

These three are probably those reported to have been spoken about by Rabbi Judah as "Shim'on, my son, the Sage; Gamaliel, my son, the President; and Hanina bar Hama, the Chairman."[12] More than likely the tomb of Rabbi Judah and his wife was left unmarked, for, as Avigad has pointed out, "the tomb at the end of the cave, built of large stones, conspicuous in its unconventional form, and famous for its importance, did not need to be marked since there was no chance of its being forgotten."[13]

---

[10] See B. Mazar, *Beth She'arim: Report on the Excavations during 1936–1940.* Vol. I: *Catacombs 1-4.*

[11] See N. Avigad, *Excavations at Beth She'arim, 1955.*

[12] Cf. *b. Ketuboth* 103, 72.

[13] N. Avigad, *Beth She'arim. Report on the Excavations during 1953-1958,* 3.63.

Catacomb 20, on the other hand, seems to have been a public burial place for other highly esteemed Jews, which category would have included many rabbinic families. In it some 130 stone and marble sarcophagi were discovered, with remains of wood, lead and pottery coffins also able to be discerned. And while most of the inscriptions in the other catacombs (other than Catacomb 14) are in Greek or Aramaic, with some also in the Palmyrene dialect from northeast of Damascus and one in Himyarite from southwestern Arabia, the inscriptions on the sarcophagi in Catacomb 20—though not always the graffiti—are in Mishnaic Hebrew.

Materials and Ornamentation
The great majority of sarcophagi found at Beth She'arim were made of limestone—some hard limestone and some soft, some white and some yellowish, some local stone (though not from the caves themselves) and some stone from the surrounding neighborhood, with some transported from farther afield. Most of the stone coffins are smooth, without any ornamentation. But many are ornamented with various reliefs in patterns taken from animal or still life. Some examples from Catacomb 20 are the Lion Sarcophagus (two lions flanking a vase or jar); the Eagle Sarcophagus (with heraldic lions, a bull's head, and stylized garlands on all sides of the coffin); the Rosette and Hunt Sarcophagus (a six petalled circular rosette with a hunting scene of a lion in pursuit of a gazelle); the Gate Sarcophagus (elaborately carved double gate with four panels, flanked by ornamental links, and two fluted columns with Ionic-type bases and capitals); the Mask Sarcophagus (the head of a bearded man with curly hair, wide-open eyes, raised eyebrows, and a closed and twisted mouth); the Acanthus Sarcophagus (decorative leaves representing the Acanthus plant); the Shell Sarcophagus (two richly ornamented shells, which represent the Arks of the Law, with patterns of interlacing circles, vine tendrils, heraldic bulls, and birds pecking at a cluster of grapes); and the Candlestick Sarcophagus (a carved *menorah*, which was also found at many places on the walls of the catacombs). Most of these reliefs incorporate motifs that were associated with death among the Jews or were common among Jewish artists.

Most interesting, however, are the marble sarcophagi found in Catacomb 20, many of which are ornamented with scenes from Greek mythology. These sarcophagi were presumably imported from abroad, for the kind of white marble used cannot be found in the region, the workmanship of the ornamentation seems better than what was then locally available, and the mythological scenes suggest Gentile craftsmen. In addition, various pieces of marble statuary have been found in Catacomb 20, which evidently were associated in some way with the marble sarcophagi—such as the hand of an Amazon woman holding the shaft of an axe; the bent leg of a mounted Amazon, showing a tunic draped above her knee and an upper strip of boot around her calf; a fragment of the head of a horse, showing the right nostril, the upper jaw and teeth; the damaged head of a woman with her hair hanging down, which suggests a wounded woman dropping her head in agony; the upper part of the torso of a woman with her right breast bare, a necklace around her neck and two bracelets on her arm, but without her head and left arm; and the figure of a winged Eros, who is seated and holding the palms of his hands with his fingers crossed on his right knee, but minus his head.

In speaking of the materials and ornamentation of the Beth She'arim sarcophagi, Nahman Avigad has observed:

> Nowhere else in Palestine have sarcophagi of this type been found, in which Jews were certainly buried. As the Beth She'arim discoveries show, there was a considerable importation of marble sarcophagi from abroad, and the purchasers were not always Gentiles; sometimes they were Jews. Even though these coffins had pagan ornamentation, they were used in caves where members of rabbinical families were buried. This proves once again the degree of tolerance shown by the Jews of Beth She'arim towards the penetration of Hellenistic influence into a great and distinguished Jewish burial centre.[14]

And Avigad aptly goes on to say:

> The tolerance of the Jews of that period in matters of fine art is explained by the fact that the various representations were deprived of their pagan character and original symbolic significance. Many symbols which had their origin in pagan beliefs had acquired a universal character. They were cut off from their original source and became conventional forms of ornament. Their use among the Jews became widespread and general, as is proved by repeated rulings of the sages on questions concerning what was permitted and what was forbidden in matters of this kind. The rabbis could not withstand the spirit of the times, caused by the spread of Hellenism, and made concessions in the interpretation of the commandment "Thou shalt not

[14] *Ibid.*, 3.33.

make unto thee any graven image" (Exod. xx, 4). They laid stress on what followed: "Thou shalt not bow down to them nor serve them." So long as there was no suspicion of idolatry, they were not strict; beyond this point Judaism permitted no compromise.[15]

Inscriptions and Graffiti

Even more interesting and significant, however, are the inscriptions and graffiti in the Beth She'arim catacombs. While some may be merely ornamental and traditional, others are to be taken as highly significant indicators of then-held Jewish attitudes toward life, death and the afterlife—particularly evidencing Jewish views regarding the immortality of the soul and the resurrection of the dead.

Frequently appearing, of course, is the *menorah* or seven–branched candelabrum, which was (and is) a common symbol in Jewish syn-agogues and tombs. It is a symbol of light and life, and so expresses hope for eternal life. It also symbolized God's compassion and forgiveness, and so has often been understood as a kind of guarantee of the soul's immortality. It appears incised on a number of sarco-phagi, is set in raised relief on some of the walls, is scratched onto both coffins and walls, and is incorporated into some of the graffiti in place of the Hebrew and Greek words for "eternal life" or the idea of "the world to come," with the result that a short semi-pictographic sentence is formed.

The use of words and *menorah* to form such semi-pictographic sentences appears not only on coffins and their nearby walls. It also appears in Catacomb 12, Room I, which served as the main passage-way into the other rooms and had stone benches along its walls for the seating of mourners. In this entrance to the complex of other rooms in the catacomb can be seen a graffito in Greek on one of the door jambs and another graffito in Hebrew close by, together with a graffito of a rather sick looking eagle. These two semi-pictographic sentences, it may be presumed, together with the dejected eagle, were the handiworks by one or more of the visitors.

The threat of divine judgment for opening a tomb—whether to place another body in it or to loot it—is frequent in both Jewish and Christians tombs, and is also a feature commonly found in the inscriptions at Beth She'arim. Usually the intruder is threatened with a denial of his portion in the world to come, as in Inscription 129:

[15] *Ibid.*, 3.35.

I, Hesychios, lie here with my wife.
May anyone who dares to open [the grave] above us not have a
portion in the eternal life (μὴ ἔχῃ μέρος εἰς τὸν βίον ἀόνιον).

Other less heinous judgments also appear, as, for example, in Catacomb 12 where two Aramaic inscriptions threaten any violator with
"an evil end" and another in Greek forbids opening the tomb "in the
name of the divine and secular law."

In Inscription 162, however, that threat of judgment is specifically
associated with God's promise to resurrect (i.e., "make alive") the
dead:

> Whoever would change this lady's place [i.e., the woman buried in
> this grave], He who promised to resurrect ["make alive"] the dead will
> Himself judge (ὁ ἐπαγγιλάμενος ζωποιῆσε τοὺς νεκροὺς αὐτὸς
> κρίνει).

This particular wording in a judgment formula, as Moshe Schwabe
has observed,

> has no parallel—not in the inscriptions found at Beth She'arim, nor in
> the inscriptions found anywhere else in Eretz Yisrael. Noteworthy
> about this inscription is the conclusive evidence it bears that belief in
> the resurrection of the dead was accepted in that period by the Jews
> who used to bring their dead to Beth She'arim for burial.[16]

Perhaps most significant for our topic of Jewish attitudes toward
immortality and resurrection, however, are two graffiti on the walls of
the eastern entrance and corridor to Catacomb 20. For after crouching
down to enter Catacomb 20 through its eastern entrance and corridor,
straight ahead one sees a Greek graffito (Inscription 193) incised on
the wall in very thin lines that are about 78 cm long and 25 cm high,
with letters that vary in height from 5 to 10 cm:

> ΘΑΡCΙΤΕ
> ΠΑΤΕΡΕC ΟCΙΟΙ
> ΟΥΔΙC ΑΘΑΝΑΤΟC
> "Be of good courage,
> Holy Fathers [or, "pious parents"]!
> No one is immortal."

The exhortation "Be of good courage" (usually θάρσι, though once
spelled θάσσι and here in the plural as θαρσῖτε) is common at Beth

---

[16] Quotation of Moshe Schwabe taken from Nahman Avigad, *ibid.*, 3.36; see
also M. Schwabe and B. Lifshitz, *Beth She'arim. II: The Greek Inscriptions.*

She'arim. The statement "No one is immortal" (whether ἀθάνατος or variantly spelled ὁθάνατος) is also common. Such a statement could, of course, be understood as a protest against viewing the human "soul" as being inherently immortal. Its use here, however, was probably only to express comfort regarding the common plight of humanity.

Looking up from this graffito, one can see another Greek graffito at the ceiling to the left (Inscription 194), which is incised in bolder lines about 90 cm long and 35 cm high, with letters that vary in height from 6 to 12 cm:

> ΕΥΤΥΧΩC
> ΤΗ ΥΜΩΝ
> ΑΝΑCΤΑCΙ
> "Good luck
> on your
> resurrection!"

"This inscription," as Avigad points out, "provides clear evidence that belief in the resurrection of the dead was widespread among Jews."[17] Further, as Avigad goes on to say regarding these two graffiti:

> Apparently the two inscriptions were incised by visitors to the catacombs, perhaps well after the burial had taken place. The fact that the inscriptions were incised at the entrance of the catacomb and not near the graves leads us to believe that these words of consolation and blessing were not addressed to any particular persons whose graves were being visited, but rather to all the deceased who were buried in this catacomb, out of esteem and affection.[18]

3. The Letters of Paul

Readers of this chapter—especially the honoree of the volume in which it was first published, Professor Peter Richardson—hardly need a lesson on "Paul and the Resurrection." Elsewhere I have written on this subject,[19] and constraints of space require that I only allude to some of the main features of those presentations. Still, some comments of a comparative nature are here necessary. In what fol-

---

[17] N. Avigad, *ibid.*, 3.95.

[18] *Ibid.*, 3.95 and 100, with intervening diagrams.

[19] R. N. Longenecker, "Nature of Paul's Early Eschatology"; *idem*, "Is There Development in Paul's Resurrection Thought?"

lows, therefore, I will simply sketch out a few of the central emphases in Paul's letters regarding the resurrection of the dead.

That Jesus believed in the resurrection of the dead is plain from Mark 12:18-27, and parallels, where the Sadducees' question about a woman who had been married to seven husbands is answered by his fourfold reply that (1) a doctrine of the resurrection of the dead is rooted in Scripture ("you do not know the Scriptures"), (2) God is able to resolve all seeming contradictions ("nor [do you know] the power of God"), (3) some type of transformation of people and relationships will take place at the resurrection ("they will neither marry nor be given in marriage; they will be like the angels in heaven"), and (4) when God establishes his covenant with his people—as with the patriarchs Abraham, Isaac and Jacob ("I *am* the God of Abraham, the God of Isaac, and the God of Jacob"), who were the paradigms of God's dealing with his people—not even death is able to bring that relationship to an end ("God is not the God of the dead, but of the living"). But that Jesus went beyond what many other Jewish teachers of his day would have said on the subject is debatable.

Nor is one able to maintain that Jesus' disciples went beyond— or, in their case, even approached—the views of resurrection that were prevalent in their day. Mark 9:10 says, somewhat enigmatically, that when Jesus spoke of the rising of the Son of Man from the dead, his disciples "kept the matter to themselves" and began questioning "what 'rising from the dead' meant" (τί ἐστιν τὸ ἐκ νεκρῶν ἀναστῆναι).

It is clear, however, that Paul taught a distinctive doctrine of the resurrection of the dead. Of all the New Testament writers, he is the one who speaks most on the topic—principally in 1 Thessalonians (4:13–5:11), 1 Corinthians (15:12-58), and 2 Corinthians (4:14; 5:1-10), but also in 2 Thessalonians (2:1-12); Romans (8:19-25; 13:11-12), and Philippians (1:21-26; 3:10-11, 20-21; 4:5). Much could be said in explication of Paul's understanding of the resurrection of the dead. Suffice it for our purposes here to highlight (1) the bases for his understanding, (2) distinctive features in his understanding, and (3) the relation he saw between resurrection and immortality.

The Bases for his Understanding
Much of what Paul thought about the afterlife and personal resurrection must, of course, be credited to his Jewish background as a Pharisee. Acts 23:6-10 represents him as claiming a Pharisaic basis for

his convictions about resurrection, and what he says on the subject in his letters strongly reflects such a background. Nonetheless, it also needs to be recognized that Paul himself considered his understanding of resurrection to have been primarily based, particularly where his views were distinctive, on the traditions he received from his Christian predecessors regarding Christ—in particular, (1) what the early Christian confessions proclaimed about Christ's resurrection, (2) what Jesus was reported to have said about a future resurrection of believers, and (3) what Paul himself inferred from such traditions regarding the resurrection of Christ's own.

What fixed and focused all of Paul's inherited thought regarding a future resurrection of the dead was for him the fact of the resurrection of Jesus Christ, and it was from this central event that his thought as a Christian proceeded. Thus in 1 Thess 4:14, for example, he argues from the Church's confession "Jesus died and rose again" to assure his converts that "even so will God bring with Jesus those who have fallen asleep in him." In 1 Thess 4:15 he argues from a "word of the Lord" (the substance of which he appears to quote in 4:16-17) that "we who are alive, who remain till the coming of the Lord, will not precede those who have fallen asleep." And in 1 Cor 15:12-58 he bases his argument for the bodily resurrection of believers in Jesus on the early Christian confession set out in 15:3b-5, which he sees as setting the paradigm for all Christian thought about resurrection generally and from which he infers a number of matters of clarification regarding the resurrection of the dead.

For Paul, the resurrection of the dead was a doctrine based in the revelation of the Jewish Scriptures and inherited from his Pharisaic past. In the time before he became a follower of Jesus Christ, he evidently had no doubt about its general truthfulness—though many questions regarding its specifics probably remained. With Christ's resurrection, however, the paradigm for understanding the doctrine had been set and certain ambiguities associated with it clarified. What earlier was founded on his Jewish instruction, therefore, became fixed and focused when seen in the light of Christ.

Distinctive Features in his Understanding
Distinctive to the New Testament's proclamation of the resurrection is the christocentric emphasis given to the doctrine: that Christ's resurrection is the basis for a future resurrection of believers; that

Christ is the agent of a believer's future resurrection; and that Christ's *parousia* is the time when that resurrection will take place. These are matters that underlie the message of resurrection throughout the New Testament. And they are features that appear also in Paul's letters.

Probably most important for our purposes here, however, is the teaching that Paul himself identifies in 1 Cor 15:51 as being an explication of an enigma or "mystery"—that is, that the resurrection of believers in Jesus will not be simply a revivification or reanimation of dead persons, as seems to have been widely thought by many in his day, but that it has to do primarily with transformation. This teaching he introduces in 15:51 by the declaration: "Listen, I tell you a mystery" (ἰδοὺ μυστήριον ὑμῖν λέγω). And he goes on in 15:51-52 to twice emphasize the point: "We will [all] be transformed" (ἀλλαγησόμεθα). This is a transformation not like that alluded to in *2 Baruch* 51:1-16, which was only so that resurrected bodies might be better suited to their places of final destination. Rather, Paul viewed it, as he says in Phil 3:21, as a transformation that will be effected by "the Lord Jesus Christ, who will transform (μετασχηματίσει) our lowly bodies," whose purpose and result will be "so that they will be like his glorious body." Through a contemplation of the nature of Christ's resurrection, therefore, it seems that Paul came to clarify his own thinking about the nature of the believer's future resurrection—that is, that much more than revivification or reanimation is involved, but that, like Jesus who was transformed when God raised him from the dead, believers in Jesus will also be transformed when they are raised from the dead, and so be like him in this respect as well.

The Relation of Resurrection and Immortality

Although relations between the concepts of resurrection and immortality were often vague in the Judaism of Paul's day—at times distinguished; at times merged—Paul seems not to have viewed them as either opposites or synonyms. They may be distinguished, yet they are always closely related in Paul's letters.[20]

---

[20] On relationships, cf. M. J. Harris, *Raised Immortal*; *idem*, "Resurrection and Immortality in the Pauline Corpus."

Murray Harris has aptly characterized Pauline thought on immortality in the following four summary points:[21]

1. Only God inherently possesses immortality (1 Tim 6:15-16).
2. Immortality is never predicated of the "soul"; "this mortal body" is destined to "put on" immortality (1 Cor 15:53-54). It is not by birth, but by grace and through resurrection that immortality is gained.
3. Immortality is a future gift (1 Cor 15:53-54).
4. The highest good (*summum bonum*) is not equated with freedom from embodiment but with the receipt of a spiritual body as a perfect instrument for the knowledge, worship, and service of God (Rom 8:23; 1 Cor 15:43-54; Phil 3:20-21). What Christians eagerly await is their "heavenly body" (2 Cor 5:2), not incorporeal bliss (2 Cor 5:2-4).

In Paul's teaching, resurrection and immortality both find their focus in the risen Christ. Resurrection involves transformation, since "flesh and blood cannot inherit the kingdom of God" (1 Cor 15:50). Resurrection also involves immortality, since believers will be "raised immortal" (1 Cor 15:52). Transformation and immortality, therefore, are coincident with the resurrection of the dead in Paul's teaching. They are both, in fact, part of the future resurrection event itself.

4. Conclusion

There were certainly differences between Rabbi Judah ha-Nassi and Paul. One thing they had in common, however, even amidst a wide diversity of opinion in their respective days regarding the fate of the dead, is that they both viewed the resurrection of the dead as a central doctrine of true religion, with its acceptance or denial having a profound effect on one's religious beliefs and ethical living.

Rabbi Judah was not only the president of the Sanhedrin and the most esteemed rabbi of his day, he was also the compiler of the Mishnah—which is the codification of the Oral Law and the foundational document of the Talmud. It is, of course, impossible to say with certainty just how the various statements within the Mishnah received their final forms. Yet Rabbi Judah ha-Nassi stands behind and can be seen in almost everything that is written in that codification

---

[21] M. J. Harris, "Resurrection and Immortality in the Pauline Corpus," 165.

of Jewish legislation and teaching. This is particularly true for what appears in *Mishnah Sanhedrin* 10:1, which reads:

> All Israelites have a share in the world to come, for it is written, "Thy people also shall be all righteous, they shall inherit the land forever; the branch of my planting, the work of my hands that I may be glorified" [Isa 60:21]. And these are they that have no share in the world to come: he that says there is no resurrection of the dead [prescribed in the Law],[22] and he that says that the Law is not from Heaven, and an Epicurean.[23]

The three matters that appear in this short list of the major tenets of Judaism that cannot be rejected without fear of losing one's "share in the world to come" are (1) the resurrection of the dead, (2) reverence for the Torah, and (3) acceptance of rabbinic authority. Three further disqualifying deviations are listed in the latter part of the passage: (4) reading extra-canonical books as though they were authoritative, (5) uttering incantations for healing, and (6) pronouncing the Divine Name. The fact that "the resurrection of the dead" appears first in this short list of central doctrines makes it abundantly clear that the resurrection of the dead was a major tenet of Rabbi Judah ha-Nassi and of the rabbinic Judaism that succeeded him.

Likewise, Paul began his longest discourse on the resurrection of the dead with the words of 1 Cor 15:12-19:

> But if it is preached that Christ has been raised from the dead [as in the confession of 15:3b-5], how can some of you say that there is no resurrection of the dead? If there is no resurrection of the dead, then not even Christ has been raised. And if Christ has not been raised, our preaching is useless and so is your faith. More than that, we are found to be false witnesses about God, for we have testified about God that he raised Christ from the dead. But he did not raise him if in fact the dead are not raised. For if the dead are not raised, then Christ has not been raised either. And if Christ has not been raised, your faith is futile; you are still in your sins. Then those also who have fallen asleep in Christ are lost. If only for this life we have hope in Christ, we are to be pitied more than all people.

Although different in many respects, here is a feature of profound agreement between Rabbi Judah ha-Nassi and Paul. How does one

---

[22] The phrase "prescribed in the Law" is omitted in some Mishnaic texts.

[23] "Epicurean" is frequently applied in the Talmud to Jews as well as to Gentiles, for it connoted one who was "free from restraint" and so not bound by rabbinic teaching.

account for it? Both men were rooted in the Scriptures (whether called the Jewish Scriptures or the Old Testament) and both were Hillelians (whether by birth and training or training alone). And both Jews and Christians have profited immeasurably from that heritage. Paul, however, was also confronted by the risen Christ, and thereafter his convictions about the resurrection of the dead were focused, fixed and developed in a manner that went beyond his Jewish heritage.

SELECT BIBLIOGRAPHY

Avigad, Nahman. *Excavations at Beth She'arim, 1955. Preliminary Report.* Jerusalem: Israel Exploration Society, 1958.

——. *Beth She'arim. Report on the Excavations during 1953–1958.* III: *Catacombs 12–23.* Jerusalem: The Israel Exploration Society and The Institute of Archaeology, Hebrew University, 1976 (from 1971 Hebrew edition).

Black, Matthew. *The Book of Enoch or I Enoch.* Leiden: Brill, 1985.

Charles, Robert Henry. *Apocrypha and Pseudepigrapha of the Old Testament,* 2 vols. Oxford: Clarendon, 1913, repr. 1963.

Charlesworth, James H. *The Old Testament Pseudepigrapha,* 2 vols. Garden City: Doubleday, 1983, 1985.

Cullmann, Oscar. "Immortality of the Soul or Resurrection of the Dead," *Harvard Divinity School Bulletin* 21 (1955/56) 5-36.

——. *Immortality of the Soul or Resurrection of the Dead.* London: Epworth, 1958.

Harris, Murray J. *Raised Immortal: Resurrection and Immortality in the New Testament.* Grand Rapids: Eerdmans, 1985.

——. "Resurrection and Immortality in the Pauline Corpus," in *Life in the Face of Death. The Resurrection Message of the New Testament.* MNTS. Ed. R. N. Longenecker. Grand Rapids: Eerdmans, 1998, 147-70.

Longenecker, Richard N. "The Nature of Paul's Early Eschatology," *NTS* 31 (1985) 85-95.

——. "Is There Development in Paul's Resurrection Thought?," in *Life in the Face of Death. The Resurrection Message of the New Testament.* MNTS. Ed. R. N. Longenecker. Grand Rapids: Eerdmans, 1998, 171-202.

Mason, Steve. *Flavius Josephus on the Pharisees: A Composition-Critical Study.* Leiden, New York: Brill, 1991.

——. *Josephus and the New Testament.* Peabody: Hendrickson, 1992.

Mazar, Benjamin. *Beth She'arim. Report on the Excavations during 1936–1940.* I: *Catacombs 1–4.* Jerusalem: The Israel Exploration Society and The Institute of Archaeology, Hebrew University, 1973 (from 1957 Hebrew edition).

Schwabe, Moshe, and Baruch Lifshitz. *Beth She'arim*. II: *The Greek Inscriptions*. Jerusalem: Israel Exploration Society and The Institute of Archaeology, Hebrew University, 1974 (from 1967 Hebrew edition).

Wise, Michael, Jr., Martin Abegg, and Edward Cook. *The Dead Sea Scrolls: A New Translation*. San Francisco: Harper & Row, 1996.

Is There Development in Paul's Resurrection Thought?

When dealing with the resurrection of believers in Paul's letters, the question inevitably arises: Is there development in Paul's thought? The question has been asked for over a century and a half, and it continues to be asked today.

The question is not, Did Paul view the Christian life in terms of growth and development? That seems to be answerable in the affirmative by appeal to such features as his illustration of the course of salvation history in Gal 4:1-3, the imagery he uses to describe believers at Corinth in 1 Corinthians 3, and the prayers he prays for his converts in Eph 1:15-23, Phil 1:9-11, Col 1:9-14, and Philem 6. Nor is it, Did Paul grow and mature in his own Christian experience? Again, that seems answerable in the affirmative by appeal to such passages as 1 Cor 13:9-12 and Phil 3:12-16.

Likewise, our question is not: Is there evidence of development in Paul's letters with regard to a number of other crucial matters at the core of his thought—such as about Jesus Christ, the Gentile mission, the nature of God's salvation, God's covenant with his people, the Mosaic law, the Holy Spirit, women in God's redemptive program, Christian ethics and lifestyle, or even about eschatology generally? Each of these matters requires careful explication (cf. *The Road from Damascus: The Impact of Paul's Conversion on his Life, Thought, and Ministry*, ed. R. N. Longenecker [Grand Rapids: Eerdmans, 1997]). And what can be said about Paul's development of thought in any of these areas cannot be claimed to apply directly to the question at hand, but only, at best, by way of analogy.

Rather, our question concerns quite specifically Paul's resurrection message. It seeks to determine the parameters of that message and to what extent his thought about the resurrection of believers may have changed during the period represented by his extant letters. Our investigation must necessarily ask regarding (1) *the circumstances* that gave rise to writing about the resurrection in his letters, (2) *the basis for his thought* about the resurrection as expressed in those letters, (3) *central features* of his various resurrection statements, and (4) *discernible shifts of focus, emphasis or expectation* in his resurrection message. (For pedagogical reasons, in fact, our discussion of the relevant passages in Paul's letters will be largely organized in terms of these four issues.) And if in our investigation certain changes or developments can be identified, we must then ask: Of what nature are they? and How does one account for them?

Development in Paul has often been identified in terms of shifts in his statements: (1) from a Jewish anthropology and cosmology in his earlier letters to a hellenistic anthropology in his later letters; (2) from Jewish apocalyptic imagery in his earlier letters to more hellenized expressions in his later letters; (3) from an apocalyptic, world-renouncing mindset to a world-affirming mindset; (4) from a collective eschatology to a personal, individual eschatology; (5) from focusing on Christ's coming (the parousia) to focusing on his own death; (6) from anticipating fulfillment "with Christ" in the future to experiencing fulfillment "with Christ" and "in Christ" here-and-now; and (7) from expecting that he himself would be alive at the time of the parousia, and so be personally involved in the resurrection without dying, to a consciousness that he would probably die before Christ's coming, and so be among those raised from the dead at the final resurrection. The data claimed in support of each of these proposals needs to be carefully evaluated as we proceed. Further, our question requires us to ask: What exactly do we mean by "development" in Paul—that is, whether dichotomous or discontinuous changes of opinion, or, in some manner, changes that occurred within a continuum of thought?; and, How are matters of "continuity" and "development" to be related when dealing with Paul's resurrection statements in his various letters?

1. *A Brief History of Pauline Developmental Theories*

The history of Pauline developmental theories can be set out in terms of two phases. The first occurred during the latter part of the nineteenth century and the first part of the twentieth, that is, from about 1845 to about 1932. The second has been taking place during the latter two-thirds of the twentieth century and into the twenty-first century, that is, from about 1932 to the present.

Phase One: 1845–1932
The second half of the 1800s was a time when ideas of development and progress were "in the air." People were conscious of achievements in science, technology, exploration, trade, and the arts, and so began to view all human endeavor in terms of progress, both quantitatively and qualitatively. More important for our purposes, a number of works were written during this time by eminent theologians representing all shades of the theological spectrum that advocated a developmental understanding of the course of Christian doctrine— usually focusing on developments after the New Testament period, though often, as well, arguing for developments throughout the Scriptures. John Henry Newman's *An Essay on the Development of Christian Doctrine* of 1845, wherein he attempted to trace the course of Christian theology from its earliest forms in the New Testament to its full-blown expression in Roman Catholicism (thereby justifying his own religious pilgrimage), was seminal for all later developmental hypotheses. But just as important were such Protestant developmental treatises (whether moderate, liberal or conservative) as Robert Rainy's *The Delivery and Development of Christian Doctrine* of 1874, Adolf Harnack's *History of Dogma* of 1886 (English translation, 1905), and James Orr's *The Progress of Dogma* of 1901.

It was Auguste Sabatier who, as a young scholar, first proposed a developmental hypothesis for an understanding of specifically the apostle Paul and who attempted to trace out what he called the "progressive character of Paulinism" (*The Apostle Paul: A Sketch of the Development of his Doctrine* [French original, 1870; English translation, 1896]). In opposition to "the orthodoxy of the past" and "the rationalistic criticism of the Tübingen School"—both of which, he asserted, denied "the existence of progress and development in Paul's doctrine," and so turned the figure of the apostle into something resembling the frigid, stone statuary of Europe's cathedrals—Sabatier took as his purpose "to write not a general biography of Paul, but a biography of his mind, and the history of his thought" (*ibid.*, v-xiv, 1-2).

A number of German scholars followed Sabatier's lead and attempted to work out a developmental understanding of Paul's thought generally. Among them were Hermann Karl Lüdemann (*Die Anthropologie des Apostels Paulus und ihre Stellung innerhalb seiner Heilslehre nach den vier Hauptbriefen dargestellt*, 1872), Otto Pfleiderer (*Der Paulinismus: Ein Beitrag zur Geschichte der urchistlichen Theologie*, 1873), and Bernhard Weiss (*Lehrbuch der biblischen Theologie des Neuen Testaments*, first published in 1868, but revised extensively through 1893). More particularly, Ernst G. G. Teichmann (*Die paulinischen Vorstellungen von Auferstehung und Gericht*, 1896) and Heinrich Julius Holtzmann (*Lehrbuch der neutestamentliche Theologie,* 1897) focused on the development of Paul's eschatological thought.

Likewise, a number of British scholars at the end of the nineteenth century added their voices in support of a developmental approach to Paul. Among them were Joseph B. Lightfoot (see particularly his "The Chronology of St Paul's Life and Epistles," which were his lecture notes of 1863 and published posthumously in *Biblical Essays* in 1893) and George Matheson (*The Spiritual Development of St Paul*, 1897). Special attention was given to Paul's eschatological development by Henry StJohn Thackeray (*The Relation of St Paul to Contemporary Jewish Thought*, 1900) and Robert Henry Charles (*A Critical History of the Doctrine of the Future Life in Israel, in Judaism, and in Christianity*, 2nd rev. ed., 1913).

Not everyone, however, understood Paul in such a fashion. On the Continent, for example, Albert Schweitzer, surveying scholarship "from Baur to Holtzmann," expressed the following opinion:

> There is in works of this period much assertion and little proof regarding the development within Paulinism. One almost gets the impression that the assumption of different stages of thought was chiefly useful as a way of escaping the difficulty about the inner unity of the system (*Paul and his Interpreters: A Critical History*, trans. W. Montgomery [London: A. & C. Black, 1912], 32).

Likewise, Johannes Weiss, pointing out the need to recognize distinctions between the early Paul (about whom we know very little) and the later Paul (about whom through his letters we know a lot), argued:

> It cannot be too much insisted upon that the real development of Paul both as a Christian and as a theologian was completed in this [early] period which is so obscure to us, and that in the letters we have to do with the fully matured man ... We cannot watch Paul's growth during these [early] years. By contrast, the 'development' which some think

they can discern in the period of the letters—ten years, at the most—is not worth considering at all (*The History of Primitive Christianity*, 2 vols., trans. and ed. F. C. Grant, *et al.* [London: Macmillan, 1937], 1.206).

In the early twentieth century, English speaking developmental approaches to Paul were also receiving a bad press. In Britain, for example, James Moffatt pointed out that "the extant letters of the apostle fall … in the late afternoon of his career" (*An Introduction to the Literature of the New Testament*, 3rd ed. revised [Edinburgh: T. & T. Clark, 1918], 62). And Moffatt went on to insist: "To arrange the [Pauline] epistles in the order and for the reasons suggested, e.g., by Lightfoot, is to confuse the parade-ground with the battlefield" (*ibid.* 170). Similarly in North America, as witness Ernest Findlay Scott's statement on the matter:

> Attempts have often been made to trace out a development of Paul's thought, as reflected in the Epistles, but this, on the face of it, is a somewhat futile task. When he wrote the earliest of these letters, Paul was a mature man, perhaps approaching fifty. He had been thinking out his message for twenty years, and had arrived at strong convictions which he was not likely now to change (*The Literature of the New Testament* [New York: Columbia University Press, 1932], 112).

Likewise, Geerhardus Vos, in an article entitled "Alleged Development in Paul's Teaching on the Resurrection" (*PTR* 27 [1929] 193-226)—in which he characterized developmental views of Paul as "consisting in the elimination of error, each successive stage of belief contradicting the preceding stage, and in turn being superseded by the following one" (*ibid.*, 193)—argued that for contextual reasons Paul did not say everything that could be said in each of his resurrection texts, but that it can be assumed that his views, though somewhat different in the various texts, were not contradictory.

Phase Two: 1932 to the Present
A second phase of developmental approaches to Paul began with C. H. Dodd's John Rylands lectures on "The Mind of St Paul: A Psychological Approach" in 1932 and "The Mind of St Paul: Change and Development" in 1933 (*BJRL* 17 [1933] 3-17 and 18 [1934] 3-44). At the beginning of his second lecture on "Change and Development," Dodd acknowledged (1) that developmental theorists of a previous generation perhaps "over-pressed the evidence in the interests of

a neat scheme of development," and (2) that "the modern tendency is to deny that the thought of Paul underwent any substantial development during the period covered by the extant epistles, and to explain the acknowledged differences as due merely to differences of aim, or to the different circumstances in which the epistles were written" ("Change and Development," 3). Nonetheless, Dodd went on to argue for "real development" in Paul's thought during his mature years, with that development being "not merely the result of the circumstances or the particular aim of the several epistles," but to have resulted, in the main, from "a significant spiritual experience which left its mark" about the time of his writing 2 Corinthians (*ibid.*, 4). And he identified that experience as being not just the stinging rebuke he experienced at Corinth, as reflected in 2 Corinthians 10–13, but principally a grave illness that left him almost dead at Troas, as referred to in 2 Cor 1:8-10 and alluded to elsewhere throughout the first seven chapters of 2 Corinthians (esp. 1:3-7 and 4:7-12)—with these two factors combining to constitute in his life a "spiritual crisis" that resulted in "a sort of second conversion," which effected a "change of temper" in his personality and ministry ("Psychological Approach," 14-17; "Change and Development," 4, *passim*).

In Dodd's understanding, Paul's "spiritual crisis" caused him to re-evaluate his outlook as a Christian missionary and to move from a world-renouncing attitude, with personal fulfillment of being united "with Christ" reserved for the future, to a world-affirming attitude, with salvific fulfillment understood in terms of the here-and-now (or, "Realized Eschatology"). Many other implications, as Dodd saw it, were also involved in this "second conversion." For example, (1) temperamentally, Paul moved from lingering feelings of resentment, frustration, self-vindication, pride, and seeking to excel (cf., e.g., 1 Thess 2:18; 1 Cor 4:21; 7:8-9; 2 Cor 12:7) to a final abandonment of any claim to achievement, success or satisfaction in his own life, in full surrender to God in Christ (as in Philippians); (2) politically, he moved from a view that believers ought not to have recourse to pagan courts (1 Cor 6:1-11) to a view that human governments exist by God's ordinance (Rom 13:1-10); and (3) sociologically, he moved from advocating a strict separation of believers from unbelievers (1 Cor 5:9; perhaps also 2 Cor 6:14–7:1) to arguing that unbelievers can do some good before God because of divine law having been written on their hearts (Rom 2:14-15) and that Christians ought to have a generous attitude toward "whatever is true, whatever is noble, whatever is right, whatever is pure, whatever is lovely, whatever is admirable" (Phil 4:8-9). Further, with regard to marriage, Dodd supposed that Paul moved from a depreciation of the value of marriage (1 Cor 7:1-9), with those who had wives being exhorted to live as though they were unmarried (1 Cor 7:29), to actually using marriage as an illustration of divine love and exhorting husbands to "love your wives, just as Christ loved the church and gave himself up for her" (Eph 5:25-33). And with regard to eschatology, Dodd argued that before his near fatal illness at Troas Paul had a parousia fixation and expected he would personally experience resurrection without dying, but that after that traumatic sickness his focus was on death, on gaining immortality at death (rather than at the parousia through resurrection), and on being now "in Christ."

While not espousing all that he proposed, a number of scholars have generally followed Dodd in tracing out developments in Paul's thought during the period of his mature Christian ministry—particularly in positing some sort of shift of emphasis between 1 Corinthians 15 and 2 Corinthians 5, but also in identifying developments in his views of Christ, the Gentile mission, the nature of God's salvation, and the church. Many of these are British scholars who have been influenced, either directly or indirectly, by Dodd—such as W. L. Knox, H. E. W. Turner, T. W. Manson, A. M. Hunter, George B. Caird, W. D. Davies, R. F. Hettlinger, J. A. T. Robinson, and F. F. Bruce. Others are Germans, who were rooted in the developmental approach of a previous generation and found in Dodd a catalyst to their thinking—such as Hans Windisch, Hans-Joachim Schoeps, Adolf Schlatter, Joachim Jeremias, and Oscar Cullmann. Still others are North Americans who have attempted to wed Dodd's developmental approach to John Knox's "Three Jerusalem Visit" chronology, and so to argue for an earlier (though more compressed) period for Paul's western mission (in the early 40s) when the apostle's thought was presumably less mature and therefore still being formed—such as Charles H. Buck, Greer Taylor, H. L. Ramsey, Frederic R. Crownfield, M. Jack Suggs, and John C. Hurd.

But though there have been many advocates of a developmental understanding of Paul during the last two-thirds of the twentieth century, there have also been many who have opposed such an approach. John Lowe's "An Examination of Attempts to Detect

Developments in St Paul's Theology" (*JTS* 42 [1941] 129-42), which was written in direct opposition to C. H. Dodd and W. L. Knox, is a classic example. For though Loewe acknowledged that Paul certainly developed in his mental history, he insisted that those developments took place before the apostle's mature thought as expressed in his letters. And though he recognized shifts in what Paul presents in his letters—which shifts could even be called inconsistencies—Loewe argued that those seeming inconsistencies should be viewed as due to (1) changes in the apostle's mood when writing, (2) differing circumstances of those addressed, (3) tensions between Jewish and Christian elements of faith, and/or (4) the paradoxical character of the gospel message itself.

Somewhat more idiosyncratically, C. L. Mearns has argued that what Paul believed and taught prior to the writing of any of his extant letters was that all of the expected eschatological events had already taken place in the experience of Jesus, but that after he encountered the problem of believers dying at Thessalonica he revised his stance to speak of events yet future ("Early Eschatological Development in Paul: The Evidence of I and II Thessalonians," *NTS* 27 [1981] 137-57). Mearns rightly latches on to certain realized eschatological features in 1 and 2 Thessalonians, which, he believes, continue to appear somewhat inadvertently amidst Paul's futuristic teachings, and which he credits to the apostle's earlier convictions. But he argues for a reshaping of Paul's early realized eschatology to a futuristic stance in the Thessalonian letters. The fatal flaws with his argument, however, have to do with (1) ascribing to Paul the belief that Jesus' resurrection was his parousia, and (2) assuming that Paul (and other early Christians) never really thought about the death of believers until confronted by the concerns of those at Thessalonica— both of which opinions seem highly unlikely.

2. *Problems in Tracing out Development in Paul*

Part of the difficulty today in even raising questions about development in Paul is that contemporary New Testament scholarship is almost exclusively concerned with the task of identifying the circumstances of each of the churches to which the apostle wrote—that is, the particular church's interests, problems, needs, misunderstandings, failures, and triumphs. These are matters that are highly relevant and important. But consideration also needs to be given to Paul's own situation and thought at the time when he wrote each letter—that is, his interests, problems, needs, hopes, fears, and maturing experience as Christ's ambassador. For the special circumstances of the various churches and the particular concerns of Paul when writing those churches can never be divorced from one another in the interpretation of what is written.

Another part of the difficulty in even considering the subject of development in Paul resides in the fact that many New Testament scholars have become wary of any synthetic, wholistic, or so-called "Biblical Theology" treatment of the apostle, preferring, rather, to deal in more modest fashion with only aspects of his thought. This saves them from dangers of an overly systematized portrayal and unfounded speculation—which, of course, are real dangers, and can never be discounted. But it also forces them to remain somewhat agnostic regarding the overall course of Paul's thought.

Yet even when one attempts to take into consideration not only (1) the situations and circumstances of the churches addressed, but also (2) the concerns and mental temper of the apostle himself in writing each of his letters and (3) the contours of the overall course of his thought, there still remain significant problems in trying to trace out developmental features in Paul's thought. Chief among these are the following:

1. That all of Paul's extant letters, however identified and whenever dated, fall within a relatively brief period of time during his later adult life (roughly speaking, somewhere between eight to fifteen years) when he was extensively engaged in ministry and when his thought might reasonably be supposed to have reached maturity;

2. That the extent of the Pauline corpus is debated, with seven letters commonly accepted but the Pastoral Epistles usually set aside and 2 Thessalonians, Colossians, and Ephesians often questioned;

3. That a relative chronology between the letters—in certain cases, also within the letters (e.g., within 2 Corinthians; perhaps also within Philippians and between 1 and 2 Thessalonians)—is a frequent matter of dispute;

4. That the pastoral and polemical nature of much of what Paul writes in his letters requires interpreters to treat his statements

more circumstantially than systematically, both as regards their subject matter and as regards their manner of argumentation;

5. That an argument from silence, which has been used frequently in support of various developmental theories, is notoriously insecure; and,

6. That the paradoxical nature of Christian truth makes it exceedingly difficult to classify Paul's thought, either in whole or in part, according to any schema of successive stages of development.

Probability debates as to whether Paul's thought on any particular subject *could* or *could not* have developed during a relatively brief period of time in his later adult life as Christ's ambassador are interesting, but not highly productive. Numerous analogies can be provided in support of either stance, and deductive reasoning does not take us very far. It is the data from his letters themselves that must be appealed to, keeping in mind the caveats listed above. And while the data on many other significant Pauline themes (e.g., Christ, the Gentile mission, soteriology, God's covenant, the Mosaic law, the Holy Spirit, women, ethics, eccesiology, and even eschatology generally) may be spread over a more expansive body of Pauline writings (whether seven, ten or thirteen canonical letters), the question of development when held to the apostle's resurrection thought is essentially confined to passages within those letters that are commonly accepted—that is to 1 Thess 4:13-18, 1 Cor 15:12-58, 2 Cor 4:14–5:10, Rom 8:19-25; 13:11-12, and Phil 1:21-26; 3:10-11, 20-21; 4:5 (in some such order). So it is to those passages that we must now turn.

3. *1 Thessalonians 4:13-18*

In 1 Thessalonians we have the earliest explicit statements about the resurrection of believers in Paul's letters, and so it is to that letter that we must turn first. John Hurd's attempt to show that the "Previous Letter" to Corinth, which is referred to in 1 Cor 5:9, contained the same type of teaching "concerning bodily resurrection" as 1 Thess 4:13-18 is interesting, informative and suggestive (*Origin of I Corinthians* [London: SPCK, 1965], 50-53, 213-40; esp. 229-33). But it remains unproven (perhaps even "not proved" in the Scottish sense of jurisprudence, which means while not guilty yet also not exonerated). Likewise, a "South Galatian" view of the provenance of

Galatians, which would allow for Galatians to be seen as the earliest extant letter of Paul, need not be invoked here. For even if Galatians was written earlier than 1 Thessalonians, as I believe (cf. my *Galatians* [Dallas: Word, 1990], lxi-lxxxviii), its few allusions to eschatology (e.g., Gal 5:5, 21; 6:8) cannot be taken as a basis for Paul's words about the resurrection in 1 Thessalonians or as detailing in any adequate fashion the nature of his early eschatological thought. At best, Galatians is only supplementary to 1 Thessalonians in matters of eschatology generally and not directly relevant when evaluating Paul's resurrection message in particular.

The Circumstances Behind Paul's Statements

It is frequently taken for granted that futuristic eschatology is the dominant theme of 1 Thessalonians and that Paul's main purpose in writing the letter was to teach and reinforce apocalyptic doctrines about the future. Such an understanding can be buttressed by appeal to 2 Thess 2:1-12 (whether written before or after 1 Thessalonians), for apocalyptic imagery is even more to the fore in that passage and Paul explicitly says that this type of teaching was part of his evangelistic preaching, even to Gentiles (cf. 2:5: "Don't you remember that when I was with you I used to tell you these things?"). But though parousia references rest easily on his lips when praising and praying for his converts in 1 Thessalonians (cf. 2:19; 3:13; 5:23), an analysis of the letter indicates that eschatology was not Paul's main concern in writing that letter. Or, as Arthur L. Moore has aptly observed, futuristic eschatology "is not the high peak" of the letter (*The Parousia in the New Testament* [Leiden: Brill, 1966], 108)—though, of course, "it is not, however, unimportant" (*ibid.*).

What was of major concern to Paul when writing 1 Thessalonians was what he speaks about in chapters 2 and 3—that is, a defense of his own and his companions' conduct while at Thessalonica, against certain charges made against them, and a message of encouragement to his converts who were facing some type of persecution. His discussions of ethics in 4:1-12 and eschatology in 4:13–5:11 seem almost tacked on as afterthoughts (cf. the colloquial expression λοιπὸν οὖν, "finally then," of 4:1, which appears to signal a transition from the main concerns of the letter to an additional topic or topics), being appended to express further concerns for believers at Thessalonica (see further my "The Nature of Paul's Early Eschatology," *NTS* 31 [1985] 85-95).

Having founded the church at Thessalonica about 49 CE on his second missionary journey, Paul was forced by Jewish opposition to leave the city after only a brief residence there—perhaps staying only three weeks, though possibly up to three months (cf. Acts 17:1-15). The church seems to have developed quickly and in a gratifying manner (1 Thess 1:3-4; 2:13), and Paul characterizes the Christians there as examples for other believers throughout the provinces of Macedonia and Achaia (1 Thess 1:7-8). But rumors discrediting him and his companions, as well as some type of persecution against believers in the city, seem to have arisen. Further, the deaths of some of these new believers, whether because of persecution or having died naturally, raised the question: Is there a resurrection hope for believers who die before Christ's parousia?

So a few months after leaving them, Paul writes back to his Thessalonian converts, probably in the spring of 50 CE from Corinth, instructing them about his own and his companions' motivations and how they should live amidst rising persecution (1 Thess 2:1–3:13). He closes this main part of his letter, which evidently expresses his major concerns in writing to his converts at Thessalonica, with what may be called a "wish prayer" in 3:11-13 (using the optative verb "may")—which type of prayer often appears as a formal closing in some of Paul's other letters (cf. Rom 15:13; 2 Cor 13:14; see also 1 Thess 5:23; 2 Thess 2:16-17 and 3:16a):

> May our God and Father himself and our Lord Jesus clear the way for us to come to you. May the Lord make our love increase and overflow for each other and for everyone else, just as ours does for you. May he give you inner strength that you may be blameless and holy in the presence of our God and Father when our Lord Jesus comes with all his holy ones.

Then as almost something of an addendum, he goes on to speak about two or three other matters that he knows were of concern to them—and which, of course, were also of concern to him: (1) their lifestyle in a pagan city (1 Thess 4:1-12); (2) the situation of believers who die before Christ's coming, and so might (presumably) miss out on the resurrection (1 Thess 4:13-18); and (3) the nearness of the parousia and a believer's proper response (1 Thess 5:1-11, with this

latter topic perhaps only to be seen as a continuation of the topic in
4:13-18).

The Basis for Paul's Statements

Paul's argument for the inclusion of the believing dead in the final
resurrection builds on two premises. The first is what appears to be an
early Christian confession, "Jesus died and rose again," as included in
4:14. The verb ἀνίστημι, "raise up," suggests something other than
Paul's own formulation, for elsewhere in his letters he usually uses the
synonym ἐγείρω, "rise up" (about forty times, and normally in the
passive) when speaking about Christ's resurrection and the
resurrection of believers. Likewise, his use of the singular name
"Jesus," which is common in the confessional portions elsewhere in
the New Testament, supports such a view, for usually Paul speaks of
"Christ," "Christ Jesus," or "Jesus Christ." Only rarely does he use
"Jesus" alone—as in Rom 8:11, 2 Cor 4:14, and 1 Thess 1:10, which
passages may also reflect portions of early Christian confessional
material, and in the latter part of our verse here (v 14b), whose
phraseology is conditioned by the confessional language of the first
part of the verse (v 14a). Further, the ὅτι that introduces the statement
"Jesus died and rose again" seems to be a *hoti recitativum*, which
would indicate that Paul is here quoting an early Christian
confessional portion.

The second premise on which Paul's argument is based is a "word
of the Lord," which seems to be set out in 4:15-17. Exactly what is
meant by ἐν λόγῳ κυρίου, "by the word of the Lord," and how this
teaching came to Paul have been hotly debated. The possibilities are
usually narrowed down to three: (1) that this "word" was a revelatory
teaching from the exalted Jesus; (2) that it was a teaching of the
historical Jesus that was not later incorporated into any of our
Gospels—that is, a so-called *agraphon* (literally, an "unwritten"
word); or, (3) that it was a deduction drawn by Paul from teachings
that were later recorded in the canonical Gospels. With Joachim
Jeremias, I believe this "word" to be an *agraphon*—that is, part of
Jesus' teaching during his ministry that was not later recorded in any
of our Gospels (cf. J. Jeremias, *Unknown Sayings of Jesus,* trans. R.
H. Fuller [from German *Unbekannte Jesusworte*, 1948, 1951; London:
SPCK, 1964], 80-83; *idem*, "Isolated Sayings of the Lord," in *New*

Testament Apocrypha, 2 vols., ed. W. Schneemelcher, trans. R. McL. Wilson [London: Lutterworth, 1963], 1.85-90).

But however we spell out the specifics of the case, it is likely that when Paul speaks about the believing dead and their relation to the final resurrection in 4:13-18, he does so on the basis of first an early Christian confession (4:14) and then by recalling one of Jesus' own words on the subject (4:15-17)—both of which he quotes and applies to the situation being addressed. From the confession he argues that since "Jesus died and rose again," the corollary follows: "God will bring with Jesus [who himself died and rose again] those who sleep in him" (v 14). And from the remembered "word" of Jesus—which in contextualizing it for his addressees he evidently substituted the expressions "the Lord himself" and "in Christ" and the pronoun "we" for what probably appeared originally—Paul highlights the following points: at the parousia (1) living believers will have no advantage over deceased believers, but rather (2) "the dead in Christ will rise first" and (3) both living and dead believers will be joined to meet the Lord and will then be with him forever (vv 15-16).

Central Features of Paul's Statements

The content of 1 Thess 4:13-18 is pastoral, with a stress on encouraging Christians who are grieving (cf. 4:18; 5:11). Central features of the passage include (1) its focus on Christ's coming, (2) its direct association of the resurrection of believers with Christ's parousia, (3) its depiction of believers being "with the Lord" as a future reality, and (4) its hint that Paul's own personal expectation was that he himself would be alive at the time of the parousia and so experience at that time the resurrection without dying—as witness the twice repeated words "we who are alive and remain" (4:15, 17).

Further, the imagery of 1 Thess 4:13-18 is highly apocalyptic—as witness such expressions as "the Lord will come down from heaven" (cf. Micah 1:3), "with the voice of the archangel" (cf. *4 Ezra* 4:36), "with the trumpet call of God" (cf. *4 Ezra* 6:23), "we will be caught up in clouds" (cf. 2 Enoch 3:1), "to meet the Lord in the air ... [and to] be with the Lord forever" (cf. 1 Enoch 62, esp. vv 13-16). Adding the imagery of 2 Thess 2:1-12 to this list, the apocalyptic nature of Paul's Thessalonian statements is heightened: "the coming of our Lord Jesus Christ," "our being gathered to him," "the day of the

Lord," "the apostasy," "the man of lawlessness," "that which restrains," and "the one who restrains."

All of this is expressly futuristic in orientation, as is also Paul's reference to his earlier preaching at Thessalonica in 2 Thess 2:5. But the presence of such futuristic features should not be taken to mean that the apostle only thought in a futuristic fashion when discussing eschatology with his Thessalonian converts. As Ernest Best has pointed out, Paul's eschatology in 1 Thessalonians also evidences a number of realized motifs—as, for example, (1) calling believers "children of the light and children of the day" in 5:5, thereby signifying that they have a new existence; (2) associating closely the indicative and the imperative of the gospel throughout 5:1-12; and (3) highlighting the close relationship of believers to Christ, as in 4:14 and 5:10—which are items that Best has rightly called "the basic structural patterns" of Paul's thought (*A Commentary on the First and Second Epistles to the Thessalonians* [London: Black, 1972], 12-14, 222). And when we add the two sets of exhortations that immediately follow the eschatological portions of 1 Thess 5:1-11 and 2 Thess 2:1-12—that is, the exhortations of 1 Thess 5:12-22 and 2 Thess 2:13-15—it becomes even more evident just how engrained these "basic structural patterns" were in Paul's thinking.

Discernible Shifts in Paul's Statements
In what follows throughout the rest of this chapter, our question will be: Are there discernible shifts in Paul's resurrection thought from what appears in his Thessalonians letters? 1 Thess 4:13-18, together with the cognate materials of 1 Thess 5:1-11 and 2 Thess 2:1-12, therefore, will function as the base for our investigation of development in Paul's letters. But here confining ourselves to the Thessalonian correspondence, it is impossible to speak of shifts in 1 Thess 4:13-18, for that is the passage from which we are working.

Yet when one considers the question of development in Paul more broadly, it needs always to be noted that the most significant shift in the apostle's thought with respect to the resurrection occurred prior to the writing of any of his extant letters, and that this occurred in connection with his conversion to Christ. For while the concept of a bodily resurrection was a rising feature within the Judaism of Paul's day, no Jew would have spoken of belief in the resurrection as being based on the fact that "Jesus died and rose again" (4:14). Nor would any Jew have repeated a "word of the Lord" that referred to the future parousia of Christ, that identified the godly dead as "the dead in Christ," or that spoke of believers being "caught up … to meet the Lord in the air" and being "with the Lord forever" (as in 4:15-17). Indeed, some fifteen to seventeen years before he wrote 1 Thess 4:13-18 Paul experienced as a result of his conversion to Christ a shift in his thinking about the resurrection of the righteous that went far beyond any shift of thought that might be found in his later, extant letters.

4. *1 Corinthians 15:12-58*

In 1 Cor 15:12-58 Paul deals with a matter that was very much on his mind and that he believed was needful for Christians at Corinth: a proper understanding of the resurrection of believers. It may be that the topic was raised by the Corinthian believers themselves in their letter to Paul and that we should understand his statements in 1 Corinthians 15 as being in response to their agenda, and so in line with his other responses in 1 Corinthians 7–14. More likely, however, this matter regarding the resurrection of believers is to be understood as reflecting Paul's own agenda—though, of course, he thought it to be a topic of great importance for his converts as well.

The Circumstances behind Paul's Statements

The church at Corinth, like that at Thessalonica, was founded by Paul on his second missionary journey (cf. Acts 18:1-18a). Unlike his stay at Thessalonica, however, his evangelistic ministry at Corinth lasted "for some time" (Acts 18:18a), probably during 50–51 CE. Later, during his third missionary journey, Paul wrote to his Corinthian converts the letter we know as 1 Corinthians, writing it toward the close of his ministry at Ephesus (cf. 16:5-9), probably in 56 or 57 CE.

We know from 1 Cor 5:9 that Paul had written the Corinthian church an earlier letter (the so-called "Previous Letter"), whose content can only be surmised (perhaps it is partly contained in 2 Cor 6:14–7:1). That Paul wrote any other letters to his converts at Corinth before writing 1 Corinthians may seem plausible, but is impossible to tell. We do, however, have 1 Corinthians, and its unity seems assured and its content known.

1 Corinthians is largely dominated in its order and form by the polemics of the situation—that is, by Paul's need to respond to reports

received from members of the household of Chloe about divisions in
the church (1:10–4:21), to rumors that were widely circulating about
certain evils in the church (5:1–6:20), and to specific questions asked
him by the Corinthian believers themselves in their letter (7:1–14:40).
In 15:12-58, however, it seems that Paul speaks to an issue that went
beyond what he was specifically told or asked about, but a matter he
knew was an issue among Christians at Corinth—a matter that he
probably knew about from being with them earlier: that of the
resurrection of believers.

Evidently some Corinthian Christians were claiming that a future,
personal, corporeal resurrection of believers in Jesus was (1) *irrelevant*, since the eschatological hope of the gospel was already fulfilled
in a believer's present, spiritual experience, (2) *impossible*, since the
corporeal body was excluded from divine redemption in Greek
religious thought—perhaps, also, in reaction to crude Jewish ideas
about resurrection as being simply revivification, reanimation or
resuscitation, and (3) even *unnecessary*, since believers were thought
to possess already an immortal soul, which, now being redeemed by
Christ, made any further action by God superfluous. Such a scenario
seems evident from a "mirror reading" of Paul's statements in the
passage. For in 1 Cor 15:12-58 the apostle sets out (1) the *fact* of a
Christian's future, personal, corporeal resurrection in verses 12-34 (as
signaled by the use of ὅτι, "that," which appears twice in v. 12), (2)
the *manner* of a Christian's resurrection in verses 35-49 (as signaled
by the use of πῶς, "how," which appears in v. 35), and (3) the
necessity for a Christian's resurrection in verses 50-58 (as signaled by
the use of δεῖ, "necessary," which appears in v. 53).

The Basis for Paul's Statements

Paul's resurrection statements in 1 Cor 15:12-58 are undoubtedly
rooted in a number of factors, both Jewish and Christian. Evident in
the substructure of the passage are (1) a Jewish anthropology, which
laid stress on the essential wholeness of a person—with both "body"
and "soul," the "material" as well as the "immaterial," being required
for true personhood, and (2) a rising Jewish understanding of a future
resurrection for the righteous, which was developing in the period of
Second Temple Judaism. This Jewish understanding of resurrection
appears to have usually taken the form of the revivification,
reanimation, or resuscitation of a deceased person (cf., e.g., 2 Macc

7:9-23; *2 Baruch* 50:1-2; *Sibylline Oracles* 4.179-91)—though, at times, it was expressed in terms of immortality (cf. *Jubilees* 26:30-31; *Wisdom of Solomon* 2:1–3:9) and even reincarnation (cf. Josephus, *War* 2.163; *Antiq.* 18.14). Also evident in the passage, however, is a Christian re-interpretation of that Jewish heritage, which saw the resurrection of Jesus as the true validation of hope for a bodily resurrection and focused on Jesus as the agent of that resurrection.

Yet what needs to be noted beyond such a general background is the fact that in 15:12-58 Paul bases all of his arguments on an early Christian confessional portion, which he incorporates in 15:3b-5:

> That Christ died for our sins according to the Scriptures;
> that he was buried;
> that he was raised on the third day according to the Scriptures; and,
> that he appeared to Peter and then to the Twelve.

In particular, Paul focuses on the statement "he was raised" (v 4; cf. also v 12) and uses it as the immediate basis for his own statements— highlighting in the process both the fact and the prototypical nature of Christ's resurrection. Thus in verses 12-34 he asserts the reality of a future and personal resurrection of believers (i.e., because Christ was raised from the dead and is the "firstfruits" of the righteous, believers in Christ will also be resurrected). Then in verses 35-49 he argues by analogy for the bodily nature of their resurrection (i.e., because Christ was transformed in his resurrection, believers will also be transformed to "bear the likeness of the man from heaven"). And then in verses 50-58, by derived implication, he presents the necessity for the resurrection of believers if they are ever to be clothed with immortality (i.e., because it was necessary for Christ to be raised, it is also necessary for believers to experience resurrection in order to gain immortality).

Central Features of Paul's Statements
A number of features of importance in Paul's argument of 1 Cor 15:12-44 can be paralleled, to one extent or another, by statements found in some of the apocalyptic writings of Second Temple Judaism and the later rabbinic materials of the Talmud. Certainly the fact of a bodily resurrection of the righteous—at times, as well, a bodily resurrection of the unrighteous—was a growing doctrine within the Judaism of Paul's day. Likewise, the insistence that it is God who is both the Creator and the Re-Creator of the righteous was a common tenet

of Judaism. And probably the seed analogy of verses 35-44a, as W. D. Davies has argued, should be considered "a rabbinic commonplace" (*Paul and Rabbinic Judaism: Some Rabbinic Elements in Pauline Theology* [London: SPCK, 1948; Philadelphia: Fortress, 1980[4]], 305).

In the talmudic tractate *b. Sanhedrin* 90b, for example, Queen Cleopatra is said to have asked Rabbi Meir whether the dead rise naked or clothed, and R. Meir is credited with replying:

> Thou mayest deduce by an *a fortiori* argument [the answer] from a grain of wheat: for if a grain of wheat, which is buried naked, shooteth forth in many robes, how much more so the righteous, who are buried in their raiment [i.e., their bodies]?

Likewise, Rabbi Eliezer in *Pirke de Rabbi Eliezer* 33.245 is represented as using the same seed analogy with the same logic to argue that the dead do not rise naked:

> All the dead will arise at the resurrection of the dead, dressed in their shrouds. Know thou that this is the case. Come and see from [the analogy of] the one who plants [seed] in the earth. He plants naked [seeds] and they arise covered with many coverings; and the people who descend into the earth dressed [with their bodies], will they not rise up dressed [with their new bodies]?

What distinguishes Paul from his Jewish compatriots on the resurrection of the dead, however, comes to the fore in verses 45-57 and has to do with two matters. The first concerns the centrality of Christ in Paul's thought, with that centrality being evident in his contrast between the first Adam and the Second Adam (vv 45-49), his allusions to Christ's parousia (v 52), and his references to the victory that God has effected and will yet effect "through our Lord Jesus Christ" (vv 54-57). So while his Jewish compatriots spoke of God as the agent and "the End" as the time of the resurrection of the dead, Paul, without denying either God or the End Time as being important, focused on Christ and his parousia when talking about the resurrection of believers.

But joined with an emphasis on the centrality of Christ is a further matter of great importance for Paul, which may also be claimed to have gone beyond what many of his Jewish compatriots were explicitly teaching and what Christians generally of his day were explicitly stating: that resurrection has to do with the transformation of a person's whole being, and is not to be thought of as merely the revivification, reanimation or resuscitation of one's former self. It is at this point in his presentation, it should be noted, that Paul speaks of giving his readers a "mystery"—that is, of explicating, as verses 51-52 have it, an enigma in Christian thinking about how the resurrection of believers should be understood:

> Listen, I tell you a mystery (μυστήριον): We shall not all sleep, but we shall all be transformed (ἀλλαγησόμεθα)—in a flash, in the twinkling of an eye, at the last trumpet. For the trumpet will sound, the dead will be raised imperishable, and we shall be transformed (ἀλλαγησόμεθα).

In biblical parlance, "mystery" (μυστήριον) does not mean a "secret" that can only be disclosed to the initiated, as in Greek thought. Rather, it signifies something "enigmatic" that was earlier only partially understood, but now has been clarified by God through a further revelation, as in Jewish thought (cf. R. E. Brown, *The Semitic Background of the Term "Mystery" in the New Testament* [Philadelphia: Fortress, 1968]). And Paul's twice repeated statement "we shall [all] be transformed" serves to highlight the importance of this feature in the explication of that "mystery."

While many of his Jewish compatriots spoke of the resurrection of the dead in terms of revivification or resuscitation, so that the righteous might live their lives on a reconstituted earth and be able to recognize one another—with some also suggesting that some type of transformation would take place at some later time, so that the righteous might then be able to live their lives in a reconstituted heaven (cf. *1 Enoch* 90:28-42; *2 Baruch* 51:1-16)—Paul speaks of the resurrection in terms of the transformation of all believers at the time of Christ's parousia. Evidently he saw in Christ's resurrection the eschatological revelation that clarifies a former enigma that had always been associated with the subject of resurrection. And so he conceives of the believer's resurrection as patterned after Christ's transformation when he was raised from the dead—for, as he says in verse 49, "just as we have borne the likeness of the earthly man [the first Adam], so we shall bear the likeness of the man from heaven [the Second Adam]."

Discernible Shifts in Paul's Statements

Writing six or seven years after having written 1 Thess 4:13-18, there is much that Paul says in 1 Cor 15:12-58 that corresponds to what he said earlier to his Thessalonian converts. His purpose in writing each of these passages, of course, differed—consoling grieving Christians in 1 Thess 4:13-18; correcting confused Christians in 1 Cor 15:12-58. But Paul's Jewish heritage (as can be seen, for example, in his emphases on God as Creator and Re-Creator, on the fact of a future resurrection of the dead, and on human personality as inseparably connected with both body and soul, as well as in his use of the seed analogy to illustrate the resurrection reality) and a common Christian re-interpretation of that heritage (as expressed, for example, in his emphases on Christ as validating the hope of the resurrection and the One who will bring about the resurrection at his parousia) are evident in both passages. Likewise, Jewish apocalyptic imagery abounds in both passages—as seen earlier in the Thessalonian materials and as is apparent also in 1 Corinthians 15: Christ is the "firstfruits" of the dead (vv 20, 23); death is "the last enemy" (v 26); Adam is the historical, natural, earthly "first man" (vv 45-49); and the resurrection takes place "in a flash, in the twinkling of an eye, at the last trumpet" (v 52).

Where Paul differs in 1 Corinthians 15 from what he wrote in 1 Thessalonians 4, and so where a discernible shift seems to have taken place in his resurrection thought, is to be found at verse 51—at that very place where he himself says he is explicating an enigma or "mystery": that resurrection has to do with transformation, not merely with the revivification, reanimation or resuscitation of a dead corpse. As Joachim Jeremias concluded in comparing Paul's statement in 15:51 with what he wrote in 1 Thess 4:13-18 and what appears in the Jewish apocalyptic writings:

> In I Thess. iv nothing is said about the change. As a matter of fact, the change at the parousia is not met within the Jewish apocalyptic literature. There, the conception is—as may be seen for example from the Syriac Apoc. of Baruch xlix–li—that the dead are raised in their earthly state. Literally, Syr. Bar. 1, 2 says "nothing being changed in their appearance." This is, as Syriac Baruch continues, to secure their identity (1. 3f.). Only after the judgment the righteous are changed.
>
> This, then, seems to be the mystery, the new revelation: the change of the living and the dead that takes place immediately at the parousia ("'Flesh and Blood Cannot Inherit the Kingdom of God' (I Cor. XV. 50)," *NTS* 2 [1956] 159).

Paul does not speculate in 1 Corinthians 15 as to the anatomical or physiological make-up of transformed believers at the time of their future resurrection. Such details, as Murray Harris points out, "were of no more consequence to Paul and the early Christians than was the geography of heaven" (*Raised Immortal,* 124). Rather, what Paul highlights in this chapter is not only that believers will be resurrected at the parousia, but also that the resurrection of believers will be patterned after Christ's resurrection—with the paradigm of Christ's resurrection being seen as having to do principally with transformation.

It is, in fact, on this point of resurrection as transformation that 1 Cor 15:12-58 evidences a development of thought over what was expressed in 1 Thess 4:13-18. And it is with respect to this teaching on transformation that one can speak of a discernible shift in Paul's statements here. Probably, it may be speculated, Paul's thought developed in the six or seven years between the writing of 1 Thessalonians and 1 Corinthians to the point where he focused not only on (1) Christ's resurrection as the basis for the actuality of a future resurrection of believers, (2) Christ's parousia as the time of that resurrection, and (3) Christ as the agent of resurrection (cf. 1 Thess 4:14-17), but also came to see Christ's resurrection as revealing the paradigm or pattern for what the believer's resurrection will be like.

5. *2 Corinthians 4:14–5:10*

2 Corinthians is a difficult writing to analyze, chiefly because of uncertainties regarding its compositional character. For while there is no external attestation in support of any partition theory, there are a number of internal features that have suggested to many that the work should be seen as composed of various Pauline letters (or, perhaps, portions of letters), which have been brought together to form our present canonical letter. These internal matters have to do with (1) the sudden changes of tone, topic, and rhetorical style in the writing, most obviously between chapters 1–7 (or, chs 1–9) and chapters 10–13, (2) the seemingly disparate character of some portions of the writing, chiefly that of 6:14–7:1, (3) the separate treatments of Titus and the brothers in chapter 8 and the collection in chapter 9, and (4) certain references to events in Paul's life and allusions to relations with his Corinthian converts that seem to suggest various times for writing what we have as 2 Corinthians—principally his statement of 13:1, "This is the third time I am coming to you"; his reference in 2:1-4 to having written the Corinthians a letter "out of great distress and anguish of heart and with many tears," after having had a "painful visit" with them; and certain allusions throughout the writing to the

varying reactions of his converts at Corinth to his person and ministry that seem to suggest various incidents or differing circumstances in their relations with one another.

There have been a number of competent scholars who have argued forcefully for the unity of 2 Corinthians, usually positing some type of "compositional hiatus" between chapters 1–7 (or, chs 1–9) and chapters 10–13. The major problem with such a view has always been: Why, then, did Paul retain the conciliatory section that speaks of his joy over his Corinthian converts' repentance (chs 1–7) in a letter that concludes in such a severe, harsh and sarcastic manner (chs 10–13)? Most scholars today, therefore, have invoked some type of "partition theory" and postulated some such order of letters as the following: (1) a "Previous Letter," which is referred to in 1 Cor 5:9 (being either no longer extant or represented to some extent by 2 Cor 6:14–7:1); (2) our present canonical 1 Corinthians (a unified letter); (3) an "Intermediate Letter," which is possibly referred to in 2 Cor 2:3-4; (4) a "Severe Letter," which now appears as 2 Corinthians 10–13; and (5) a "Conciliatory Letter," which now appears as 2 Corinthians 1–7 and was written about 57–58 CE—with, perhaps, chapters 8 and 9 appended to that final letter.

We need not here get bogged down in the current critical debates regarding the composition of 2 Corinthians. The integrity of what is written—that is, that Paul is the author of all that we have in 2 Corinthians—is not in question. It is primarily only the historical order of the "Conciliatory Letter" (chs 1–7) and the "Severe Letter" (chs 10–13) that is of any importance for a discussion of development in Paul. And even that is not of overwhelming significance for dealing with Paul's resurrection thought, for most of the explicit data on the topic of resurrection in 2 Corinthians is contained within chapters 1–7.

The Circumstances Behind Paul's Statements
However we relate the various sections of 2 Corinthians to one another, it seems obvious that Paul's relations with his Corinthian converts were often strained. Even if chapters 10–13, with their clear indications of a breakdown in relations, are ignored, there still runs throughout chapters 1–7 a refrain of difficulty and distrust between Paul and his converts—as, for example, in his reference to a former "painful visit" (2:1), his statements about the distress caused by that visit (2:2-4), his allusions to grief caused by someone in some parti-

cular situation at Corinth (2:5-11), and the various hints throughout these chapters that he was aware of a growing unhappiness among his converts regarding his ministry (e.g., 3:1-3, *passim*).

Of more importance for an understanding of the circumstances behind Paul's resurrection statements in 2 Corinthians, however, is the traumatic situation that he speaks about as having taken place "in the province of Asia"—at some time when he was away from Corinth and probably shortly before writing what he wrote in (at least) chapters 1–7. He refers in 1:8-11 to that situation as a time when he was "under great pressure, far beyond our ability to endure, so that we despaired even of life"—when, in fact, he "felt the sentence of death" and experienced "deadly peril." And he continues to allude to that situation elsewhere in chapters 1–7, principally in 1:3-7 and 4:7-12.

The Basis for Paul's Statements

The basis for Paul's resurrection statements in 2 Cor 4:14–5:10 must, first of all, be judged to be his Jewish heritage as reinterpreted by his basic Christian convictions, with that background evidently being common to all early Jewish believers in Christ. Such a commonality of background is evident in 4:14-18, where he says, "The one who raised the Lord Jesus from the dead will also raise us with Jesus and present us with you in his presence" (v 14,)—which seems to echo early Christian confessional material. Likewise, it is evident when he exhorts believers to allow "thanksgiving to overflow to the glory of God" (v 15,), not to "lose heart" (vv 16-17,), but to fix their eyes "not on what is seen, but on what is unseen" (v 18,).

More particularly, however, Paul's statements in 2 Cor 4:14–5:10 need to be seen as motivated by certain difficulties he had encountered with believers at Corinth and by a traumatic personal experience he had "in the province of Asia" sometime shortly before writing, which he refers to directly in 1:8-11. Evidently that latter experience was a situation unlike anything he had experienced before, for his reaction of distress and despair (cf. 1:6-11) seems quite different from how he responded to the litany of sufferings he sets out in 2 Cor 11:23-27—imprisonments, floggings, beatings, stripes, stonings, shipwrecks, perils from bandits, persecutions by both Jews and Gentiles, opposition by believers who proved false, being hungry, cold and without proper clothing—because of which, he says, he was "exposed to death again and again," but in which he gloried as a servant of

Christ. C. H. Dodd's guess that it was a near-fatal illness at Troas is as good as any. But whatever it was, it seems to have caused Paul to contemplate his own death in a new way and to change his thinking about whether he himself would be alive or dead at the time of Christ's parousia.

Central Features of Paul's Statements

Admittedly, the explicit terms "death" (θάνατος), "resurrection" (ἀνάστασις), "transformation" (ἀλλαγή; cf. the verbs ἀλλάσσω and μετασχματίζω), and "immortality" (ἀθανασία, ἀφθαρσία, or ἄφθαρτος) do not appear in 2 Cor 4:14–5:10. Nonetheless, the ideas represented by these terms are very much to the fore in this passage by the use of synonymous expressions. Certainly "wasting away outwardly" (4:16) and "the destruction of our earthly tent" (5:1) refer to death; while "he [God] will also raise us with Jesus" (4:14) and "we have [proleptically?] a building from God, an eternal house in heaven, not built by human hands" (5:1) have in mind the believer's resurrection. And with almost as much confidence, it can be affirmed that "swallowed up" and "life" in the purpose clause "so that what is mortal may be swallowed up by life" (5:4) allude to the believer's transformation and immortality, respectively.

A number of scholars understand Paul in 2 Cor 5:1-10 to be primarily focused on death, rather than Christ's coming, and to be principally concerned with the state of believers in an interim period between death and the parousia. They argue that under the catalyst of a hellenistic anthropology, Paul here develops a view of the intermediate state wherein a believer's personal "self" acquires immortality at death and so gains at that time conscious fellowship "with Christ" (in line with Dodd's "realized" interpretation); yet they also argue (going beyond Dodd) that Paul in this passage visualizes believers as having to await final fulfillment "with Christ" at the parousia, at which time they will then experience the resurrection of their bodies (cf., e.g., A. Plummer, *A Critical and Exegetical Commentary on the Second Epistle of St Paul to the Corinthians* [Edinburgh: T. & T. Clark, 1915], 160-61; J. Dupont, *ΣΥΝ ΧΡΙΣΤΩι: L'union avec le Christ suivant saint Paul* [Louvain: Nauwelaerts; Paris: Desclée de Brouwer, 1952], 135-91; L. Cerfaux, *The Christian in the Theology of St Paul* [London: Chapman, 1967], 191-212, 223). But such statements as "he [God] will also raise us with Jesus" (4:14), "we have [proleptically] a building from God" (5:1), and the Spirit guarantees "what is to come" (5:5) suggest that Paul's focus throughout this passage—even though personally weighed down by an intense realization of his own mortality—is still firmly fixed on the resurrection of believers that will occur at Christ's parousia.

There are, indeed, a number of exegetical issues in 2 Cor 4:14–5:10 that cry out for treatment if one were to attempt a full exegesis of these verses. Further, certainly such expressions as "at home in the body we are away from the Lord" and "away from the body [we are] at home with the Lord" (5:6-9) sound fairly hellenistic. On the other hand, the apostle's opposition to hellenistic anthropology is highlighted by his revulsion to being "found naked" or "unclothed" at death (5:3-4)—that is, to existing as some disembodied soul or spirit that only awaits a future embodiment.

Probably more important to note in this passage, however, is the sequence of ideas presented: (1) death ("wasting away outwardly"; the destruction of our "earthly tent"); (2) resurrection ("he [God] will also raise us with Jesus"; "we have a building from God"); (3) transformation (mortality "swallowed up"), and (4) immortality (post-resurrection "life"). Such a sequence suggests how these concepts were related in Paul's own mind—both logically and chrono-logically—at the time when he wrote 2 Corinthians (or, at least when he wrote chs 1–7). And that sequence stands as a paradigm for how their relations should be understood by us today.

In 1 Cor 15:50-54 Paul insisted that immortality is neither a quality inherent to human beings nor a condition bestowed on them by God at creation: "Flesh and blood (σὰρξ καὶ αἷμα, which is a locution for humanity in its finitude and frailty) cannot inherit the kingdom of God," for humans decay (are "perishable") and die (are "mortal"). "Only God is immortal" (ὁ μόνος ἔχων ἀθανασίαν), as the doxology of 1 Tim 6:16 declares. Angels, of course, are also im-mortal, having been created as immortal beings by an immortal God. But no person is said elsewhere in the Pauline letters to be immortal, whether inherently, by creation, or at death. And 2 Cor 4:14–5:10 need not be interpreted as a shift in Paul's central focus—that is, from immortality as a result of resurrection and transformation at Christ's parousia to immortality as gained by believers at death. Rather, though with an increased consciousness of his own mortality, the sequence of events in 2 Cor 4:14–5:10 continues to be: (1) death, (2) resurrection, (3) transformation, and then (4) immortality.

Discernible Shifts in Paul's Statements

While we must deny any essential shift of focus in 2 Cor 4:14–5:10—that is, from a focus on Christ's parousia and the resurrection of believers to a principal interest in death and some type of soulish immortality at death—there yet remain two features that can be seen as subsidiary shifts in Paul's statements in this passage. These shifts have to do with (1) his change of language from dominantly apocalyptic to more metaphorical, and (2) his expectation regarding how he himself would fit into the scenario he envisages. For while the language of 1 Thess 4:13-18 and 1 Cor 15:12-58 is literal and highly apocalyptic, that of 2 Cor 4:14–5:10 is metaphorical—"a building from God," "an eternal house in heaven," "a house not made with hands," "not to be found naked," and "not to be unclothed but to be clothed [with our heavenly dwelling]"—and without apocalyptic symbolism. And while in 1 Thess 4:15-17 Paul associates himself with those who will be alive at Christ's coming, throughout 2 Cor 4:14–5:10 he identifies himself with those who will die before the parousia.

"It is clear," as William Baird has pointed out, that in 2 Cor 4:14–5:10 "Paul's eschatological language has undergone change"—although that change, as Baird goes on to insist, should not be seen as "a gradual development out of Jewish into Hellenistic forms," for "major eschatological concepts have remained relatively constant" in the passage ("Pauline Eschatology," 327). Such a change may be posited to have come about because of Paul's "increasing concern for the past and the present" (*ibid.*). For although his earlier writings incorporate concerns regarding the present (e.g., Gal 5:1-12; 6:7-10; 2 Cor 10:3-4; 11:12-15), and his later letters reflect a continued interest in the future (e.g., Rom 8:19-25; Phil 1:10; 2:16; 3:10-11, 20-21; 4:5), Paul's principal concerns in writing 2 Corinthians 1–7 had to do with circumstances in the present—which had been motivated by the stinging rebukes of his Corinthian converts and by some traumatic, near-death experience that he faced shortly before he wrote these chapters.

Paul's thought in 1 Corinthians 1–7 appears to have become "increasingly personal" and more realistic with respect to his own death (cf. again Baird, *ibid.*). It is not, therefore, too surprising to see in 2 Cor 4:14–5:10 his identification with those who will die before the parousia—that is, a change in his personal expectation as to how, exactly, he himself would be related to the parousia. Yet, even with such a change of expectation, Paul's focus on Christ's coming and the resurrection of believers at that time seems to have remained constant.

6. *Romans 8:19-25; 13:11-12*

Paul's letter to Christians at Rome, while in many ways the heartland of Christian theology and piety, has always been a difficult letter to analyze and interpret. In large measure, understanding Romans has been difficult because of uncertainties as to (1) the identity and situation of its addressees, (2) the "dual character" of its contents (i.e., the presence and distribution of both Jewish and Gentile features), and (3) the purpose of Paul in writing.

There is little doubt, however, regarding the letter's provenance. Rom 15:14-32, which is the "Apostolic Parousia" or travelogue section of the letter, sets out the details quite clearly: that it was written (1) at the close of Paul's mission in the eastern part of the Roman empire (vv 19-23), (2) during his final, three-month stay at Corinth (v 25), ; cf. Acts 20:2-3), and (3) just prior to returning to Jerusalem with a collection for the impoverished believers of that city (vv 25-27, 30-31)—and that after his trip to Jerusalem, he planned to visit the Christians at Rome; and then, with their assistance, to continue his mission in the western part of the empire on to Spain (vv 24, 28-29). The letter can, therefore, be dated sometime during the spring of 58 or 59 CE, since Acts 20:6 tells us that Paul, traveling to Jerusalem by land through Macedonia, was again back at Philippi during Passover.

It would be somewhat pedantic to try to retain our pedagogical fourfold outline of "the circumstances," "the basis," "central features," and "discernible shifts" in discussing the eschatology of Romans. Some of these matters for Romans are hotly debated. Each of them, in fact, would require an extensive discussion beyond the limits at our disposal for any proper treatment.

It is only the last of the four, that regarding "discernible shifts in Paul's statements" in Romans, that is of concern for our present purposes. Suffice it here to say that the notion that Paul made substantial changes in his eschatology from the time he wrote 1

Thessalonians or 1 Corinthians to when he wrote Romans (i.e., over the course of eight or nine years, from about 50–58/59 CE)—in particular, any change in his central focus with respect to the resurrection of believers—is confounded by a comparison of his statements in Romans to those in 1 Thessalonians and 1 Corinthians.

Certainly the cosmic eschatology of Rom 8:19-22 puts an end to any theory that Paul shifted from a collective eschatology in his earlier letters to a personal, individual eschatology in his later letters. Similarly, references in Rom 8:23-25 to the "groaning," "eager waiting," and "hope" of believers for "our adoption as sons"—that is, "the redemption of our bodies"—oppose any view that Paul shifted his focus from resurrection and transformation at Christ's parousia to simply death and subsequent immortality.

Likewise, it needs to be noted that the language of Rom 8:19-25 has a distinctly apocalyptic flavor, similar to the imagery of 1 Thess 4:13-18 and 1 Cor 15:12-58. Further, the eschatological climax to the exhortations of Romans 12–13 that appears in 13:11-12—"The hour has come for you to wake up from your slumber, because our salvation is nearer now than when we first believed. The night is nearly over; the day is almost here!"—puts an end to any theory that Paul shifted in his later letters from a sense of imminence regarding Christ's coming (as in 1 Thess 4:14-18) or from a sense of urgency regarding living for God in light of the nearness of the parousia (as in 1 Thess 5:1-11; cf. also 1 Cor 7:29-31).

7. *Philippians 1:21-26; 3:10-11, 20-21; 4:5*

Philippians is a particularly difficult letter to evaluate in terms of a developmental hypothesis. Scholars in the past often took it to be a composite of two or three letters—for example, 4:10-23 being one letter, 1:1–3:1 plus 4:4-7 another letter, and 3:2–4:3 plus 4:8-9 another. On such a view, one must first determine the respective situations and relative chronologies of the various parts of the composite writing before attempting to trace out the development of any of its themes. But partition theories for Philippians are usually seen today as being, in the words of Werner G. Kümmel, "totally unconvincing" (*Introduction to the New Testament*, trans. H. C. Kee [Nashville: Abingdon, rev. ed., 1975], 333; see also 332-35), and deservedly so.

More serious is the question of the letter's provenance and date. For while Phil 1:12-26 indicates quite clearly that it was written from prison, the question remains: Was it written from Ephesian imprisonment (sometime during 53–57 CE), Caesarean imprisonment (about 58–59 CE), or Roman imprisonment (about 60–62 CE)? Issues regarding provenance usually have to do with (1) the number and nature of the journeys between Philippi and Rome reflected in the letter, and (2) the kinship of the contents and rhetoric of the letter to Paul's other letters, particularly to material in Galatians and 2 Corinthians. Cogent arguments can be mounted in support of each of these postulated situations and times of writing. And, obviously, whatever is accepted with respect to the provenance and date of Philippians has a profound effect on how one relates its themes, rhetoric and language to the other Pauline letters.

Phil 1:21-26, together with 2 Cor 5:1-10, has often been interpreted as evidencing a shift away from an apocalyptic mindset, which focused on a corporate resurrection of believers at Christ's parousia, to a more hellenistic concern for the individual person, which focused on death and immortality. In Phil 1:21-23, for example, Paul writes: "For to me, to live is Christ and to die is gain. If I am to go on living in the body, this will mean fruitful labor for me. Yet, what shall I choose? I do not know! I am torn between the two: I desire to depart and be with Christ, which is better by far." But, as William Baird points out, "the shifts in eschatological language in II Cor. v and Phil. i do not primarily involve a change in Paul's idea of the time of the end, but a change in Paul's understanding of his own relationship to the end" ("Pauline Eschatology," 327).

Both 2 Corinthians 5 and Philippians 1 reflect Paul's ambiguity as he faces the prospect of his own death—that is, as he is anxious about certain traumatic, near-death experiences—and so he desires "to depart and be with Christ." His reactions are similar in the two passages, though the circumstances were probably different (i.e., a near-fatal illness in 2 Corinthians; a possible judicial sentence of death in Philippians). Indeed, such similar reactions may suggest a particular period in Paul's life when this type of reaction, for some reason, was more common. Or, conversely, they may reflect only a similarity in Paul's responses at different times in his ministry when he was faced with near-death situations. It is precarious to identify Paul's reactions to a potential judicial sentence of death as having taken place sometime shortly after his writing of 1 Corinthians 15 (as per the Ephesian imprisonment theory), or at a later time that was roughly coordinate with his writing of 2 Corinthians 5 (as per the Caesarean imprisonment theory), or sometime later still after the writing of Romans (as per a Roman imprisonment theory)—though, for reasons set out by Dodd ("Change and Development," 5-26), I personally favor the third option.

Nonetheless, however Phil 1:12-26 is evaluated, it cannot be said that Paul's hope for Christ's coming and the resurrection of believers that will take place at that time is in any way abated in Philippians. For in 3:10-11, in what is probably his most revealing autobiographical statement, Paul speaks of wanting "to know Christ and the power of his resurrection and the fellowship of sharing in his sufferings, becoming like him in his death, and so, somehow, to attain to the resurrection of the dead." And in 3:20-21 he says: "Our citizenship is in heaven. And we eagerly await a Savior from there, the Lord Jesus Christ, who, by the power that enables him to bring everything under his control, will transform (μετασχηματίσει, "he will refashion" or "change the outward form of ") our lowly bodies so that they will be like his glorious body." So while the ringing affirmation of 4:5, "The Lord is near!" (ὁ κύριος ἐγγύς), has often been taken in a spatial manner (e.g., "Christ is always present among his people"), in context it should undoubtedly be understood primarily in temporal terms to mean: The parousia of Christ is imminent, and that fact should affect the believer's attitudes and actions!

8. Conclusion

What, then, can be said to our question "Is there development in Paul's resurrection thought?" A number of proposed shifts are unable to be validated. This is particularly so with regard to claims that he shifted (1) from a Jewish anthropology in his earlier letters to a hellenistic anthropology in his later letters, (2) from a world-renouncing mindset to a world-affirming mindset, (3) from a collective eschatology to a personal, individual eschatology, or (4) from a focus on Christ's parousia and the resurrection of believers to a primary concern with his own death and subsequent immortality. Yet three shifts in Paul's thought about the resurrection of believers seem to be evident in his letters.

The first has to do with what he himself identifies in 1 Cor 15:51 as an explication of an enigma or "mystery"—that is, that the resurrection of believers is not simply the revivification, resuscitation or reanimation of dead persons, but has to do primarily with transformation. For, as he says twice in 1 Cor 15:51-52, "We shall (all) be transformed" (ἀλλαγησόμεθα); and again in Phil 3:21, "He [i.e., 'the Lord Jesus Christ'] will transform (μετασχηματίσει) our lowly bodies so that they will be like his glorious body." Evidently, while contemplating Christ's own resurrection some time after writing 1 Thessalonians 4–5 and before writing 1 Corinthians 15, Paul came to understand not only Christ's resurrection as the basis for the actuality of a future resurrection of believers, Christ's parousia as the time of that resurrection, and Christ as the agent of resurrection, but also to view Christ's resurrection as an eschatological revelation that clarified and set out the nature of a believer's resurrection.

Another shift seems also able to be seen in the resurrection statements of Paul's letters in his use and non-use of apocalyptic imagery. For while the language of 1 Thess 4:13-18 and 1 Cor 15:12-58 is highly apocalyptic in nature, that of 2 Cor 4:14–5:10 and Phil 1:12-26 is devoid of apocalyptic imagery. This might, of course, be only a matter of circumstances, for Paul in Rom 8:19-25—which was certainly written after his letters to his Thessalonian and Corinthian converts—uses a number of apocalyptic expressions in his compacted, cosmic portrayal of the resurrection hope of both believers and all creation. Nonetheless, there does seem to be something of a reduction in Paul's apocalyptic imagery and expressions as we move from his earlier to his latter letters.

Likewise, there seems to be a shift in his letters regarding his own expectation vis-à-vis Christ's parousia and the resurrection. For while in 1 Thess 4:15-17 he associates himself with those who will be alive at the parousia, throughout 2 Cor 4:14–5:10 he identifies with those who will die before that event. And probably he so identifies himself, as well, in Rom 8:19-25, which is set in the context of "suffering" and "glory," and Phil 1:21-26, which reflects the possibility of a judicial death sentence.

Nonetheless, whatever shifts of thought, mood, or personal expectation might be postulated, it needs to be emphasized and enunciated clearly that the focus of Paul's teaching regarding the resurrection of believers was always on Christ's parousia and the resurrection of believers that would then take place. And it is this resurrection message that remains constant in his teaching.

SELECT BIBLIOGRAPHY

Baird, William. "Pauline Eschatology in Hermeneutical Perspective," *NTS* 17 (1971) 314-27.

Barrett, C. Kingsley. "New Testament Eschatology," *SJT* 6 (1953) 136-55.

Benoit, Pierre, and Roland E. Murphy, eds. *Immortality and Resurrection*. New York: Herder, 1970.

Charles, Robert Henry. *A Critical History of the Doctrine of the Future Life in Israel, in Judaism, and in Christianity*, 2nd rev. ed., London: Black, 1913.

Dodd, C. H. "The Mind of St Paul: A Psychological Approach," *BJRL* 17 (1933) 3-17; repr. as "The Mind of Paul: I," in *New Testament Studies*. Manchester: Manchester University Press, 1953, 67-82.

———. "The Mind of St Paul: Change and Development," *BJRL* 18 (1934) 3-44; repr. as "The Mind of Paul: II," in *New Testament Studies*. Manchester: Manchester University Press, 1953, 83-128.

Furnish, Victor Paul. "Development in Paul's Thought," *JAAR* 38 (1970) 289-303.

Gaffin, Richard B., Jr. *The Centrality of the Resurrection: A Study in Paul's Soteriology*. Grand Rapids: Baker, 1978.

Harris, Murray J. *Raised Immortal: Resurrection and Immortality in the New Testament*. London: Marshall, Morgan & Scott, 1983; Grand Rapids: Eerdmans, 1985.

———. *From Grave to Glory: Resurrection in the New Testament*. Grand Rapids: Zondervan, 1990.

Hurd, John C., Jr. *The Origin of I Corinthians*. London: SPCK, 1965.

Lightfoot, Joseph B. "The Chronology of St Paul's Life and Epistles," in *Biblical Essays*. London: Macmillan, 1893, 215-33 (posthumous publication of 1863 lecture notes).

Lincoln, Andrew T. *Paradise Now and Not Yet: Studies in the Role of the Heavenly Dimension in Paul's Thought, with Special Reference to his Eschatology*. Cambridge: Cambridge University Press, 1981; repr. Grand Rapids: Baker, 1991.

Longenecker, Richard N. "The Nature of Paul's Early Eschatology," *NTS* 31 (1985) 85-95.

Matheson, George. *The Spiritual Development of St Paul*. London: Hodder & Stoughton, 1897.

Moore, Arthur L. *The Parousia in the New Testament*. Leiden: Brill, 1966.

Perkins, Pheme. *Resurrection: New Testament Witness and Contemporary Reflection*. Garden City: Doubleday, 1984.

Plevnik, Joseph. *Paul and the Parousia: An Exegetical and Theological Investigation.* Peabody: Hendrickson, 1997.

Stanley, David M. *Christ's Resurrection in Pauline Soteriology.* Rome: Pontifical Biblical Institute, 1961.

Thackeray, Henry StJohn. *The Relation of St Paul to Contemporary Jewish Thought.* London: Macmillan, 1900.

INDEX OF AUTHORS

INDEX OF BIBLICAL REFERENCES

APOCRYPHA

PSEUDEPIGRAPHA